Stress & Trauma Handbook

Stress & Trauma Handbook

Strategies for Flourishing in Demanding Environments

John Fawcett, editor

World Vision

John Fawcett has worked in Christian humanitarian work for nearly 15 years. Since 1996 he has focused on the psychological stress and trauma experienced by front-line humanitarian workers. He has worked closely with Christian and secular NGOs, as well as the United Nations, and acted as an advisor to organisations seeking to provide effective support services for humanitarian staff. He has written extensively on this issue and is a regular presenter of research findings at international conferences. Presently he is an independent consultant to NGOs in the areas of stress and trauma management, and NGO security preparedness. Fawcett lives in Phnom Penh, Cambodia.

Printed in the United States of America.

10 09 08 07 06 05 04 03   5 4 3 2 1

Published by World Vision International, 800 West Chestnut Avenue, Monrovia, California 91016–3198, U.S.A.

Editor in chief: Edna Valdez. Senior editor: Rebecca Russell. Copyediting and typesetting: Joan Weber Laflamme/jml ediset. Cover design: Judy Walker. Cover art: Judy Walker.

ISBN 1–887983–52–X

♻ This book is printed on acid-free recycled paper.

contents

108470

Appendices:
Resources for Individuals and Organisations

Introduction

The humanitarian effort: dreams of transformation

This is not a book about survival. It is about living. It is about growing and thriving in some of the most important, challenging and exciting work in the world. Stress management is not merely about finding the tools to help people cope with the daily grind and to make it through the night. In the context of complex humanitarian emergencies and the rigours of life in developing nations, aid workers arrive on the scene expecting to enhance life, not just to neutralise pain. Humanitarian work is, after all, a celebration of life, not homage to death and despair.

Humanitarian aid professionals need and deserve care and treatment when their own bodies and souls are faced with crisis. Humanitarian workers do not set out to have careers of depression, trauma, sorrow and grief. Nor do they agree with contemporary cynics who decry the value of any assistance offered to those in need. International aid is a challenge to the power not only of hunger, war and poverty, but also of cynicism. Faith-driven or secular, the workers who bring aid to individuals, families and communities are the living embodiment of a human conviction that wrongs not only *must* be righted, but they *can* be righted.

Humanitarian personnel work in increasingly dangerous environments, often in close proximity to military units. UN statistics show that aid staff are more likely to be killed in the line of duty than peace-keeping soldiers. With increasing polarization politically and religiously around the world, aid workers often find themselves targets and suffer accordingly. Even in developed nations, emergency personnel suffer the consequences of politically motivated terrorist acts. The very high numbers of New York Police and Fire Department staff killed on September 11, 2001, are proof of that.

Too often stress and trauma management methods, techniques or even discussions are avoided by aid personnel out of fear. Fear that an acknowledgement of stress infers agreement that the horrors seen and experienced will triumph over good works accomplished. Fear that despite our best intentions, and all our efforts, wrongs will outnumber rights, and refugees will outnumber the settled. Many people think that if aid organisations or individuals begin to examine the nature, extent and depth of the stressors facing their staff, they will have no option but to close up shop and go home. The bad things out there are truthfully quite dangerous, and it is sensible to be cautious and to manage expectations with integrity.

But protection against the major impacts of traumatic stress is not only possible – it is critical for all humanitarian and welfare agencies. New research detailed later in this book reveals that much stress results from organisational decisions and structures. A significant method of protecting staff against serious stress injury is to work on improving organisational factors such as management capacity and team functioning. For the last five years World Vision International, the world's largest international Christian humanitarian organisation, has been developing a comprehensive programme to provide staff with the support and care necessary to ensure continued health and safety. This book was developed as part of that strategy and documents some of the research now accumulating.

Human beings are valuable. Secular and religious people alike agree to this. Additionally, World Vision believes that people are created, sacred beings in relationship with a loving and all-powerful creator-God. If every human life is sacred because we are made in the image of God, if each person is valuable because God cherishes us and intends to give us a future and a hope, then a Christian initiative to help manage stress in humanitarian work must do more than promote survival. Beyond protection, we must create space to grow, flourish and develop. Hope is central to World Vision's stress and trauma initiative, despite the reality of pain and loss, of grief and suffering. We do not believe it is sufficient merely to train people to cope with such processes. Survival of suffering is the first step; flourishing and growing in healthy communities built on foundations of mutual respect and honour are the ultimate outcomes of a comprehensive stress and trauma management strategy.

Stress management techniques often focus on providing protection for good things by keeping bad things out. In other words, stress management skills often are designed to create a barrier through which only limited harm can enter. This "barrier" approach is similar to trying to plant a garden in a hostile environment by setting a strong fence around a favoured vegetable or flower patch to keep predators and insects out. The first challenge to this approach is obtaining materials for the fence. The second is building a fence, which takes time and energy away from care and attention to the garden. A single gardener is torn between the need, first, to build the barrier to protect the plants and to care for the plants themselves, and second, to access new resources for both the barrier and the garden.

Many aid workers intuitively shy away from this type of approach. They hear a covert message that they do not internally have the resources to protect themselves and so must spend precious time and money obtaining those resources. Then, barriers are themselves problematic. A major motivation for doing this work is a result of being touched somewhere inside. Their "hearts" have been moved by the evidence of great need. This provides a lot of the energy to do what must be done. A process that appears to create a barrier between the evidence in front of their eyes and the heart of their motivation appears not only threatening but also counterproductive.

Experienced fieldworkers also know that there is no barrier strong enough or deep enough to stop the "bad things" from getting through to the heart. The monsters of the killing fields take up residence in daydreams and nightmares, and no amount of ploughing will remove them. Even moving far away from the source of the beasts is not sufficient. Such monsters follow through the years, across the oceans, into the suburbs and on into old age and retirement. Building fences, in the end, does not appear to solve the problem.

From spiritual and psychological perspectives, the dichotomous view of reality is a problem, because monsters, the "bad things", also exist inside our own hearts. The garden is not all good and life-giving on the inside and the outside world all bad and destructive. Field experience reveals that, were circumstances only a little different in my own life, I might be figuring as perpetrator and/or victim. As I stand before the evil of Cambodia, of Rwanda or of Kosovo, this truth becomes very clear. Most of the perpetrators are very similar to me, with similar ideals, similar goals, even similar theologies, living similar lives. There are monsters in my heart as well, and in the night they cry out to those who have acted against their friends and communities. Any effort to build a wall to keep the monsters out results, in the end, in caging the beasts already within the garden.

Effective stress management, then, is not mainly about keeping harm out; rather, it is about learning to live with beasts and, in the end, to tame them. This means the garden may appear to be a wilder place, at least in the beginning. There will be less control and more observation and maybe containment. Instead of a structured, formal place with no stressful weeds or insects, the healthy heart is dynamic, open to new "plants", full of buzzing things, exchanging seeds with the rest of the world. There will still be a need for discipline. A landscape where one predator overwhelms all the habitat quickly falls into ruin. Likewise, a garden where a fast-growing creeper is allowed to cover all other vegetation will collapse and decay. But appropriate discipline expends more energy tending to and directing a garden's inhabitants rather than suppressing and denying reality. The result is a much more interesting and attractive landscape, capable of enduring and thriving within, rather than in spite of the local environment.

This book maintains that the objective of stress and trauma management is not merely to protect local and expatriate staff but to encourage them to grow, flourish and sow the seeds of well-being among colleagues and communities in which they work and live. Protection from stress and trauma does not come about as a result of going out and shopping for new items to provide protection. Instead, effective stress and trauma protection involves recognising the strengths and resilience already inherent in our lives and applying these in a fashion that becomes our own contribution, a statement of our belief in the triumph of life over death. A healthy heart, or spirit, or soul or whatever term is used to define the core of who we are, is in itself the greatest protection against stress and trauma damage. This is more substantial than merely a feeling of lightheadedness. A healthy heart is rooted in real life relationships, real knowledge and skills, and real professional activities.

One of the most effective ways both to protect and to flourish is to maintain excellent social relationships within and outside the work environment. Among colleagues and friends, family, community members and the wider global village, we can build common understandings and common strength. Going it alone, or being independently strong, is not sufficient, according to experience and research. Our recent studies present solid evidence of this, but in these pages we will also provide an overview of the most highly regarded texts and sources currently available.

In addition, we have included anecdotes and case-study accounts that bring these compelling research findings to life. The evidence indicates that most international humanitarian aid workers actually do quite a good job at looking after themselves and maintain very healthy lifestyles when compared to the average educated Western citizen.

New information describes how the most stressful events in humanitarian work have to do with the organisational culture, management style and operational objectives of an NGO or agency rather than external security risks or poor environmental factors. Aid workers, basically, have a pretty shrewd idea what they are getting into when they enter this career, and dirty clothes, gun shots at night and lack of electricity do not surprise them. Inter- and intra-agency politics, inconsistent management styles, lack of team work and unclear or conflicting organisational objectives, however, combine to create a background of chronic stress and pressure that over time wears people down and can lead to burnout or even physical collapse.

Our findings suggest that strong relationships afford the best protection in traumatic and stressful environments. If true, then it may be most productive to use this book in group or team settings. In cases where this is not possible, recommendations, checklists and assessments have been prepared for use by individuals, as well as teams. Nevertheless, the full organisational benefit of attention to stress and trauma management will be gained when learnings and techniques are applied to groups or teams. Programme objectives and organisational plans will be more achievable where aid workers have strong social relationships, are members of cohesive teams, are blessed with consultative leadership, and are adequately skilled to do the job for which they have been employed.

Of course, some successful career aid workers may, at this point, argue that they have survived and even thrived during many years of individual front-line work. Such people may be disinclined to read further. However, it appears that the most successful individuals in humanitarian work do have strong interpersonal relationships with a small but very close group of peers or family members that helps keep them strong. Work peers may or may not be employed by the same agency, and family members may meet face to face too rarely. But the strength of a relationship is not only in the number of contact events; it is also a function of how deep those contacts are when they occur. Although more and more teams are being employed in major relief efforts, there are still tasks best completed by highly skilled individuals, experienced in the art of self-care and able to operate in virtually any kind of environment. Even then, however, it is possible to surround such specialists with supportive teams or groups, thus reinforcing the benefits of interpersonal social relationships.

Another interesting research finding reported later in this book is that people working in front-line emergency relief situations appear to experience degrees of stress symptoms similar to those shown by those living and working in supposedly less stressful development-focused environments. Guns, bombs and civil war appear to carry similar stress and trauma risk levels as battling chronic poverty, corrupt politicians, poor water supplies and lack of schooling for local children. This is not, of course, to deny the reality that war zones are intrinsically dangerous places. Nevertheless, stress symptomology appears somewhat uniform across a wide range of humanitarian fieldwork environments. Perhaps this is not a new claim. However, the research reported herein gives increased detail to our understanding of the fairly high potential for stress and trauma damage that aid workers face in all humanitarian work, no matter where it is performed.

Effective stress management is a holistic practice, requiring more than piecemeal attempts at prevention and protection. Health, which is after all the objective of stress management, addresses all that it means to be human. We are spiritual, physical, cognitive beings who live in a web of social relationships in the context of an ecological environment in which we both act and are acted upon. If the research reported here is correct, then it may well be our relationships that save us, rather than our knowledge and skills. Above all other factors, we seem to be dependent upon the strength and nature of our relationships with one another, with the earth on which we live, and with the God who created us.

This book is divided into three parts. Part I is a general introduction to the nature of stress and how stress affects human functioning. The particular focus is on stress in humanitarian work but is relevant to almost all aspects of life. Part II establishes the foundation of this book. During the past three to four years World Vision International has intentionally sought to understand the causes and effects of stress and trauma in humanitarian work, how stress affects the lives of staff and their families, and what individual and organisational actions might be taken to reduce the impact of stress and strain. Part II reviews some of the practical field research undertaken by World Vision and makes suggestions based not only on theory but also on applied fieldwork and more than 50 years' experience in humanitarian efforts around the world. In Chapter 3 Dr Graham Fawcett presents a developing model of stress and strain in order to assist our understanding of why some things work to reduce strain and others appear to fail. In Chapter 4 Dr Cynthia Eriksson and her colleagues summarise portions of a major global study looking at the lives and experiences of international field staff. Then, in Chapter 5, Dr Graham Fawcett examines in some depth research findings relating to the protective nature of social relationships in humanitarian work. Part III seeks to apply our present understanding of the research to practicalities of everyday humanitarian work. The authors are convinced that unless learning and insight can be applied, tested and evaluated in the environments in which the need is found, the information is essentially useless. Therefore we have included chapters with recommendations for individuals and for organisations on how to mitigate the impact of stress and strain amongst field staff and their family members. Finally, the book concludes with a series of appendices and a recommended reading list.

Throughout the book are brief vignettes that are indeed the voices of humanitarian workers. Not all are World Vision staff, but in all cases we have protected the confidentiality of NGO staff and the communities they serve by changing their names and any details that might endanger ongoing work. We have tried to quote accurately, apart from these changes. None of the remarks comes from the research detailed in Chapter 4, as this would have breached conditions set up for the research.

It is important to note that this research is ongoing, and final analysis of data is not complete. Indeed, so rich is the data collected that it is expected to take some years to complete this task. There is also an increasing body of literature in this area, although compared with other populations, humanitarian workers are considerably underserved. More research will enhance our understanding of stress and will further assist with the protection and safety of humanitarian personnel worldwide.

What is new in this volume is the emphasis on what works on the ground in international humanitarian work. Much of the literature relating to stress management has arisen out of Western first-world environments. The advice is not always easy to follow in the middle of a coup or an earthquake. Principles for maintaining a healthy lifestyle, however, are similar wherever a person lives and works. It is becoming clearer which activities might work best in the kinds of places common to relief and development work.

The number of people worldwide presently employed in humanitarian work is huge and is increasing every year. Objectives have become more defined, and approaches more structured and professional. Relief staff today are more often in the front line alongside, or even ahead of, military forces. The neutrality afforded aid workers in the past has been compromised, and the death and injury count amongst fieldworkers continues to rise. Agencies now spend large amounts of money recruiting and preparing staff for service internationally – a significant investment in skill and experience. Potential loss of such investment, aside from moral and ethical issues, has quite rightfully driven NGOs to reassess security arrangements and to focus intentionally on provision of adequate support services for staff. Stress and trauma management is a key component of any organisational strategy to ensure the health, well-being and continued productivity of field staff.

Protection and prevention are always more cost effective than treatment, especially considering that a person who experiences severe burnout may never be able to return to front-line fieldwork. But organisations and individuals who view stress management merely as a way to protect existing assets by erecting containment measures miss the point. Containment is not what humanitarian work is about. Life, which international aid work affirms every day, is about growth, learning and transformation. A comprehensive organisational stress management strategy will identify outcome objectives relating to flourishing rather than containment. The vision at the heart of this book is that of humanitarian workers enabled to experience their own growth and development as they care for themselves and the great needs of those to whom they are responding.

A note on checklists
Some chapters conclude with a series of checklists and questions that aid workers and agency management may find useful in assessing stress levels, designing stress management programmes, preventing serious traumatic disability, and improving working conditions for personnel. These lists are assuredly not comprehensive and make no pretence of being

diagnostic. While many are useful for personal assessment by individuals, we strongly recommend that these questions be addressed in social and organisational contexts in which group interaction plays a major role in the process of addressing stress and trauma. As previously stated, and repeated often in this book, strong social relationships, good team dynamics and sound consultative leadership styles contribute significantly to health and well-being in humanitarian work. Using these checklists as a basis for group or collegial conversations could provide a framework for enhancing this protection.

Part I

How stress affects aid organisations and staff

chapter 1

What is stress and how does it affect aid workers?

It has been five weeks since I last had a decent night's sleep. Three to four hours a night is all that is possible. The refugees just keep coming, even in the night when the roads outside the camp are in the hands of the rebels. They come crying, cradling their dead and dying children, dragging their exhausted parents or aunts or brothers. Some have lost limbs to the arrogant drunkenness of the jungle children. Most of the women and girls have been raped, many more than once. The air is thick with dust or mud, sometimes both at the same time. My sleeping bag is now in tatters, but it hardly matters. I don't spend much time there. I'm not thinking straight right now. It's hard to remember which day this is. I do know there are not enough medical supplies for the numbers already here, let alone those I hear entering the camp today. My stomach, my back and my legs ache. At times I wonder if I have malaria or something worse. I profoundly hope that today, just for one day, that crazy Brit will stop whistling while he bandages wounds and dispenses antibiotics. Tracy told me yesterday I was . . . suffering too much from stress. Ha! What did she expect? A picnic? OK, let's go, another day in paradise.

—MELIKA, FROM THE NETHERLANDS, WORKING IN ANGOLA 2000

Maintaining health in the face of life's extremes is always difficult. Dealing with stress is a learnable skill summed up in the phrase *stress management.* The implication inherent in this term is the universality of stress and the appreciation that all human beings experience stress to varying degrees. Most stress is not overwhelming. It is, in fact, part of being alive. Rather than trying to create a stress-free existence, most credible advice centres on the concept of management. While stress may be unavoidable, the amount and nature of the stress experienced can be modified.

Success in stress management is often measured in terms of a reduction in pain and suffering from the negative impact of stress. When we think of stress in terms of pressure or influence, it is easy to see that every component of life contains elements of stress. Any alteration to the present is a change, and change brings pressure or stress. Even positive change brings stress. In itself, stress is neither positive nor negative. Although there is a tendency to consider stress as something negative, something to be removed, a more healthy appreciation of stress is to view it as a neutral phenomenon. How we respond to stress is less often so neutral.

In *Emergency Services Stress*, Jeffrey Mitchell and Grady Bray offer this useful definition of stress: *"Stress is a state of psychological and physical arousal that comes about as a result of a threat, challenge or change in one's environment."* Taking a vacation, for example, is generally regarded as a positive activity with positive benefits. However, a vacation does involve change from the daily routine. Planning, expenditure, and travel required to have a successful vacation can be stressful, and people are sometimes surprised to discover the negatively stressful consequences of an activity that is supposed to result in reduced stress. Most people are aware of the tradeoffs in taking a vacation. People with extremely complex and demanding employment often choose to forgo a vacation, because they realise that the changes in work productivity would be more negative than the positive gains in being away from the office for a period of time.

A further confusion exists in the way we talk about stress. Although technically stress is a term used to describe a cause, we often talk of stress as something we experience; we say that we feel stressed, but that is a result rather than a cause. When pressed, we might describe a particular event that caused us to feel the way we do. Or we might claim to feel stressed because of a whole raft of events, some of which may have been building up over weeks, months and even years. There is certainly a negative connotation to this use of the word *stress*. Yet the way we feel about an event (a change) is deeply personal and can be described quite differently depending on who we are and what we are anticipating.

Consider this example. A business executive steals millions of dollars from his company colleagues and loses it gambling. It is likely that the business associates will describe their feelings on learning the news as "stressful" or "stressed", implying or stating an increased anxiety or even depression. There is a negative change. The business editor of the local newspaper, however, may be exhilarated by the change, seeing in this situation an opportunity to break a major story, advance a career and become better known. This is a positive change for the editor. For all parties there will be stress to manage, but whether it is negative or positive depends largely on where the individuals stand in relation to the change.

To clarify the differences, I define *distress* as *a psychological and physical arousal for which routine stress management is inadequate over time.* Some changes bring both negative and positive stress results. A well-loved child graduating from high school and departing the family home for university study brings change. Stress – both positive and negative – will be experienced by all parties. Leaving home is a natural event; making a new life is an exciting and longed-for step; and separation from parents is both welcomed and grieved. The mix of emotions in such normal family changes can be tiring, exhilarating and confusing.

Humanitarian workers face complex stresses every day. Humanitarian work is all about change – either planned change in the context of project designs or unplanned change requiring response in emergency disaster situations. Successful humanitarian work is about managed change, or managing changes. People who choose this career often do so because they are energised by change itself, viewing change as an essential part of their life experiences and therefore to be both anticipated and welcomed. Humanitarian workers are experienced in managing the impact of change and, by inference, the effects of stress. The ambiguity and evolution of relief and development environments provide much of the enthusiasm and energy sought by humanitarian workers.

And yet questions raised increasingly in the past decade surround the higher reported incidences of negative stress experiences in humanitarian work. Has the work become more stressful? Has there been more change? Have the changes become larger and more complex? Are disasters today so much worse than those of 50 years ago? Or could it be that the people entering humanitarian work do not have the capacity to manage the changes and stresses of this work? Do we have a recruitment problem?

Most likely, honest answers involve combinations of all of the above. The challenge, therefore, is in determining which components of stress management are personal (or individual), which are organisational (or group, or family), which are environmental (situational), and which of these can be influenced and which need to be lived with.

Important Stress Definitions

Because stress has become such a popular point of discussion in everyday life, many terms used in technical discussions are relatively well known. Still, for this book to be of most use, it is necessary to provide descriptions of those terms and phrases early on.

Stress, as defined above, occurs at a time of change. We experience stress in physiological, cognitive, behavioural, social and spiritual ways.

Distress can be described as strain; it occurs when stress causes an individual to move away from his or her normal healthy functioning towards a less healthy state.

Stress management is a term that now comprehensively refers to any and all actions (preventative or curative) taken by individuals, communities, organisations and even countries to reduce incidences of distress and to enable individuals and groups to cope with stress.

Stressors, stress factors, causes of stress, are those single, multiple or complex events (changes) that bring about either stress or distress (strain).

Day-to-day stress is the term given to normal, anticipated events that occur regularly and with which we cope. Getting to work every day, paying the bills, and so on, are stressful, but once handled, are considered behind us. Most people cope with day-to-day stress.

Chronic stress is the result of single, multiple or complex events (changes) that become repetitive or never ending. This can be a form of day-to-day stress, but generally it refers to an environment in which the ability to cope with repetitive stress factors has diminished and distress (strain) begins to rise. Chronic stress is a likely experience of humanitarian aid workers, and in its extreme form appears to differ very little from Post Traumatic Stress Disorder (PTSD) (see below). Recent research suggests, in fact, that PTSD (or something very similar to PTSD) in humanitarian work is most likely to be caused by high levels of chronic stress rather than exposure to single critical events. Humanitarian workers appear to have very low levels of PTSD associated with critical traumatic events but seem to develop the range of symptoms associated with PTSD through chronic and cumulative stress.

Cumulative stress is similar to chronic stress in that the stress becomes ever present. The slight difference is that cumulative stress generally refers to an increasing number of stress factors on top of each other, further reducing ability to cope or deal with the distress. Alternatively, cumulative stress may also refer to a situation where the number of stress factors remains the same but their intensity or demands become greater, thus increasing strain.

Burnout is generally used to describe results of prolonged strain, either chronic stress or cumulative stress. Burnout is a result, not a cause. When individuals' coping strategies have not been sufficient to handle strain over a period of time, a set of identifiable symptoms often emerge, leading to burnout. Although people experience burnout in unique ways, generally symptoms cluster around physical health concerns (heart, back pain, stomach complaints, cancer, etc.), mental health concerns (depression, anxiety, suicidal thinking, etc.), relationship concerns (marriage breakup, workplace conflict, etc.) or spiritual concerns (loss of faith, inability to attend religious occasions, etc.). Burnout is a serious condition from which recovery may be long term and problematical unless managed carefully.

Flameout describes a kind of temporary burnout with a very rapid onset. It may be experienced at the conclusion of a particularly difficult period, maybe a high-intensity relief assignment or something similar. Often flameout is experienced as an almost overwhelming weariness, excessive desire for sleep, lethargy, difficulty in thinking clearly, excessive sadness or grief, failure to admit to loss of functioning and an inability to see oneself objectively. The popular understanding of the stress related ulcer is probably related to flameout. Because with sufficient rest flameout is usually somewhat temporary, some people view flameout as less damaging than burnout. However, incidents of flameout should be treated seriously. Often such an experience is indicative of a high degree of chronic stress and, unless significant adjustments occur, the long-term prognosis is not good.

Post Traumatic Stress Disorder is the most commonly referred to condition under the general grouping of *Acute Stress Reactions* (ASR). Despite its increasing usage in popular media, PTSD is one of the least understood of the stress and strain conditions. Utilised, as it has been, as a plot factor in

TV and movie scripts, PTSD has unfortunately come to refer to almost all kinds of distress and strain. Everyone can, it is assumed, "get" PTSD from such common experiences as having a tooth filled or being in an argument with one's boss. For the purposes of this book, a professional understanding of PTSD and other ASRs will be used. An ASR (which includes PTSD) is something that afflicts an individual who experiences an event that is so overwhelming that any "normal person" would be unable to cope. Such events therefore are restricted to those that are personally life-threatening or where a person is in a setting where others are at major risk. For a clinical diagnosis of PTSD, precipitating events on this order of magnitude must be clearly identified.

Secondary traumatization, or secondary stress, is another relatively well-known condition. Generally, this phrase refers to strain or distress experienced as a result of someone else's direct exposure to trauma or significant stress. First identified among health professionals such as counsellors, social workers and medical practitioners, it is now well established as a very real risk for humanitarian workers of all kinds. Listening to survivors of natural or human-contrived disasters, hearing accounts of colleagues who have been through "hell", taking photographs or videos of disasters in the making, are all commonly understood causes for the onset of secondary traumatization. Use of the term *trauma* in this context is technically viewed as being more serious than *stress*, in that trauma is connected to diagnosis of PTSD and other ASRs. Hearing distressing stories may be painful and may induce stress, but this process does not always result in a traumatic response. Trauma, as described above in the section on PTSD, is by definition overwhelming and disabling.

Psychological debriefing or Critical Incident Stress Debriefing (CISD) is a process that has, through its associations with PTSD, become relatively well known to the general public, and in the process, become somewhat misunderstood. CISD is a well-constructed therapeutic intervention for groups of people exposed to a single shared traumatic event. Developed by Jeffrey Mitchell and his colleagues, CISD has been very widely used in Western cultures, especially among emergency personnel, fire departments and police forces. In recent years intense professional criticisms of CISD have been voiced, most particularly when CISD is indiscriminately applied to survivors of complex humanitarian emergencies, aid workers and cultures other than those originating from a European base. This book is not intended to detail this debate, which is still very much in progress. An interested reader need only look at the proceedings of such institutions as the International Society for Traumatic Stress Studies (www.istss.org) to gain a fuller understanding of the complexities of the debate.

The broader concept of psychological debriefing may be of use to humanitarian workers, one that encompasses a wide range of potentially helpful mental health interventions for those affected by stress, strain and trauma. When the word *debriefing* is used, it must be clear whether the process referred to is psychological or operational. Many agencies utilise a process of operational debriefing that is a review of operational outcomes or actions during or after a field assignment or deployment. Although such a process may in fact have positive mental health results, the purpose of an operational debriefing is to enhance attainment of agency objectives, not to provide an opportunity for stressed employees to process their own stress reactions.

Defusing, or *psychological defusing*, is another term with fairly wide provenance. The idea of defusing is intuitively connected to the work undertaken by de-mining experts or those dealing with unexploded bombs. Defusing is a skill that renders an explosive safe by removing its ability to detonate. Psychological defusing, then, is a process that is expected to drain away accumulated stress and strain to remove the psychological detonator inside a strained or distressed individual. The objective of such defusing is to anticipate the potentially destructive onset of PTSD and enter a process in which, through a time-limited and immediate group discussion of the critical incident, the possibility of survivors developing PTSD is reduced. Again, much discussion is currently under way in the professional literature regarding the efficacy of psychological defusing, but many organisations promote a form of the process on the basis that it doesn't appear to do any real harm and may do some good.

A Note on Clinical Diagnosis

The above descriptions are provided only as a way for the reader to categorise stress and stress reactions in general. They cannot take the place of a properly conducted clinical diagnosis. Any and all clinical diagnosis, and subsequent treatment, must always be performed by an appropriately qualified and trained specialist. Instruments and tools available in this book and through other sources can be used to assist in attaining self-knowledge and making basic self-assessments of stress levels, burnout and fatigue. However, these are only indicators and cannot substitute for professional assistance. Those who have concerns about their state of physical, mental or spiritual well-being should always seek professional advice and assistance. Conversely, any agency or organisation that has staff employed in environments in which incidences of potential stress, strain, distress or trauma are high must make available to all staff ready access to appropriate health professionals. Success in protecting staff from disabling stress responses is a partnership between employer and employee. It cannot be left to only one party.

I've been in relief work for about 20 years now, I guess. Started with orphans, as we called them back then, and progressed on to more challenging assignments. I suppose I've been at most of the major disasters in the last ten years. Cambodia, Rwanda, Sierra Leone, Kosovo, Palestine, the hurricanes and earthquakes in Latin America, the starvation in the Horn of Africa, HIV/AIDS, the cholera epidemics. Probably more. They become a bit of a blur over time. Sure I've been stressed. I've cried at the death, the suffering, the pain. At times at the hopelessness of it all. I've looked after myself. I exercise as much as I can; I eat healthy foods; I take time out for reading novels, listening to music, dancing and taking vacations at the beach. I spend a lot of time in prayer, but then I always have, from my youth, and I continue that today. Basically I have slept well at night. Of course there are some places where sleeping is very hard. Rwanda was probably the worst. Occasionally I have had nightmares, but only for a day or so. I don't need to take sleeping pills either.

But lately, over the past year, something strange has been going on, and I don't know what it means. There is this dream, which repeats over and over again. It's not a nightmare, and it doesn't leave me scared or frightened. In the dream I am in one of those orphanages of long ago. And there are children in the beds and on the floor. Some are very ill. But they are not the focus of the dream. There is an old woman. She is there every time this dream arrives. Sometimes she walks in; sometimes she is just there. She comes up right close to me and stops. She never says anything. She just stands in front of me as if she has a question for me. But she never asks it. Sometimes, after I wake up, I feel angry that I wasn't able to stay asleep to hear the question! It feels important, but I don't know the reason. Why don't I dream of the camps in Rwanda? What I saw there was much, much worse than the orphans. What does the old woman want to ask? Why does the dream come back and back?

—Angus, from Scotland, working in Gaza City in 2001

Chapter 2

A living sacrifice: the body's responses to stress in traumatic environments

One of the more enduring myths held to by humanitarian workers and soldiers alike is that a truly strong person will be able to remain both psychologically and physically relaxed during times of high stress, that such an individual will experience none of the normal physical responses to a stressful incident or environment. Unfortunately for aid workers (and soldiers) there is very little substance in this belief. While it is possible to become more controlled in certain circumstances, it is virtually impossible to remove all of the physiological reactions to stress.

Habituation or being more able to cope with an environment is very real, however, and needs to be acknowledged. Aid workers who have lived for many months or years in Chechnya may find checkpoints more tedious than traumatic. For them, physiological responses to yet another group of bearded young men toting AK47's may be considerably lower than that of a first-time visitor to Chechnya. But it would be inaccurate to believe that the moderate nature of the response is less harmful than a full-blown physical panic attack. The human body is a wonderful creation, and it is capable of absorbing much strain, but too much can be very dangerous.

At times of stress the human body automatically responds by increasing production of some hormones and chemicals, by cutting production of others, by heightening the activities of some organs and functions, and by slowing down or even ceasing others. The specifics of these actions will be detailed below, but the overall effect of this physiological response is to increase the momentary efficiency of the body to help meet and deal with perceived threat or challenge. This is generally a very good thing, because it markedly increases chances of survival in life-threatening situations.

There are, however, two general groups of people among whom things can go wrong. In the first, individuals have little or no awareness of what the body is actually doing. Some people appear to lack, for whatever reason, insight into their bodily functions; they seem to have no awareness of heart rate, restricted breathing, tightened muscles and other stress responses. Because they are unaware, they are unable to utilise their own bodies to assist in coping with a difficult situation. Lack of this type of awareness can lead to such apparently sudden conditions as heart attacks, strokes and physical collapse. This group can be greatly helped through a comprehensive stress management education programme.

The second group includes people who have been aware of their physical responses to stress and strain but now claim they "feel nothing". Often people hear this claim in connection to the emotions or feelings of the claimant. "Feeling nothing" is believed to be some kind of reduced affective ability. While this may well be part of the situation, emotions and hormones are very much linked in reality. If an individual has experienced such a high degree of strain or distress or even trauma that the linkages among sensing, emotions, hormones and other bodily functions are compromised, then there is indeed a major problem. Reports of long-term or permanent lack of feeling should result in referral to mental health professionals.

This is different from experiences that commonly occur among people in the heat of a highly stressful event. Countless individuals seriously wounded in wars or natural disasters have quite literally not felt the pain at that time and have continued to perform their duties with a high degree of success. This, as we will see soon, is a natural part of the body's brilliant protection strategy. Once the event is over, however, these people will become aware (if they do not die) of how seriously injured they are. The concern expressed above is for those people who have been through events, have been in and out of field countries over a period of years, and who claim no matter where they are at present, to "feel nothing".

We came across the convoy about midday. I guess there were about 20 vehicles in all, most old farm tractors towing trailers. It was a bit hard to tell because they had been so badly hit by artillery shells. They were still burning when we arrived. Most of the people were women and children, with a few older men as well. Most of them were dead, blown across the roadway and into the wheat fields. Clothes, belongings, shoes and animals strewn everywhere. Some were still alive but very badly injured. I am a reporter, so I took up my camera and began filming. The scene was horrific, the smell appalling and the crying and moaning made my flesh crawl. But in circumstances like that I am professional. I put those things to one side and get on with the job. These are the pictures of war. If you can't deal with it, then you shouldn't be there. I get angry with the people who commit these crimes, but I am not responsible. My job is to bring help by telling the world what has happened. I feel good that my pictures can stop the fighting and make peace. I do not have nightmares.

—ROLANDO, FROM MOZAMBIQUE, WORKING IN CHECHNYA IN 2001

As far as is known at present, physical or physiological responses to stress are cross-culturally similar. There may be moderation dependent on cultural learning and expectation, but it appears that the physical mechanisms are common to all human beings.

The body is continually manufacturing and processing a huge number of hormones and chemical products. This is not a book about endocrinology, so a reader who wishes to understand more on this subject is referred to more professional literature. However, some significant hormones, for our purposes, need to be introduced here.

Cortisone Production

Cortisone and adrenaline account for about 80–90 per cent of the body's response to stress. When stress is experienced, the cortex of the adrenal gland increases production of both cortisol and cortisone. Both these hormones are very useful in counteracting pain and inflammation of body tissues. Reduction in experienced pain can be very useful in a high-stress situation, when a person needs to be able to focus on solving the problem or just getting out alive. However, these hormones are very powerful and if levels of production become high and remain high, eventually parts of the body's immune system begin to break down. A simple example of a reduction in efficacy of the immune system is the common cold. Many relief workers seem to be almost constantly dealing with minor colds or chest infections. Other very common stress-related conditions include cold sores and mononucleosis. Some put this down to frequent international travel, others to allergies, but few seem aware that it is more likely a result of a compromised immune system due to continual high levels of corticol hormones in the bloodstream.

While a cold may seem a small price to pay for dealing with complex humanitarian crises, degradation of the immune system, over time, will almost invariably lead to much more serious complications such as stomach ulcers, high blood pressure and heart conditions. The connection between chronic stress and cancer is not yet clearly proven, but these other conditions are themselves serious enough to address. Humanitarian workers should view persistent or frequent colds as a warning sign.

Adrenaline Production

Adrenaline and noradrenaline are also produced by the adrenal glands, and at quite high levels very quickly after the onset of stress. These hormones affect the heart and blood supply very quickly indeed, inducing the heart to pump blood quicker, raise blood pressure and prepare the body to move fast if needed. The effect of this is to increase blood flow to the brain, so that thinking is sharpened, auditory and visual senses are enhanced, and muscles all over the body are ready to contract. This response has popularly been named the fight-or-flight response, as it appears to bring the body to a point where the brain can decide either to run away from the danger or to do combat with the threat.

Obviously such a response is very helpful in an emergency. However, as with all chemicals, prolonged exposure to adrenaline is quite toxic to the body. Increased blood flow to the head, muscles and stomach means reduced blood flow to other parts of the body. Temporarily this can be managed, but in the long term, parts of the body not obtaining an adequate supply of blood will deteriorate. Increased blood supply to the stomach may help with rapid digestion, but the increased production of stomach acid over time leads to ulcers. Continued adrenaline presence in the bloodstream will also increase cholesterol production, decrease removal of cholesterol, and increase the deposition of plaque on arterial walls. All of these conditions are associated with heart disease.

Until recently it was assumed that the fight-or-flight response was the same in both men and women. However, a UCLA study in 2000 highlights significant differences between genders.[1] Researchers at UCLA noted that when stressed, women produce a hormone called oxytocin. Release of oxytocin creates what the research team named a tend-and-befriend response, which counteracts the fight-or-flight response. This response encourages women to care for children and to be in close proximity to other women. When this occurs, production of oxytocin increases again, thus reinforcing the effects. Apparently, high levels of testosterone produced in men under stress counteract any oxytocin production, leading to the suggestion that there may be significant differences in reactions to immediate stress between genders. On reviewing studies that identified the fight-or-flight response, the UCLA researchers found that virtually all the subjects in those studies were men, a factor apparently unnoticed until the present. Although these findings are very recent, they are of such significance that mention of them needs to be made here. It would seem logical to assume that overproduction of oxytocin, as with other hormones, contains elements of risk. At this stage no information on possible detrimental effects of oxytocin overproduction is available.

Endorphin Production

In an age when physical fitness is almost obsessively pursued by some, the phenomenon of runners' "endorphin high" is widely known. Endorphin is, in fact, almost identical to morphine in chemical makeup and has much the same effect on the body. Endorphin (like morphine) is an extremely potent painkiller and, at times of high stress, removal of pain increases the potential for survival or success. Like morphine, endorphins also create a feeling of well-being, lightness, even a euphoria approaching carelessness. Soldiers and veteran fieldworkers sometimes talk with amazement about being involved in extremely dangerous situations and at the same time feeling almost "high", exhilarated and energised while dodging bullets.

One challenge the body faces is that it is not possible to produce endorphin at a high rate for any extended length of time. While the first thing an aid worker might become aware of is reduction in euphoria, studies have shown that chronically depleted endorphin levels can lead to increased arthritis pains and severe headaches. Another significant result of extended endorphin production is lessening of the pain relief, as well as lowered euphoria. The process is almost exactly the same as that which occurs with habitual morphine (or opiate derivative drugs) usage. To achieve the same effect, dosages need to be higher each time. For aid workers, the connection between a high-stress environment and feeling great is an experience that can obviously be repeated. The phenomenon of the "aid junkie" is partly attributable to an endorphin addiction. The problem of habituation means that often the only way to continue the experience is to seek increasingly dangerous situations or to begin to take drugs that complement or enhance the effects of endorphins. Caffeine in the form of coffee or sodas is the most popular drug in the aid community, although other, sometimes illegal substances are also used.

The problem with pain and pain relief is that once we have learned that certain chemicals or experiences reduce pain, there is a natural tendency to seek other methods of relief. The body is a wonderful manufacturer of pain-relief drugs, but the inherent design is to limit production of such drugs in order to protect the long-term viability of the body. When cultural imperatives against the need to experience pain are added to the mix, it is not unexpected that people who work in potentially painful environments will actively seek pain relief. Manufactured-drug usage is relatively high amongst humanitarian workers, especially in emergency relief situations. Most usage is not at very high levels, but many humanitarian workers regularly consume legal over-the-counter medications for minor pain relief or to assist in sleeping. Prescription pain and sleep medications are also popular, and anecdotal evidence and personal observation confirm that alcohol and marijuana consumption is higher than anyone would wish in the aid community.

It is interesting to observe, however, that despite the apparently quite high levels of self-medication amongst international aid workers, incidences of significant drug abuse or addiction appear to be very low. Recent research indicates that aid workers are generally very good at looking after their personal health, and it may be that use of legal and illegal drugs by humanitarian workers is self-controlled.

There is still not enough research evidence to be conclusive however.

Testosterone and Progesterone Production

When one's life is under ongoing threat, the desire or practicality of sexual reproduction moves far down the list of priorities. The physiological imperative to reproduce is very strong and is in part maintained through production of testosterone in men and progesterone in women. In times of stress, however, production of these hormones is reduced, or in extreme situations, even halted. While reduction in the desire for sexual intercourse may seem to be marginal among concerns for good health in areas of humanitarian crisis, there are implications, both for those who have sexual partners and those who do not.

Reduction in hormone production in women can significantly affect the ovulation cycle. Evidence suggests that regular periods contribute to reduction in cancer risk and that early onset menopause may bring increased cancer risk. Long-time single female aid workers sometimes speak with relief of lowered libido and reduction in the intensity of periods. While this may appear to be a positive occurrence, if a significant physical change is occurring at an early age, it would be wise to have a professional checkup to prevent permanent damage.

Often production of sex hormones is the first hormonal effect to occur and may be the last to recover. Highly stressful situations are necessary to produce endorphin highs, but chronic weariness is sufficient to reduce libido. Many emergency relief workers are chronically tired, even if they refuse to acknowledge being stressed. Being tired is certainly reason enough not to be interested in sex, but if lack of interest continues, it may be connected to reduced sex-hormone production due to stress. Veteran fieldworkers often ascribe lowered sexual drive to age. However, evidence is fairly conclusive that age itself has very little to do with libido levels. Rest and relaxation (the so-called cruise remedy) has been shown to be quite effective in restoring testosterone and progesterone levels – even for couples in their 70s.

While some may argue that reduction in testosterone levels in some male humanitarian workers may be a pleasant relief, there are down sides. Apart from the physiological impact of lowered hormone levels, reduction in libido for both men and women can significantly affect their relationships. We shall see later in this book that social support and family relationships are the most protective factors for humanitarian workers. Sexual dysfunction because of lowered hormonal levels as a result of stress will almost always negatively affect the ability of a social network to provide support.

This book intentionally focuses on personal stress management skills. However, it is worth noting here that a change in behaviour or physical functioning in almost any area should be a signal to a relief worker that it is time to assess the level of stress being experienced. In this instance the key factor to be aware of is the extent of change from previous behaviour. Generally, hormones associated with sex are produced at very constant rates once puberty is complete and prior to menopause for women. All things being equal (excluding major illness or disabilities), people should retain relatively constant levels of libido throughout life. Significant changes, especially chronic ones, are indicators that something may be wrong. For humanitarian workers these indicators point to stress levels that have become chronic. It is time to reduce stress.

Increased Acuity in the Senses

This has already been referred to in sections above, but because this consequence of stress is so obvious, and apparently so beneficial, it merits a section of its own.

Naturally, an increase of the ability of the senses to function at a higher level is a result of the increases in hormones and blood flow brought about by the onset of stress. The first impact is that the brain is able to concentrate much more closely and intently, and for longer periods. The ability to multi-task increases markedly, and juggling many responsibilities at once becomes easier. This author's personal experience of war zones on a number of occasions can be typified by one memorable morning. With mortar attacks in the distance and a rebel advance on the outskirts of town, the project manager was observed using three VHF radios, two cell phones and a UHF radio all at once – while leading a grant-proposal-writing meeting. Not only was the manager performing all these tasks at once, but no one in the room noticed anything out of the ordinary until some weeks later, when the pressure was off and the team was sitting around a local bar laughing about the incident.

On other occasions, after departing conflict zones, it has been the author's experience (confirmed by others) that those in the same agency who were not in the war environment, appear to be moving as slow as snails, not able to make a decision quickly enough, and seem generally lacking in awareness of what is going on. Most often, a couple of good nights' sleep and leisurely breakfasts result in more matched "speeds", but the experience can be disconcerting.

Physically the senses of hearing, eyesight, touch, taste and smell are enhanced. This is why memories of these events are often so clear and why, unlike more general experiences, such memories can seem to be three-dimensional, almost like being there again. Any experienced fieldworker can bring to mind any one of a number of times when the air seems crystal clear; the smoke from fires is still in the nostrils; and the sound of horses, motorcycles, or wood-chopping echoes in the ears, or perhaps the soft crump of artillery drawing closer through the trees. Such experiences are so profoundly alive that all others sometimes seem lifeless and of less value.

Another side effect of such enhancement is increased incidences of vivid dreaming about these events. Severely traumatised persons often experience recurring nightmares of traumatic events, to the point where the dream may replicate, or even exceed, the initial incident. Sometimes memory of the event can be so intrusive that a daytime "flashback" can occur. This very vivid "waking dream" can be extremely disconcerting. Triggers for such experiences may be as simple as a smell or noise. Any person who experiences flashbacks or recurring nightmares long after the actual incident should seek professional assistance.

There are other drawbacks to increased acuity. Increased acuity actually places the senses under enormous pressure, and eventually they become less efficient. People can actually lose their sense of smell, taste can diminish, and hearing loss may occur. The sense of touch can also be affected so that actual physical contact is not felt. While under stress, enhanced muscular power is matched by significant loss of fine motor control. It may be possible to run faster and lift heavier loads, but the ability to drive well or handle sensitive equipment is diminished. Under stress, people often drop objects or fail to see items directly in front of them. Enhanced ability to sense potential danger is matched by a very sharp focus. Unfortunately, this results in lack of awareness of other things occurring in the situation and can lead to serious mistakes.

While the ability to act in the present is enhanced, there may be loss of memory functioning, and, because of this, group decision-making capacity is generally reduced. In a time of crisis, it is possible to observe a highly stressed group moving about rapidly, holding short and intense conversations, taking actions, but not being particularly effective in attaining objectives. Emergency relief programmes in highly stressful environments are often characterised by intense activity, occupying most hours of the day and night. However, objective analysis of outcomes tends to indicate that within a very short time frame (less than a week) such activity is not achieving objectives and may even be adding to the problems. It is generally much more effective for a front-line relief team to restrict activity to more realistic hours following the first week at the crisis site.

Summary

International aid workers need to be constantly aware of the state of their physical health. It is strongly recommended that for front-line fieldworkers, a full physical checkup be conducted on an annual basis. Workers should be monitoring themselves for signs of changes in physical condition and ability. These changes may be indicators of potentially serious hormonal or physical conditions. Many relief workers attribute changes to frequent relocations, jet lag, difficult living or sleeping conditions or environmental challenges such as heat or cold. While this may be accurate, such a lifestyle will increase overall stress levels, with all the potential consequences described above.

Employing agencies must not leave the task of regular medical checks to individual staff. One of the direct consequences of stress is, over time, diminished ability to make accurate and objective decisions. When this result is coupled with the very strong personal motives for entering this work in the first place, it is hardly surprising that humanitarian workers often view the action of sacrificing themselves for the sake of the mission as an honourable and acceptable price. Employers need to see this attitude for what it really is – a sign of stress-related poor judgement. Therefore, employers must create a set of protocols and policies that will ensure all staff have regular medical assessments on at least an annual basis. One way to accomplish this would be to attach such a process to the annual performance assessment conducted in most organisations. Proof of the medical assessment (though obviously, for confidentiality, not the contents of the assessment) would need to be furnished by the employee to complete the performance-assessment process. A further step could be to require the medical specialist to make a formal recommendation on whether an employee is fit for front-line fieldwork or not.

Care and support of individuals is a joint responsibility for both employer and employee. But the agency bears the greater responsibility. Apart from documented evidence that high stress affects individual ability to make good decisions, field staff are an aid agency's only real assets. Often organisations make the mistake of assuming that money in the bank or a fleet of vehicles or other property makes up its assets. But these things can be easily replaced. Staff, on the other hand, determine the success or failure of any relief or development initiative. Staff are the only asset of sustainable value, and it is therefore essential that employers take primary responsibility for ensuring that staff are kept healthy and functioning.

Gerald lives in Pristina, Kosovo, but would prefer to be permanently in the smaller town his project operates from, on the border about 50 km up the road. For safety reasons his NGO won't let him, but whenever he can, he sneaks out of the office and drives up the road past the burnt-out tanks and troop carriers, past the NATO checkpoints and into the town, a town on the edge of hell. His room overlooks a pleasant green field, which ends in pretty forests bursting with spring growth. The forest runs up a slight hill. From the top of the hill snipers occasionally fire down into the streets. Gerald's window is plainly visible from the hill top, but he prefers the relative quietness of this place over the craziness of Pristina. He also has links with this town. One day some months ago a Serbian tank rolled over a mother and daughter in the street. Gerald helped scrape up the remains with a spade and assisted in laying out the bodies in a local warehouse until the family could take them for burial. He says the bodies were so flat they were easy to move, once they were detached from the road, that is. In the local school, where he sometimes helps out, Gerald has had many discussions, some quite animated, with the teacher who refuses to remove the extensive bloodstains from the classroom walls. Pitted with bullet holes, the walls are streaked with dark stains. Teaching occurs every day, and the teacher insists that the pupils, most of whom are younger than 10, should be daily reminded of the atrocities committed on their fathers and uncles and brothers. On weekends Gerald likes nothing better than to gather together groups of these children and, with a colleague, drive his Land Cruiser up into the achingly beautiful hills where they play for hours in mountain streams and sleep in the long grass. Gerald's colleagues often refer to him as being somewhat "strange" and detached, not really a mixer, a loner. He says that he is alive.

—GERALD, FROM THE UK, WORKING IN KOSOVO IN 2000

Note

[1] S. E. Taylor, et. al., "Female Responses to Stress: Tend-and-Befriend, Not Fight-or-Flight," *Psychological Review* 107/3 (2000): 411–29.

Part II

Studies of stress in humanitarian work

chapter 3

Preventing trauma in traumatic environments

GRAHAM FAWCETT

Introduction

It seems entirely possible that the potential and serious psychological effects of traumatic episodes among aid workers may be largely mitigated or fully prevented. There is recent evidence that, indeed, substantial numbers of those who experience trauma actually grow psychologically as a consequence. Mitigation, prevention and growth are accomplished by focusing on organisations' efforts in selection, training and team building of aid workers. Such an approach reduces stress levels and also promotes the general health, effectiveness and productivity of teams working in highly stressful situations.

Graham Fawcett is a clinical psychologist who has served with Youth with a Mission UK and Ireland since 1989. He has co-chaired YWAM UK's public policy group since 2000. Also serving on the boards of Tear Fund UK and Inter-health, he has developed a keen interest in how people can flourish in stressful and traumatic settings. He has consulted to World Vision since 2001 in organizational stress management. Fawcett lives and works within a YWAM community in England with his wife, Janet, and son, Samuel.

The model he describes in this chapter emerged from a meeting commissioned by World Vision in October 2000 and has been developed further since then. Fawcett wishes to express his gratitude for the valuable input of John Fawcett, Bev Irwin, Hector Jalipa, Nicole Kamaleson, Lincoln Ndgoni and Janelle Richards, together with many hundreds of World Vision staff who have given up valuable time to engage with and, it is to be hoped, benefit from the implications of the model.

John Fawcett argues that scarce funds should be committed to field support and to reducing stress levels, because preventing traumatic injury is considerably cheaper than treating the impact of trauma.[1] He also notes that professional staff are a growing scarce commodity (due to increasing demand for their services by an ever-increasing number of NGOs and governmental agencies) and that no NGO can afford to lose staff through preventable causes.

For a Christian agency such as World Vision International there is the additional biblical imperative of honouring staff as people made in the image of God and therefore seeking to ensure the best possible pastoral care. Many agencies operationalise this through signing up to Codes of Best Practice such as those represented by the International Committee of the Red Cross Code of Conduct and the People in Aid Code of Best Practice in the United Kingdom.

Fawcett goes on to note the inherent assumption that the psychological needs of expatriate and local staff are similar following a traumatic incident, and that talk therapy is assumed to be the best means of meeting their psychological needs. In light of work by D. Summerfield and by G. Fawcett, it seems improbable that Western talk therapy methods are relevant to non-Western populations.[2] However it appears quite possible that methods of preventing stress in the first place would be more universally relevant.

The Common-Sense View of Stress

The common-sense view of stress is that shown in Figure 3–1. Broadly speaking, the health, effectiveness and productivity of a team are seen to be outcomes of the external stressors and strains that a team is under. Should those stressors, in the guise of a traumatic event, be severe or overwhelming, then the team's overall ability to function at any level may be compromised or eliminated. To outline the most credible literature to date, there are two possible incapacitating reactions to extreme stressors recognised internationally – an

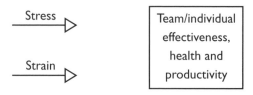

Figure 3-1

Acute Stress Reaction (ASR) or Combat Stress Reaction (CSR) lasting up to a month (Appendix A) and Post Traumatic Stress Disorder (Appendix B) with the same symptomatology but lasting longer than one month. Handled correctly, the majority of cases of ASR are considered self-limiting. Significant loss of day-to-day functioning may be experienced. The most productive form of treatment to date is Critical Incident Stress Debriefing (CISD) whilst remaining at or near the site of the trauma and, for aid workers, remaining actively engaged in their day-to-day duties. PTSD is regarded as a more chronic and treatment-resistant psychiatric problem, which requires removal from active duty not merely from the particular project but from any future situation in which chronic stress or traumatic stress is a possible feature.

Bowman demonstrates that a traumatic event, per se, does not account fully for why some people go on to become traumatised.[3] Her conclusion is that as little as 9 per cent of the variance between those experiencing a traumatic reaction following a critical incident and those who do not experience a traumatic event is due to the event itself. Put another way, Busuttil states that only 25 – 52 per cent of people experiencing trauma will go on to develop PTSD.[4]

Understanding, prevention and treatment of extreme stress reactions have been researched extensively by military psychologists. A summary of the findings is outlined by Noy in a review of the publicly available literature.[5] He concludes that when soldiers' resources are depleted due to prolonged exposure to intensive threat and stressors, and when the social support network, unit leadership and cohesion have all collapsed, then the risk of CSR increases. The severity of CSR varies with the type of stressor:

Intensive condensed stressors coupled with team collapse are associated with high rates of CSR. Given the military nature of the literature, it is unlikely that aid workers will be exposed to the very extreme stressors implied by the term 'intensive condensed stressors'.

Prolonged moderate stress is associated with a smaller number of CSR referrals. Somatic symptoms predominate, including difficulty in sleeping, irritability, poor concentration, hyper vigilance, exaggerated startle response and motor restlessness.

This intermediate stress tends to lead to fatigue and to removal from the field for somatic reasons.

Sporadic stressors lead to the least CSR casualties and tends to precede behaviour disorders, disciplinary cases and administrative removals.

Secondary stressors and strain factors include dehydration in hot climates, hypothermia in cold climates, physical exertion, sleeplessness, poor diet, lack of communication and lack of support from loved ones. These secondary stressors have been well researched in a correlational study by Eriksson and colleagues linking stressors to burnout and depression.[6] The study corresponded with the findings of Noy regarding reported stressors. Additional stressors reported by a majority of international aid workers in the study included team conflict (53 per cent) and feeling powerless to change the situation (52 per cent). Separation from loved ones was reported by 68 per cent of participants in the study.

Prevailing stressor levels as measured by recent life events are considered to account for less than 10 per cent of the variance between those who experience PTSD and those who do not.

The conclusion, therefore, is that acute and intense stressor levels do affect the overall level of stress reactions, but that they are a poor predictor of which particular individuals and which particular teams will experience either ASR or PTSD. Busuttil points out that moderate levels of PTSD may relate to low levels of exposure to traumatic situations as well, and asks whether simply "being there" is enough to put some people at risk.[7] He does not offer any defining variables for that subgroup, but it is likely that the factors outlined below would identify such a population.

Behavioural Approaches to Stress

Busuttil has outlined the case for a behavioural approach to the issue (Figure 3–2).[8] Behavioural approaches include stress-related behaviour as the critical measure of the effects of trauma, rather than more general measures of health and team effectiveness. For the purposes of the behavioural approach, it is these stress-related behaviours which may then be modified to ameliorate the effects of the stressors. Whilst Busuttil can find little evidence to support the effectiveness of this approach, the indicator of stress related behaviour is retained in the current model as a more direct measure of levels of stress in the team and their impact on the general health, effectiveness and productivity of the team.

FIGURE 3-2

Stress-related behaviour ranges in intensity from anxiety-related behaviour (such as sleeplessness, loss of appetite, feeling anxious) through to PTSD or ASR.

Coping Strategies

CISD aside, the psychological literature pertaining to stress management is well developed and focuses on coping strategies. These are defined as cognitive or behavioural responses taken to reduce or eliminate psychological distress or stressful conditions.[9] Most approaches deal with strategies oriented to approaching and confronting the problems and strategies oriented to avoiding directly dealing with the problems. Approach strategies include problem solving, information seeking, negotiation and optimistic comparisons associated with improved outcome. Avoidance strategies include denial and withdrawal associated with psychological distress, particularly beyond the initial crisis period. (Figure 3–3).

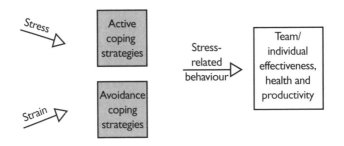

FIGURE 3-3

Eriksson's study suggests a portfolio of approaches to positive health as a way of ameliorating stress-related behaviours. These include abstaining from smoking and drinking alcohol, low intake of caffeine, seven hours of sleep per night, and exercise. These mechanisms do serve as protective mechanisms in chronically stressful situations and can be both selected for and also trained up within a management framework.[10]

The significance of religious coping or spirituality is poorly researched, and no reliable literature exists on the impact of religiosity on symptomatology during or following a traumatic event. This is extraordinary given the findings of Eriksson's study that 75 per cent of participants reported that they put their trust in God, seek God's help, find comfort in religion and pray more than usual during stressful experiences.[11] Presumably the participants are finding some utility in religious behaviour, even if the literature by and large discounts this behaviour as unworthy of consideration.

Resilience

The concept of resilience has been posited as a partial explanatory variable for who does and who does not experience PTSD and other stress reactions. Rutter has defined resilience as people's genetic makeup which in part creates the environment they experience.[12] From that perspective, people both select environments and shape them.

Resilience is a combination of protective factors and interactive processes. Protective factors refer to influences that modify, ameliorate or alter a person's response to some environmental hazard that predisposes to a maladaptive outcome. It is not necessarily synonymous with a positive or beneficial experience. For example, a particularly hazardous experience may toughen an individual. Interactive factors are the notion that any factor on its own may not have an effect on psychiatric risk, but that psychiatric risk rises sharply when several adversities co-exist (Figure 3–4).

John Fawcett points out that resilience literature is beginning to hint that prolonged exposure to trauma may not increase general resilience, as has been thought, but rather may lead to people becoming more vulnerable to the development of traumatic symptoms.[13]

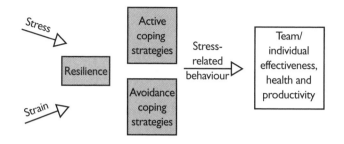

FIGURE 3-4

Resilience and Past Mental Health

Past mental health problems almost certainly contribute to decreasing the resilience of individuals. Protective selection criteria are reported in the literature in a very narrow way, and it may be that recommendations will settle down to a more realistic level after further study. Currently, the advice being given on the basis of the available literature to reduce the risk of PTSD is to reject anyone who has any history of any mental illness whatsoever[14]. Those with a history of PTSD, even in remission, are considered particularly vulnerable. These recommendations are now publicly available, and it is for individual agencies and team leaders to decide whether, or to what extent, to abide by them. This is significant for World Vision staff, with the Eriksson study reporting 85 per cent of World Vision participants reporting personal exposure to trauma.[15]

It seems likely that these recommendations will be modified in the future. They are too broad and are currently based on simple correlations between crude, global diagnoses (depression, eating disorder) and the incidence of PTSD. In time, more helpful criteria will probably be generated which will more precisely take account of what it is within a history of mental illness that makes people vulnerable to PTSD. In the meantime, assessment by a mental health professional is essential for those at high risk of encountering trauma who also have any history of mental health problems.

Youth with a Mission UK has adopted less rigorous selection criteria, as follows:

1. No history of any psychotic disorder (e.g. schizophrenia, manic depression). Family history is queried.
2. No episodes of depression or anxiety within the previous two years. Candidates should have been off all medication and out of counselling or therapy for a period of two years.
3. No history of eating disorders within the previous five years.
4. No history of any PTSD or ASR.

The risk arises of applicants faking on the medical sections of their applications in order to enhance their chances of acceptance. Anecdotally, the author has evidence of this occurring. Three issues arise. The first, and least relevant, is that of agency vulnerability to litigation. The organisational stress management literature currently reads that prior mental health problems increase the likelihood of PTSD or ASR. Not to screen for those or at least inform the candidate of the risks leaves the agency open to potential litigation for negligence. For those agencies adopting a human resource (HR) approach to selection, the issue is one of cross-checking information received and ensuring that candidates' medical histories are confirmed with respect to prior psychiatric conditions. This is unlikely to succeed fully. Candidates may not have presented their difficulties formally for medical assistance; there may be no psychiatric or counselling systems to report difficulties to (due in some counties to scarcity of resources or, indeed, the perceived irrelevance of some stress reactions). There will be creative HR responses to these issues aimed primarily at candidate safety, recognising that candidates in aid work are often highly motivated to help others with scant regard to their own health and safety.

Many faith agencies will adopt a more cooperative approach, seeing selection of a candidate as a partnership comprising the candidate, the agency and, if applicable, the sending church and the candidate's supporters.[16] To that end, the issue is less whether candidates are "up" to the job, but rather whether the community within which candidates have their roots are in agreement with their application.

Resilience and Personality

Personality, as measured by standardised tests, does not predict vulnerability to PTSD or ASR and, as such, is not considered a component of resilience. However, Busuttil has suggested that resilient people may, in fact, avoid combat or front-line tasks in the military through certain personality traits such as higher levels of assertiveness and social competence, which is suggestive of similar behaviour in aid workers with respect to potentially hazardous duties.[17]

Resilience and Information Processing

A further possible component of resilience lies with the information-processing theory of PTSD. This is strongly suggestive of otherwise normally functioning people experiencing a traumatic episode which overwhelms their capacity to process the incoming information. Horowitz suggests that active memory storage has an intrinsic tendency towards repeated representations of its content and that this tendency continues indefinitely until the storage of the particular contents in active memory is terminated.[18] The termination of active contents in active memory occurs when cognitive processing has been completed; in effect, active memory contents follow an automatic "completion" tendency. This is the key theory underlying much of CISD.

Assuming that a major factor in the onset of PTSD is cognitive overload, then any way of reducing that load will facilitate processing of information. To that end, practising and rehearsing routine tasks which are likely to accompany a traumatic event will mean that the novelty of those tasks will diminish and they will become more or less routine and automatic. As a consequence, the amount of cognitive effort required to carry out the tasks will be markedly diminished. This will leave more processing capacity for other aspects of the traumatic event and may mean that emotional and cognitive reconciliation processes are less likely to become "stuck".

In a key development of his theory Horowitz identifies key components of what may "block" the information processing of events in general and traumatic events in particular. He emphasises personal cognitive style, patterns of conflict, and avoiding and coping mechanisms.[19]

The following examples of cognitive styles that increase the probability levels of a stress reaction are taken from reports by aid workers during debriefing with the author:

- Irrational but enduring attitudes such as "wishing makes it so", or "one must always be loved by another in order to survive". For example, an aid worker may have the underlying motivation of helping others in order to feel loved; the very rebels she is trying to help attack and kill colleagues, and she is left with the extreme dissonance of not being loved by the very people she was trying to be loved by.
- Incompatible sets of wishes and values whose content is associatively similar to the traumatic event that has been experienced. For example, an aid worker may have a heightened sense of justice and be working with an internally displaced population (IDP). Despite their best efforts, the IDPs remain starving and homeless so the government may make a political point. These

entirely preventable deaths result in traumatisation for the aid worker unable to reconcile her passionate need for justice with the helplessness she feels.

- Habitual use of information-distorting control processes that lead to pathological defences such as projection, splitting, or extreme repression. Front-line aid workers dealing with acute relief situations often report for debriefing with a breathtakingly relaxed attitude towards the horrors they have encountered and seem hardened to the reality of what they saw. They may claim that they have to become immune to the horror in order to "do the job". In fact, they may be merely putting off the inevitable confrontation with the horror they have experienced. This avoidance can lead to pathological behaviours such as drug abuse, aggression, nightmares, and so on and interfere substantially with resolution of their thoughts and feelings.

- Excessive preoccupation with fantasy-based reparations of defences. For example, staff who witness the deaths or injury of colleagues or beneficiaries may become preoccupied with fantasies of revenge by themselves or by powerful proxies. These fantasies become ever more fantastic and vivid, and disable the cognitive processing necessary to resolve the trauma.

- Self-concept that views the self as bad, damaged, worthless or incompetent. Rare amongst aid workers who make it to the field is the personality that is fundamentally flawed and unable to help others, since the sense of self is so compromised. Less rare are personalities seeking to help others due to unresolved issues of receiving insufficient nurturance themselves, those looking to help others in order to build a sense of worth, and those overcompensating for their own sense of incompetence. Such candidates are often weeded out at the interview stage or psychiatric evaluation stage, but some do get through. When a traumatic event is

encountered, their lack of self-worth may lead to a
sense of helplessness or a neurotic sense of validation;
for example, "bad things happen to me and I deserve
them. . . . Being held by rebels was God's punishment
for my past bad deeds".

Resilience and Social Support

Currently the best available definition of resilience is that
offered by Saigh and Bremner.[20] Using structural equation
modelling, the authors identify resilience for men and
women as hardiness, functional social support and successfully negotiated stressful life events. In addition, men need
structural social support. Other studies reported by Saigh
are strongly suggestive of the necessity of family cohesion
and satisfaction with social support. Taken together, these
factors distinguish PTSD cases from non-PTSD cases.

Social support is central to the understanding of traumatic
stress prevention. There are two forms, structural support
and functional support.

Structural social support relates to the size of the friendship network, together with its density and interconnectedness. These influence the impact that social interac-
tions have on network members in well documented domains
of physical and mental health. The size of the network is of
less importance than its density and interconnectedness –
that is, the extent to which several people in an individual's
network also know one another.

By contrast, functional support specifies aspects of social
support that are beneficial to individuals. These include
attachment, social integration, opportunity for nurturance,
reassurance of worth, sense of reliable alliance and guidance.

Differences between the approaches may be gender
specific in part.[21] Male networks tend to foster increased
risk-taking and instrumental problem solving. Female
networks tend to emphasise emotional support and information exchange.

In defining resilience in this fashion, Saigh and Bremner move away from defining it in purely personal terms; they define *resilience* as individual characteristics embedded in a social framework. In general, however, the mechanisms and dynamics pertain either to an individual's ability to cope or to some measure of the intensity of a stressful incident and its duration. The joint predictive ability of these factors is helpful but unable to account fully for the overall phenomena of ASR/PTSD.

The overall thrust of the current literature is that, whilst the factors above are components of any understanding of stress reduction, the greatest percentage of the variance between those experiencing and not experiencing a severe stress reaction is accounted for by psycho-social variables.

Social Support Factors

Both Green and colleagues and Rutter make much the same point.[22] For Green, psycho-social approaches place much emphasis on the interaction among traumatic experience, the individual's characteristics and the environment. The process of the event takes place in an individual and a social context and is an interactive process. Environmental concerns include social support, protectiveness of family and friends, attitudes of society, intactness of the community and cultural characteristics.

Rutter further points out that a person's response to any stressor will be influenced by his or her appraisal of the situation and capacity to process the experience, attach meaning to it and incorporate it into the individual's belief system.[23]

Janoff Bulman follows through on Rutter's thesis and outlines three fundamental assumptions that she asserts people believe about the world in which they live:

1. Personal invulnerability, less likely to become ill, etc.

2. Perception of the world as meaningful; the world is orderly, comprehensible, predictable and controllable. Decent people who are appropriately cautious do not understand why this has happened to them specifically.
3. Perception of oneself as positive. Most believe they are worthy decent people. They have relatively high levels of self-esteem.[24]

Bulman suggests that intense trauma shatters these assumptions. This leads to a negative self-image dominated by a self-perception of being weak, helpless or needy, feeling frightened and out of control. All this, in turn, leads to a loss of self-esteem. She goes on to suggest the need to redefine the event, to find meaning and change behaviour from a victim mentality.

Lovell has found some experimental evidence to support the ideas of Janoff Bulman amongst aid workers who were also Christian.[25] His work suggests that workers who have rigidly held beliefs are particularly vulnerable to experiencing a fundamental shattering of their belief structure after a traumatic experience and then going on to experience a loss of self-esteem. Graham Fawcett suggests that Christians with rigidly held beliefs relating to the efficacy or prayer and the sovereignty of God are particularly vulnerable to a shattering of their belief structure.[26] John Fawcett points out that this may then lead to accusations of sin or faithlessness in conservative Christian circles, thus adding to the individual's sense of psychological pressure.[27]

In an extension of the Janoff-Bulman line of reasoning John Fawcett reports the work of Higgins which suggests that resilience is a function of a person's strength of "faith" in self, the goodness of people, the goodness of God, the future and a sustaining religion.[28] As such, faith needs to be separated from religiosity when considering resilience as a protective mechanism against psychological damage following trauma.

Barrett and Mizes demonstrate that social support accounts for about 33 per cent of the variance between those experiencing PTSD and those who do not.[29] It is clear that social factors play a major part in determining stress reaction vulnerability to traumatic events (Figure 3–5).[30]

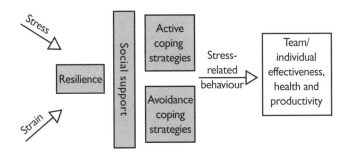

FIGURE 3-5

The military literature identifies two critical aspects of social support – team cohesion and consultative leadership style.

Team cohesion can be described loosely as the ability of a team to give and receive affection amongst its members. It has been defined more formally by military psychologists as the bonding together of soldiers (aid workers) in such a way as to sustain their will and commitment to one another, the unit (team) and mission (project) despite combat (project) stress. Alternatively, the thing that enables a person to keep going in the face of danger is the near presence or presumed presence of a comrade.[31]

Cohesion is facilitated by a common social background, shared experiences which become the glue holding the work group together (leaders need to be involved as well), confidence in the ability and determination of leaders and peers to support group members during traumatic and difficult events, and a clear and meaningful group mission.

Consultative leadership style refers to those in charge needing to lead by example, that is, acting out the kind of responses that will safeguard both physical and mental health, such as calm responses. Team leaders need to maintain objectivity and discipline when dealing with those in their charge; that is, team members need to feel treated fairly, justly and reasonably. The team leader needs to know the team members personally – not intimately necessarily but certainly enough that the team members are more than just cogs in a machine. Those in charge need to be subject to the same adverse conditions as the people in their charge, both in the everyday activities of living as well as exposure to danger. Finally, the leaders must be willing to place the needs of their staff before their own needs.[32]

Trust in commanders is then defined as a function of professional capability or technical competence, credibility as source of information, together with the amount of care and attention paid to staff. Trust in leaders in peaceful situations is defined as belief in professional competence of the team leadership, belief in the credibility of the team leader, and the perception of how caring the team leader is. By contrast, in highly stressful (traumatic) situations, "good" leaders are defined by their competence.

One further factor is also important with respect to team leadership. The determinants of morale for a team include biological factors such as health, food (quality and quantity), rest, sleep, clean and dry clothes, shelter and washing facilities. However, this is measured not so much by the absolute level of these provisions but by the relative level. If everyone is in the same state, including the team leader, then the group is better able to bear the privations.

Social support may thus be expressed as a high level of unit cohesion and a high level of trust in effective leadership, which instigates a sense of optimism and hope for survival.

There is a negative relationship between level of morale and confidence in leadership before a traumatic episode and the resultant prevalence of ASR.[33] Noy summarises the military literature in strong terms: "The causation of CSR relates only to situational factors: battle stressors, unit cohesion and trust in the commander. Recovery relates mainly to personality variables and also to previous life events."[34]

By extension we can therefore conclude that the major factors that mitigate against the onset of ASR (and therefore PTSD) in aid workers are primarily team cohesion and well-defined attributes of team leaders. Although aid workers are exposed to significant stressors, which may include traumatic incidents, the intensity is different from soldiers in combat, and thus the absolute level of traumatic stressors may be of secondary importance.

Figure 3–5 summarises the complete picture. The health, effectiveness and productivity of a team is a direct function of stress-related behaviour. Stress-related behaviour is influenced by coping strategies which may reduce its incidence or maintain and possibly increase its incidence. Stressors and strain are experienced to the extent that social support is absent within a group of people with lessened resilience. Little social support and weakened resilience account for by far the greatest variance between those teams or individuals who experience PTSD or ASR and those who do not.

Post Traumatic Growth (PTG)

A recent stream of research is examining the phenomena of individual renewal and the rebirth of nations.[35] Possibly the most dramatic city-wide phenomenon of PTG has been the emergence of New York in the immediate aftermath of September 11 as a calmer, friendlier and less frenetic place to live.

A long-term process measured in decades, PTG is the phenomenon involving a proportion of those encountering and surviving trauma who go on to experience growth in their perception of self, interpersonal relations and philosophy of life. They cast themselves as survivors rather than as victims, and learn better how to be emotionally intimate with trusted others. They experience an enhanced sense of compassion as they recognise similar pain in others and empathise accordingly. Priorities change with the sense of being given a second chance and wanting to treat that gift with care. Fundamental existential questions cease being academic or trivial and are faced more honestly, though not necessarily resolved. Many report a sense of spiritual development, a sense of a greater connectedness to the transcendent, and a greater appreciation and commitment for their chosen religious tradition or beliefs.

How to enhance the possibility of PTG is the subject of complex, continuing research.[36] Strongly implicated are the survivor's social and family support networks, community groups and resources and, finally, personal resilience. No studies have yet been conducted to determine the extent to which these factors contribute to the overall variance between those who experience PTG and those who do not. However, it is the author's hypothesis that the contribution of social support will be consistent with its contribution to preventing symptoms, and thus will be a significant contributing variable.

Implications

The following recommendations relate to selection, training and team building with respect to factors known to be protective of PTSD or ASR and enhancing of the possibility of PTG.

Selection

1. Standardised personality tests do not distinguish between PTSD-prone individuals and those who are not

prone. However, the use of tools such as Myers-Brigg or DISC would be useful as a means to enhance team cohesion.

2. A full psychiatric history, including that of the immediate family, is necessary. Indications of any psychotic episodes, eating disorders or recent depressive or anxiety-related disorders should be referred for psychiatric evaluation in the context of field placement. Presently the literature suggests that any previous history of PTSD or ASR should be regarded as an exclusion factor for any field placement where trauma is a significant possibility.

3. Through interview, the applicant can be assessed for evidence of coping skills and belief systems. The content of the belief system is less relevant for these purposes than the flexibility with which it is held.

4. The ability to secure and retain a good social support network (defined above) can be assessed using the tool in Appendix C of this chapter or through interview.

5. Life events in the year prior to applying should be audited using a standardised tool. At interview or as part of the paper application, candidates should be asked how they have handled these transitions successfully. Evidence of a lack of transition or a pattern of failing to handle life events successfully should be considered as partial grounds for excluding candidates.

6. Leaders require assessment in additional areas related to their consultative leadership style. In particular, they should be assessed on their competence relative to their team, rather than on an absolute level of competency. Team leaders should be perceived as more competent than their team in stressful times, an essential factor in credibility. Leaders should also have good relational skills as measured by their ability to get to know team members as people.

Training

1. Realistic professional training is the key element in enhancing people's information-processing capacity in crisis.

Such training gives individuals the chance to see what a situation is like and how they react. They gain an understanding of how to handle the relevant equipment in a variety of situations (for example, how to start the four-wheel drive in the dark, where the radio is kept, how to get into the safe for team funds). Particular cross-skill competencies are gained apart from the core competencies, for example, first aid, use of radio, driving, use of fire extinguishers, and so forth. Extensive use of simulations is suggested both as a way of skill enhancement and also as a way of building individuals' cognitive capacity to handle a traumatic incident.

2. Induction training should include orientation to adverse stressors and how to cope practically, emotionally, spiritually and physically. Such training would include an overview of the importance of team cohesion, morale and its components, coping strategies, leadership issues, security issues and relevant applied theologies of suffering to lay out a model of the environment World Vision is expecting as best practice.

Team Building

1. Team building aims to enhance group cohesion as one of the primary protective factors in preventing PTSD. To that end, simulations and exercises are powerful team building tools, provided they are conducted with the full participation of relevant team leaders.

2. During induction courses, significant time should be allocated to informal networking and relationship building.

3. Serving or working with a predictable and known group of people is demonstrably protective of PTSD. Aid workers in general and relief workers in particular have a very high turnover of colleagues, and it seems probable that this would heighten the risk of a stress reaction. Therefore consideration needs to be given to the formation of reasonably stable groups of workers for multiple tours of duty in relief work,

rather than the current practice of putting people together, more or less at random, for varying lengths of time in different projects, thus causing instability in the teams and significantly heightened vulnerability to PTSD.

In 1993 we were living in Phnom Penh, Cambodia. There was still a lot of violence in the country, and life was pretty dangerous at times. We were watching TV one night, some drama movie on satellite TV, and the movie was just at the point where the bad guy was going to be revealed through some piece of skilled detective work. So we were all sitting there, focused on the flickering screen. Just as the tension heightened, a gun battle broke out in the street outside our house. AK47's at first, then some heavy calibre 50mm stuff. We all leapt to our feet at once and dived straight for the remote control so we could turn the volume up and not miss the punch line of the movie. It was a little crazy. There were bullets bouncing off buildings and cars up and down the road, and here we were, anxious not to miss the last few lines of a movie. We did this kind of thing quite often really. At night, if there was shooting outside, we could just roll over, identify the type of gun, and then go back to sleep without a problem. We wondered, was this habituation? Or denial? Burnout? Or just plain old acceptance?

—EDDIE, FROM AUSTRALIA, WORKING IN CAMBODIA IN 1993

Appendix A: DSM-IV Criteria for PTSD

A. The person has been exposed to a traumatic event in which both of the following were present:

1. The person experienced, witnessed, or was confronted with an event or events that involved actual or threatened death or serious injury, or a threat to the physical integrity of self or others.
2. The person's response involved intense fear, helplessness or horror.

B. The traumatic event is persistently reexperienced.

C. The person must persistently avoid stimuli associated with the trauma or experience a numbing of general responsiveness not present before the trauma.

D. The person must experience persistent symptoms of increased arousal not present before the trauma

E. Symptoms must have lasted at least a month. The diagnosis is specified as acute if duration of the symptoms is less than three months and chronic if longer than three months. Delayed onset is specified if the onset of symptoms occurs at least six months after the stressor.

F. The disturbance causes clinically significant distress or impairment in social, occupational or other important areas of functioning.

Appendix B: Diagnostic Criteria for Acute Stress Disorder (DSM-IV)

A. The person has been exposed to a traumatic event in which both of the following were present:

1. The person experienced, witnessed, or was confronted with an event or events that involved actual or threatened death or serious injury, or a threat to the physical integrity of self or others.
2. The person's response involved intense fear, helplessness or horror.

B. Either while experiencing or after experiencing the distressing event, the individual has three or more of the following dissociative symptoms:

1. a subjective sense of numbing, detachment, or absence of emotional responsiveness
2. A reduction in awareness of his or her surroundings (e.g., "being in a daze")
3. de-realisation
4. de-personalisation
5. dissociative amnesia

C. The traumatic event is persistently reexperienced in at least one of the following ways: recurrent images, thoughts, dreams, illusions, flashback episodes, or a sense or reliving the experience; or distress on exposure to reminders of the traumatic event.

D. Marked avoidance of stimuli that arouse recollections of the trauma (e.g., thoughts, feelings, conversations, activities, places, people).

E. Marked symptoms of anxiety or increased arousal (e.g., difficulty sleeping, irritability, poor concentration, hypervigilance, exaggerated startle response, motor restlessness).

F. The disturbance causes clinically significant distress or impairment in social, occupational or other important areas of functioning or impairs the individual's ability to pursue some necessary task such as obtaining necessary assistance or mobilising personal resources by telling family members about the traumatic experience.

G. The disturbance lasts for a minimum of two days and occurs within four weeks of the traumatic event.

Appendix C:
Social Support Questionnaire (short form)

The SSQ is a guide rather than a standardised assessment tool. There are no norms available. The tool is used as an indication of the quality of social support for an individual and as a basis for discussion. The two parts of the scale (A and B) follow:

A. The number of available people the individual feels he or she can turn to in times of need in each of a variety of situations.

B. A listing of relationships held generally:

1. Whom can you really count on to distract you from your worries when you feel under stress?
2. Whom can you really count on to help you feel more relaxed when under pressure or tense?
3. Who accepts you totally, including your best and worst points?
4. Whom can you really count on to care about you regardless of what is happening to you?
5. Whom can you really count on to help you feel better when you are generally "down in the dumps"?
6. Whom can you really count on to console you when you are very upset?

The degree of satisfaction with the perceived support available in both parts may be measured on a five-point Likert scale using the poles "very dissatisfied" to "very satisfied" to indicate the individual's subjective evaluation of his or her social support.

Scores on both A and B are negatively correlated with depression and anxiety.
Scores on A are positively correlated with extroversion.
Scores on B are negatively correlated with neuroticism.[37]

Notes

1 John Fawcett, "Managing Staff Stress and Trauma," in *Complex Humanitarian Emergencies*, ed. M. Janz and J. Slead (Monrovia, Calif.: World Vision, 2000).

2 D. Summerfield, *The Impact of War and Atrocity on Civilian Populations*, Relief and Rehabilitation Network Paper 14 (London: ODI, 1996); G. Fawcett, reported in S. Cavill, "Psychology in Practice: Welfare of Refugees," an interview, *The Psychologist* (British Psychological Society) (2000): 13, 552–54.

3 Marilyn Bowman, *Individual Differences in Post Traumatic Response* (London: Laurence Erlbaum, 1997).

4 W. Busuttil, "Interventions in PTSS: Implications for Military and Emergency Service Organisations" (master's thesis, University of London, 1995).

5 S. Noy, "Combat Stress Reaction," in *Handbook of Military Psychology*, ed. R. Gal and A. D. Mangelsdorff (Chichester: John Wiley, 1991).

6 C. Eriksson et al., "WVI and Headington Program Occupational Stress and Trauma Assessment," paper to WVI (October 2001).

7 Busuttil, "Interventions in PTSS."

8 Ibid.

9 C. J. Holahan and R. H. Moos, "Life Stressors and Mental Health: Advances in Conceptualizing Stress Resistance," in *Stress and Mental Health: Contemporary Issues and Prospects for the Future*, ed. W. R. Avison and I. H. Gotlib (New York: Plenum, 1994).

10 Eriksson et al., "WVI and Headington Program Occupational Stress and Trauma Assessment."

11 Ibid.

12 M. Rutter. "Resilience in the Face of Adversity: Protective Factors and Resistance to Psychiatric Disorder, *British Journal of Psychiatry* (1985), 147, 598–611.

13 John Fawcett, "Managing Staff Stress and Trauma."

14 Graham Fawcett, *Ad-Mission: The Briefing and Debriefing of Teams of Missionaries and Aid Workers* (Great Britain: YWAM, 1999).

15 Eriksson et al., "WVI and Headington Program Occupational Stress and Trauma Assessment."

16 Implicitly the government of the candidate as well; governments are increasingly reluctant to be the health insurers of last resort (see Graham Fawcett, *Ad-Mission*). Chapter 2 has a fuller discussion of these points.

17 Busuttil, "Interventions in PTSS."

18 M. J. Horowitz, "Intrusive and Repetitive Thoughts After Experimental Stress, *Archives of General Psychiatry* 32 (1975): 1457–63.

19 Ibid.

[20] P. A. Saigh and J. D. Bremner, *Post Traumatic Stress Disorder* (Boston: Allyn and Bacon, 1999).

[21] R, H. Kaplan and S. L. Hartwell, "Differential Effects of Social Support and Social Networks on Psychological and Social Outcome in Men and Women with Type II Diabetes Mellitus," *Health Psychology* 6 (1987): 387–98.

[22] B. L. Green, J. P. Wilson and J. D. Lindy, "Conceptualizing Post Traumatic Stress Disorder: A Psycho Social Framework," in *Trauma and Its Wake*, vol. 1, *The Study and Treatment of Post-traumatic Stress Disorder*, ed. C. R. Figley (New York: Brunner/Mazel, 1985).

[23] Rutter, "Resilience in the Face of Adversity."

[24] R. Janoff Bulman, "The Aftermath of Victimisation: Rebuilding Shattered Assumptions," in Figley, *Trauma and Its Wake*, vol. 1, *The Study and Treatment of Post-traumatic Stress Disorder*.

[25] D. M. Lovell, *Psychological Adjustment Amongst Returned Overseas Aid Workers* (D.Clin.Psy. thesis, University of Wales, Bangor, 1997).

[26] Graham Fawcett, *Ad-Mission.*

[27] John Fawcett, "Managing Staff Stress and Trauma."

[28] G. Higgins, "Resilient Adults," *Overcoming a Cruel Past* (San Francisco: Jossey Bass, 1994).

[29] T. W. Barrett and J. S. Mizes, "Combat Level and Social Support in the Development of PTSD in Vietnam Veterans," *Behaviour Modification* 12 (1988): 100–115. Combat exposure accounted for 15– 20 per cent of the variance.

[30] The same study demonstrated that combat exposure accounted for less than 20 per cent of the variance.

[31] Gal and Mangelsdorff, *Handbook of Military Psychology.*

[32] Ibid.

[33] Noy, "Combat Stress Reaction."

[34] S. Noy, "Stress and Personality as Factors in the Causation and Prognosis of Combat Reaction," in Gal and Mangelsdorff, *Handbook of Military Psychology.*

[35] R. G. Tedeschi, C. L. Park and L. G. Calhoun, *Posttraumatic Growth* (Mahwah, N.J.: Laurence Erlbaum, 1998).

[36] J. A. Schaeffer and R. H. Moos, "The Context for PTG," in Tedeschi et al., *Posttraumatic Growth.*

[37] I. G. Sarason et al., "Social Support Questionnaire (Short Form)," in I. G. Sarason and G. R. Pierce, *Handbook of Social Support and the Family*, Plenum Series on Stress and Coping (New York: Plenum Publishers, 1996).

chapter 4

Occupational stress, trauma and adjustment in expatriate humanitarian aid workers

CYNTHIA B. ERIKSSON, JEFFREY BJORCK
AND ALEXIS ABERNETHY

Introduction

The environment of humanitarian aid, by definition, includes stressful experiences and exposure to traumatic life events. The purpose of a humanitarian mission is to facilitate relief and growth in areas of the world suffering from natural or human-made disasters. It is no surprise, therefore, that expatriate aid workers commonly confront devastating poverty, criminal violence, maltreatment, large-scale and small-scale natural disasters and war in a culture that is not their own. Researchers now identify humanitarian aid work as an occupation involving inherent risk of exposure to stress, traumatic events and the possible consequence of trauma-related psychological distress. Researchers and aid agencies are particularly interested in understanding the experience of staff in order to inform human-resource strategies in selection, training, ongoing staff support and emergency debriefing.

Cynthia B. Eriksson received her Ph.D. in clinical psychology from the Graduate School of Psychology at Fuller Theological Seminary in 1997. She is currently an assistant professor of psychology at Fuller and co-directs the Headington Program in International Trauma. She has participated in trauma training and research in

This chapter describes the assessment procedure and the results of the World Vision International – Headington Program Occupational Stress and Trauma Survey. World Vision International partnered with the Headington Program in the Graduate School of Psychology at Fuller Theological Seminary[1] to design an assessment to expand upon World Vision International's knowledge of current staff needs, experience of stressors and level of personal functioning. The information gathered was used to inform human-resource policy and undergird the agency's staff support programme. We believe that this information will also inform other NGOs as they seek to address the needs of both expatriate and national staff.

The following is a common story:

> Robert is a project manager who has worked with World Vision for eight years. He is married and has one son, who is five years old. Robert's wife and extended family are happy that he works for World Vision; however, his wife is saddened by the travel

Liberia, Japan, Cambodia and the United States. Her research examining the traumatic exposure and reentry distress of international relief and development workers was published in the *Journal of Traumatic Stress*.

Jeffrey Bjorck is a licensed clinical psychologist, researcher and associate professor of psychology. Since receiving his Ph.D. from the University of Delaware in 1991, he has served on the faculty of Fuller Seminary's School of Psychology. Bjorck's published works include empirical journal articles on stress, faith and coping.

Alexis Abernethy, associate professor of psychology at Fuller Theological Seminary, is known for her expertise in the relationship between health-related outcomes and spirituality. In addition to her experience in teaching, consulting, service and administration, Abernethy has researched and published widely on cross-cultural competence, spirituality and health, cultural competency, anger management, religion and psychotherapy, and group dynamics. Abernethy holds a B.S. in psychology from Howard University and an M.A. and Ph.D. in clinical psychology from the University of California at Berkeley.

schedule his position requires. His job entails extended periods of separation, and the travel is often in areas of high security risk.

In his travels and project work Robert has come face to face with violence. Recently he was threatened by a group of men who accused him of showing political alliance to a rebel organisation because of the ethnic background of the recipients of the agricultural programme in the area. Robert's friendships with local staff have been rich and rewarding. However, his grief is great when he hears of these friends enduring physical harassment, burglary, threats and sometimes murder. He often finds questions about suffering and loss at the centre of his prayers to God.

Yet, with all of this human suffering, Robert's greatest stressor is his relationship with his immediate supervisor. The two men disagree on a few key issues of management and communication. Robert values autonomy in his planning, but his supervisor expects that decisions will be made in a group. While both men are Christians, they have had difficulty reconciling their differences in the work setting. Robert noticed that he has started to spend more time in travel. The travel keeps him autonomous but also keeps him apart from his family. This creates a difficult bind.[2]

Robert's story puts a human face on a number of critical findings from the World Vision International – Headington Program Occupational Stress and Trauma Survey. Separation from family due to work responsibilities was the most difficult stressor reported by participants. Staff also commonly reported experiences involving real suffering, violence and personal threat. In addition, the work environment itself was often a source of considerable stress. In contrast to the inevitable stress of living in a humanitarian aid environment, the research shows that organisations and agencies can mitigate a number of work-related stressors: (1) team conflicts; (2) lack of direction from management; (3) lack of recognition for work; (4) performance of tasks outside of one's training; and (5) criticism by authority figures who could not or did not act to better the situation themselves.

Staff participating in the assessment described both areas of stress and their current emotional functioning. Results of the assessment indicate that staff support is not a luxury that can be discarded. All of the participants were working in WVI offices around the world. One would assume that all were functioning adequately in their day-to-day lives, sufficiently to maintain a job and complete the interview. The vast majority of participants also reported strong spirituality and active lives of faith. However, when these men and women responded to specific questions about symptoms of depression, post-traumatic stress and burnout, 30 per cent to 50 per cent of them received scores indicating a moderate to severe level of emotional distress. These results demonstrate the strong motivation that pushes these staff to do their job and respond to the needs of the recipient community. The question raised by these findings is: Who responds to the aid worker's needs?

Published Research Background

To develop a clear and comprehensive assessment, the authors met with representatives of World Vision International to identify key areas of interest and need. In addition, published literature provided the foundation for a conceptual model that guided the assessment.

Only a small number of empirical research studies have been published identifying levels of exposure to trauma common among aid workers, as well as factors associated with emotional distress reported by staff. One study conducted in the late 1990s by Cynthia Eriksson surveyed

North American aid workers from five evangelical Christian aid agencies. The participants had recently returned from field locations, and the study identified a range of life-threatening events confronting aid workers directly or indirectly. The most common events staff workers faced were "being threatened with serious physical harm by someone"; "life-threatening illness or chronic condition"; "being within the range of gunfire, being shot at"; and "road accidents."[3] One-quarter to almost one-third of staff in this study had personal experience of these events. Several reported significant emotional distress related to PTSD. Approximately 10 per cent of the participants could be diagnosed with PTSD, and an additional 19 per cent reported clinically significant PTSD symptoms. Both personal and vicarious experience of life-threatening traumatic events was significantly related to the report of PTSD symptoms. In addition, participants' report of social support was found to buffer the experience of post-traumatic distress; staff with high levels of exposure and low social support reported higher levels of symptoms than those reporting high exposure and high social support.[4]

Another study by researchers from the Centers for Disease Control and Prevention assessed expatriate and national staff from several international aid agencies during their work in the complex humanitarian emergency in Kosovo. This study followed a rigorous epidemiological model of assessment, and researchers interviewed hundreds of aid workers. These staff reported a high percentage of traumatic stressors during their work, the most common including "a situation that was very frightening"; "verbal or physical threats to life"; "hostility of the local population"; "armed attack or robbery"; and "handling dead bodies."[5] This study also identified chronic stressors such as separation from family, lack of access to means of communication outside the field, inadequate living and working conditions, team conflicts, poor management and low pay for extremely difficult work. Participants in this study reported low levels of PTSD; only 2 per cent of expatriate and 7 per cent of national staff met diagnostic levels using a conservative measure of the disorder. However, aid staff did report high levels of depression, anxiety and alcohol use.[6] In addition, staff reporting exposure to more than 6 traumatic events were significantly more likely to report high levels of anxiety symptoms.

Conceptual Model

Understanding staff's experience and adjustment in traumatic environments requires a complex perspective that takes several variables into account. The studies described above demonstrate that there are aspects of the environment (the stressful event, the organisational culture) and aspects of a person's own history and choices (social support, coping strategies) that influence that person's well-being. The model below represents the theoretical framework guiding the WVI-Headington Program Occupational Stress and Trauma Assessment. The model emphasises the influence of environmental factors on staff adjustment. These variables may be altered by the individual or the organisation: practical health behaviours, spirituality, coping styles, social support and support from God. Staff's experience of their work environment is separated into work-related stressors and two aspects of WVI's organisational structure: (1) the ethos or culture of the organisation and (2) the staff's sense of support from the organisation (see Figure 4-1).

Lines and arrows connecting the groups of variables represent a hypothesised relationship where overall adjustment of staff is influenced by factors present before the work experience (background), by the experience of chronic and traumatic stress on the field, and mediated by organisational and individual resilience variables.

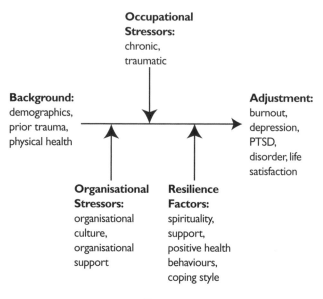

Occupational Stressors:
chronic, traumatic

Background:
demographics, prior trauma, physical health

Adjustment:
burnout, depression, PTSD, disorder, life satisfaction

Organisational Stressors:
organisational culture, organisational support

Resilience Factors:
spirituality, support, positive health behaviours, coping style

FIGURE 4-1

Survey Method and Participants

To reach as many expatriate staff as possible, the first set of survey questions was distributed as an e-mail attachment to all World Vision International middle-management staff in field locations. One hundred and one staff responded.[7] The e-mail survey included questions about types of chronic and traumatic stressors that staff experienced on their field locations.

The second phase of the survey included a more complex set of questionnaires that assessed several personal and organisational factors including health symptoms and behaviours, depression, coping, traumatic stress symptoms, social support and burnout. This survey was completed as a telephone interview. To attain a sample population as representative as possible, participants were randomly selected from the WVI staff list. Those randomly chosen received e-mails describing the research project and emphasising the organisational commitment to staff support. Several staff did not respond to the recruitment e-mails. It is not clear whether there were difficulties in receiving the e-mail message, or whether the staff member was too busy or disinclined to respond. Staff working in areas of high security risk had the lowest response rate (30 per cent). The urgent nature of high security relief and shorter project lengths may have contributed to this percentage. The response rate among staff working in areas of moderate security risk was 77 per cent; and 52 per cent of those working in a low security risk area responded positively to the recruitment e-mail. Among all the staff who responded to the recruitment e-mail, only 16 refused to participate (8 per cent of the recruited sample). Doctoral students in clinical psychology administered the telephone interview, which required approximately 60 to 90 minutes to complete.

The expatriate aid workers who responded to the e-mail survey and the telephone interview represented a wide range of cultural and ethnic backgrounds – 35 different countries of birth and 37 different first languages were represented. Almost half of the staff were Caucasian; one-third were black; one-sixth were Asian; and a small percentage represented mixed or other racial backgrounds. Two-thirds of participants were male, and one-third were female. The majority of staff were married; however, approximately 10 per cent were married but living apart from their spouse due to their work. The average age of staff participating in the e-mail survey and interview was 41. They had been working with World Vision an average of eight years. The group was highly educated; 45 per cent of participants held a master's degree.

Work Environment

Chronic and Traumatic Stressors

Typical humanitarian aid work sites are areas of multifaceted need. Whether that need results from a complex humanitarian emergency such as war or ethnic conflict, or from a natural disaster, the extent of damage, lack of resources and compromised infrastructure create a work environment rife with chronic stressors.

A list of common stressors was developed from published materials on stress and stress management for humanitarian aid workers.[8] Staff responded to this list according to whether they were currently experiencing the stressor, and if so, how much distress they felt in relation to the stressor. The list can be sorted into five conceptual categories (see Figure 4-2).

The sixteen situations described in the table were quite common; for each situation at least 75 per cent of the participants indicated that they were currently experiencing that stressor. Separation from family was the most commonly reported problematic stressor; almost 70 per cent indicated that they experienced moderate to extreme stress related to being separated from family due to work. Half of the staff participants expressed moderate to extreme stress related to (1) feeling powerless to change the external situation; (2) travel difficulties, threatening checkpoints, rough roads; and (3) conflicts between team members.

Many staff participants wrote in chronic stressors in their field environments that had not been included in the questionnaire. These responses centred on the following issues: (1) workload and deadline stress; (2) cultural tensions and language difficulties; (3) pressure and criticism by a funding source; (4) management difficulties (both being managed and managing others); and (5) local bureaucracy.

Unfortunately, many stressors mentioned in the survey may be impossible to change; these may represent the difficulty of the humanitarian aid environment. However, key situations related to organisational functioning might be more amenable to modification by the agency:

1. team member conflicts
2. lack of management direction

Interpersonal	Physical environment	Organisational	Community/host country	Existential
• Separation from family due to work responsibilities • Conflicts between team members	• Travel difficulties, threatening checkpoints, rough roads • Excessive heat, cold or noise • Shortages of resources • Housing/privacy problems • Vehicle mechanical problems	• Lack of direction from management • Lack of recognition for work • Being asked to perform duties that are outside one's professional training • Criticism of work by agency authorities	• Feeling hostility from the host country/environment • Being watched or under surveillance • Oppressive leadership in the community • Criticism of work by media or community members	• Feeling powerless to change the external situation

Figure 4-2

3. lack of recognition for work
4. tasks outside of professional training
5. criticism by agency authorities
6. workload and deadline stress
7. management difficulties

Aid agencies have an opportunity to benefit staff directly by paying renewed attention to these areas of management and staff relationships.

In addition to chronic environmental, social and organisational stressors, humanitarian aid workers may become direct or indirect targets of violence or trauma in their work. The survey of exposure to traumatic stressors was adapted from a similar study.[9] The original list of traumatic events was adapted from measures of community violence and war trauma exposure.[10] Participants were asked to indicate their experience of several possible events listed (for example, "being chased by a group or individual," "damage or loss due to natural disaster," or "life-threatening illness or limited access to medical care"). According to their reports, the three most common experiences of trauma are road accidents, being threatened with serious physical harm by someone, and being near gunfire. Six staff out of ten indicated that they had experienced a traumatic event firsthand in their current field location.

Perhaps one might assume that staff travelling to communities of need would be aware of the potential threat to their health and physical well-being. Assessing these risks must be part of the decision to work for an NGO. However, actually living through an event when one believes one's life will be lost is a qualitatively different experience from an intellectual awareness of risk. Facing the man with the knife or struggling with an illness in a community with no doctor makes the threat real. It is striking to note that one-quarter of staff completing the survey indicated that they had experienced at least one life-threatening experience during their current assignment.

Another significant challenge in humanitarian aid is indirect experience of trauma. The nature of the work requires repeated confrontation with suffering, violence and maltreatment that staff witness or hear about happening to someone they know and care about. These experiences of "secondary exposure" can have a profound effect on morale, worldview and emotional adjustment of staff. Almost nine out of ten participants in the e-mail survey indicated they had witnessed an event or heard about something traumatic happening to someone they knew personally during their current assignment. Many staff reported seeing mass graves in the communities where they work, as well as seeing children die due to maltreatment. In addition to the suffering inherent in the work of child advocacy, several expatriate staff identified the pain of watching national staff co-workers face painful tragedies: staff family members killed or abducted, illnesses and even the murder of national staff.

Organisational Culture

An important part of the work environment is the way an organisation creates its own internal culture of service and demonstrates whether support of staff is a valued component of policy. This organisational context can offer staff a network of practical support, as well as personal support, offering meaning and value to the work accomplished. Five survey questions were created based on hypothesised organisational factors associated with staff resilience and vulnerability.[11] Three statements queried staff experience of practical support: (1) WVI supports me; (2) WVI encourages me to use vacation and sick leave; and (3) WVI encourages me to work together with other NGOs. The remaining two statements offer a small glimpse into the "culture" of work and service within the organisation. They ask for responses to the following: (1) Programmes and Partnership policies are followed too rigidly; and (2) WVI values the number of people served at the expense of service quality.

World Vision staff completing the interview indicated a strong sense of support from the organisation. Almost 90 per cent agreed with the statement, "WVI supports me. " The vast majority of staff also felt encouraged to take appropriate leave time and to cooperate with other organisations. However, a little more than half agreed with the statements regarding the difficulty of following policy rigidly and valuing numbers over quality. One staff member wrote, "[There is] incongruence between professed institutional core values and actual practice."

Adequately assessing an organisation's culture is difficult, at best. Practical support demonstrated by encouragement to care for oneself and to work cooperatively is easily endorsed. It is more subjective to consider issues of unspoken culture. Perhaps the participant's statement above offers the organisation the most salient advice: to be very intentional about professed values and policies. Humanitarian aid workers must struggle with the meaning of suffering and injustice as they make choices about food distribution or medical supplies. When inevitable compromises must be made, the professed values and policies become a foundation (or at least a small rock) to stand on. At those moments, congruence between organisational practice and professed values becomes most critical. Core values represent the meaning behind the work. Congruence is the responsibility of every staff person but also of the organisation. Managers and administrators have a responsibility to be thoughtful and honest with the values expressed and the task of living out those values day after day.

Organisations with a professed Christian or faith-based value system face the challenge of avoiding hypocrisy. A staff member working in a region of the world that was not predominantly Christian commented about the need to balance Christian faith with professionalism. In this particular case, staff hired from the local area were not given opportunities for advancement or professional training if they were not professed Christians. This is a complicated example of organisational policies coming in conflict with a broader valuing of people.

Personal Background and Current Resources

In considering factors that may influence a staff person's experience of chronic and traumatic stress exposure inherent in aid work, one of the first issues is the individual's own life and background. Staff come to their work with their own history of experience, their own ways of choosing to cope with difficult experiences, and their own spirituality.

Prior Experience of Trauma

Prior experience of traumatic events, especially abuse as a child or experience of sexual assault, can have a marked affect on the emotional well-being of any individual. Entering a profession that requires confronting the trauma of others may trigger one's own memories of hurt and betrayal. Staff participating in the telephone interview responded to a series of questions to assess exposure to earlier trauma not associated with fieldwork.

For this assessment, staff were asked to indicate the frequency of experience for the following three areas: unwanted sexual experiences;[12] domestic violence or threat of violence;[13] and injury in childhood due to parental discipline.[14] Forty-three percent of interview participants indicated a history of at least one unwanted sexual experience; 22 per cent had experienced violence or the threat of violence in a romantic relationship; and 17 per cent had experienced an injury in childhood related to parental discipline. It is important to note that the reported unwanted sexual experiences represented a range from unwanted display of nudity to sexual assault. This rate of exposure to trauma may seem surprising. However, the percentage of staff reporting these experiences were comparable to other populations of professionals and ministry workers in the United States. Perhaps a key to understanding risks associated with prior trauma among helping professionals is not whether early experience of trauma occurred, but to what extent the person has addressed hurt and memories connected to that history. Earlier painful experiences may contribute to a person's sense of empathy or compassion for others, but they can also create difficult patterns of denial, overgeneralised fear and mistrust.

Physical Health

Just as individuals bring emotional history to their work, they also bring a history of physical health and disease that affects their health status and functioning. For some individuals, emotions they experience due to personal issues or work-related stress may contribute to development of physical diseases such as hypertension or physical problems such as obesity and headaches. Individuals' perceptions about personal health provide invaluable information about the burden or resilience they may experience related to disease or physical difficulty.

To assess staff participants' perceptions of their own health, we used the five items from the Medical Outcomes Study 36 item Short Form (SF-36).[15] These items provide individuals with an opportunity to rate their health in general terms and in comparison to others. For example, respondents rate the following question on a five-point scale: "In general, would you say that your health is (excellent, very good, good, fair, poor)?" Participants reported being in good health on average. This would suggest that these staff were not burdened by health difficulties.

Interestingly, even though staff reported generally good health, they also reported experiencing stress-related physical symptoms (back pain, stiffness, fatigue and headaches) in response to the symptom subscale of the Physical Health Spectrum.[16] These symptoms may be early warning signs of health problems beyond normal aging. Stress management training and positive physical habits such as exercise and relaxation may help reduce these symptoms, which often are related to tension and fatigue.

Social Support – Help from Others

When considering an individual's overall well-being, it is important to bear in mind that no person lives in a vacuum. The extent to which one perceives personal and/or professional relationships as positive and helpful (for example, believing that one could readily obtain help from others when needed) can influence overall functioning. Such social support has been shown to be positively associated with physiological[17] and psychological[18] health and well-being. Conversely, lack of social support has been linked with greater levels of depression and psychological distress.[19] As mentioned earlier, previous research indicated that high levels of social support buffered effects of high exposure to traumatic events in a sample of humanitarian aid workers during reentry to their home culture.[20]

The Social Provisions Scale used in this assessment measured participants' perceptions of support by querying the following areas: availability of assistance, emotional closeness, respectful relationships, recognition of skills and competence, guidance from others, shared interests, and support of another person.[21] Participating staff generally reported a strong perception of support. Only a very small number of participants reported scores suggesting the experience of isolation or ambivalence about support in their field assignment. Staff participants also estimated how many people who support them are people that they work with, and 48 per cent of staff indicated that half or more of their supportive relationships are with co-workers. These reports suggest that an aid organisation has an important opportunity to provide support and enhance resilience through its teams that are created in projects and offices.

Healthy Behaviours

There is general acceptance across medical and mental health fields that physical health and mental health are intricately interrelated. Exercise and other healthy habits have been associated with reduced stress and reduced depression. Positive health behaviours are also an area of resilience that can be increased in practical ways. The organisation can provide opportunities and resources, but it is individuals who need to take the steps to incorporate the habit (or reduce a negative habit!) in their own lives.

For this assessment, positive health habits were measured by adapting a series of questions from the Behavioral Risk Factor Surveillance System Questionnaire 2000.[22] We focused on eight specific behaviours:

1. No smoking
2. Eating five or fewer servings of junk food per week
3. Eating both fruits and vegetables
4. Rarely eating when emotionally upset
5. Getting at least seven hours of sleep per night
6. Drinking 14 or fewer servings of caffeine per week
7. Exercising three or more times per week
8. Not driving aggressively

The great majority of staff reported more than half of the habits listed above. However, almost all participants reported at least one area where they might improve. The eight areas above are listed in the order of their prevalence as reported by staff. The two healthy habits that seem to be the most difficult for staff to sustain on the field are regular exercise and avoiding aggressive driving. Understandably, circumstances in the field may make it difficult to follow these habits regularly: certain foods may not be available, exercise equipment or security issues may limit physical exercise, or driving conditions may require assertive or aggressive tactics. Yet staff can be encouraged to commit to as healthy a lifestyle as possible, with the knowledge that these physical habits can benefit their emotional health.

Coping

When considering the impact of behaviour on health and well-being, coping behaviours are clearly relevant. Specifically, how one copes with particular stressful events, as well as with chronic ongoing stressors, relates directly to psychological adjustment. Two leading coping researchers, Lazarus and Folkman, classified coping behaviours as either problem-focused (that is, resolving or managing a problem) or emotion-focused (that is, managing the emotions aroused by a problem). A wide range of behaviours belong within each of these two categories, and some behaviours can fall into both categories, such as religious coping (discussed below).[23]

When responding to the COPE, a measure of coping styles,[24] staff indicated that they utilise two problem-focused coping strategies most frequently when confronting a stressful event: (1) strategising, or coming up with a plan, and (2) taking actions to do something about the stressor. It is important to note that denial, a coping strategy considered less adaptive, was reported infrequently among these World Vision participants.

Spirituality

Spirituality has been defined in many ways. Some definitions emphasise relational dimensions of spirituality and view spirituality as a transcendent relationship with that which is sacred in life.[25] Spirituality is also related to religiousness; this may include organised religious activity such as attending church, more private religious activity such as private devotions, or a more subjective acknowledgement of the importance of religion.[26] Spirituality and religiousness have been viewed as a protective factor.[27] Because church attendance may be related to a number of factors, including an individual's physical ability to get to church (a critical issue in many remote aid environments), more recent work has begun to focus on subjective religiousness and spirituality.

The Spiritual Transcendence Index is a scale developed to measure a dimension of an individual's spirituality that might be associated with health. Spiritual transcendence refers to an individual's perceived connection to sacred experiences, people and/or objects; this connection provides meaning and helps the individual transcend life's difficulties.[28] One sample item is, "I experience a deep communion with God. "Participants in this study had high scores on spiritual transcendence. This finding suggests that spirituality provides meaning for this staff. Their scores were higher than a community sample and were closer to scores obtained from clergy and seminary samples. Participants who scored higher on spiritual transcendence also obtained higher scores on their general perceived health. This finding is consistent with other research demonstrating a relationship between spirituality and health perceptions in graduate students attending a seminary.[29]

Given the significance of spirituality for participants in this study, it is also important to consider the potential spiritual aspects of their general resources. For example, the concept of general social support is concerned with the impact of interpersonal relationships but does not include the possibility of a relationship with God. Similarly, the general concept of coping focuses on what most people usually do in response to stressors, but it typically does not consider how a person's faith might inform these actions. Thus the current study examined both of these issues.

Religious Support – Help from God

For a spiritual person, both faith community and God can be viewed as unique support resources, above and beyond general social support. Fiala, Bjorck and Gorsuch studied such religious support resources and found that persons who feel more supported by God, their congregation and their church leaders typically experience better psychological adjustment.[30] Moreover, the positive relationship between religious support and adjustment was found even after controlling for effects of general social support. This suggests that religious support is not merely equivalent to general social support in a religious context. Instead, it appears to be a unique resource. This distinctiveness is perhaps most evident regarding support perceived as coming from God. Whereas support from a religious congregation might be considered analogous to support from members of a civic organisation or from one's neighbourhood, support from God has no theoretical parallel within the context of general social support. Some researchers have suggested that focus on a higher power (for example, God) might be the distinguishing factor of religious organisations.[31] Moreover, there is empirical evidence for the idea that support from God can be a resource. For example, Maton found that in high stress-situations (such as grieving the death of one's child), persons who perceived God as supportive reported less psychological distress than those who did not perceive God in this way.[32]

The recent study of WVI participants also confirms the importance of perceived support from God. When completing a measure of perceived God support, this group generally voiced strong agreement with the personal experience of a supportive God.[33] A small group of staff reported scores that indicated some ambivalence about their experience of support from God as described by the questionnaire items (for example, "I have worth in the eyes of God," "God cares about my life and situation"). Differences in scores may represent language, cultural or denominational differences in understanding one's relationship to God. The World Vision staff participants represented 22 different Christian denominations, from Pentecostal to Roman Catholic. However, as a whole group, the average score showed agreement with the experience of support from God in life circumstances.

For persons holding positive views of God, support from God could be seen as beneficial both directly and indirectly. Directly, for example, Jolley and Taulbee found that those who feel more supported by God report having enhanced self-concept; and Kirkpatrick, Shillito and Kellas found that such persons also felt less lonely.[34] Indirectly, feeling supported by God presumably expands the range of potential adaptive coping responses to include religious forms of coping. Indeed, persons reporting a positive God concept have been shown to have more ability to cope effectively with stressful events. Koenig and colleagues found this to be true for older adults, and Park and Cohen found it to be the case among college students.[35]

Religious Coping

Religion's importance to coping is well documented. For example, Bjorck and Fiala found that religious college students who perceived God as a supportive, guiding force tended to have more favourable outcomes when coping with stressful events than those who did not.[36] Moreover, even persons who are not generally religious often cope by turning to God when facing stressful events, seeking support or solutions. Bjorck and Cohen found that undergraduate college students who were not particularly religious still planned to rely at least somewhat on religious coping when facing very stressful events.[37] McCrae studied a general population adult sample and found that faith was often cited as a coping resource, and McCrae and Costa found that these same adults ranked faith as the most effective coping strategy.[38]

In contrast to the general population, persons who see faith as central to their lives view religious coping as even more important, and such coping can be a significant help in times of stress and trauma. For example, Pargament and colleagues found that, among Christian church members, using one's positive relationship with God as a basis for coping was associated with better emotional functioning. Such coping strategies included, for example, "[Taking] control over what I could, and [giving] the rest up to God," "[using] Christ as an example of how I should live," and "[realizing] that God was trying to strengthen me."[39]

As stated earlier, much coping research classifies coping strategies as being either problem focused or emotion focused.[40] Problem-focused coping methods are used to resolve a stressful situation directly (for example, pursuing treatment for illness). Emotion-focused methods are used to improve one's emotional state regarding a situation that may not necessarily resolve (for example, choosing to look on the bright side). Rather than falling neatly into either category, however, religious coping incorporates elements of both. For example, one might seek God's guidance as a collaborator in resolving a problem. Alternately, to find emotional support and relief from distress, one might confess sins, pray to God for comfort, or turn to one's faith community. In general, a growing number of empirical studies suggest that such religious coping strategies are generally an adaptive response to life stress.[41]

Religious coping can be particularly useful when facing extreme life stressors. For example, Pargament, Smith, Koenig and Perez found that adaptive forms of religious coping were associated with stress-related growth among Oklahoma City church members after they experienced the Oklahoma City bombing.[42] Given that international relief workers often encounter extremely stressful events and environments, it is likely that religious coping is a strategy that should be cultivated, particularly among those serving in a religious context (for example, as part of a faith-based NGO). The importance of religious coping is supported by the World Vision study of international relief workers, in which religious coping was cited as one of three most frequently utilised strategies when facing life stress.

Adjustment and Mental Health Risks

Burnout

Burnout and *stress* are common terms in service occupations. The concept of burnout was developed to address occupational stress and distress experienced by persons working in helping professions. Work that requires consistent attention to the needs of a person, or a group of people, can create a situation of prolonged emotional investment, ambiguity and frustration. Work in a chronically stressful and emotionally charged environment can create burnout.[43]

The Maslach Burnout Inventory-Human Services Survey (MBI) is a measure of this job strain.[44] Three separate scales measure Maslach's hypothesised three aspects of the burnout syndrome: emotional exhaustion (EE), depersonalization (DP), and lack of personal accomplishment (PA). The EE scale rates feelings of being exhausted by one's work and emotionally overextended. The DP scale measures calloused feelings of numbness towards those one serves. The PA scale assesses positive feelings of competence and achievement regarding one's work. Burnout is indicated by higher scores on EE and DP and lower scores on PA.

Maslach and Jackson have established cutoff scores for the MBI subscales that indicate low, moderate and high risk for burnout. The majority of staff responding to this assessment are at low levels of risk for job-related burnout. However, a significant minority showed moderate or high risk: 40 per cent for depersonalization and 49 per cent for emotional exhaustion. In addition, almost one-quarter of the staff scored at high risk for burnout related to a lack of personal accomplishment. The average scores for the three subscales in the WV participant group were comparable to a normative sample of medical professionals, teachers, mental health workers, and social service staff.[45] These results suggest that aid work can create a significant risk for job-related strain, similar to the risk already identified in other high-stress, human service professions.

Depression

Earlier research has identified depression as a significant mental health risk for humanitarian aid workers.[46] The Center for Epidemiological Studies – Depressed Mood Scale (CES-D) assessed participants' symptoms over the previous seven days.[47] The CES-D included symptoms such as sadness, low self-esteem, appetite and sleep problems, loneliness, hopelessness, fatigue, difficulty concentrating and withdrawal from activities or relationships.

Fifteen percent of participants reported levels of symptoms that could be considered in a clinical range, or high risk for depressive disorder. This percentage of high risk is similar to what was reported by Cardozo and Salama (2002) in their assessment in Kosovo.[48] These results indicate that a small but important group of staff needs support for depression or discouragement in fieldwork.

PTSD

As mentioned earlier, PTSD has been an area of recent investigation in the humanitarian aid context. Psycho-social programmes have been developed in international settings to care for victims of war, terrorism and natural disasters, and NGOs have begun to recognise that their own staff may develop PTSD symptomatology while working in environments of danger and suffering. PTSD may develop after one experiences a traumatic event, and PTSD symptoms are both physiological and emotional. Symptoms cluster into three categories: (1) reexperiencing the event through nightmares, flashbacks or intrusive images; (2) avoidance evidenced by withdrawal, numbing or actively avoiding reminders of the event; and (3) hyperarousal, demonstrated by jumpiness, irritability, tension or sudden episodes of fear.[49]

As one might imagine, managing PTSD symptoms in a humanitarian aid context may be quite challenging. The work situation might include constant reminders of the loss of a friend, an earlier mugging, or the death of a child due to lack of resources. Aid workers struggling with PTSD might find themselves thinking about an earlier event when they do not want to; they may have serious problems sleeping; they may also have intense fear reactions that could jeopardise their safety in high security risk areas.

In this survey the Los Angeles Symptom Checklist was used to assess PTSD symptoms.[50] Thirteen percent of staff reported high levels of symptoms that would warrant a diagnosis of PTSD. An additional 33 per cent indicated a moderate level of symptoms, indicating that nearly half of those completing the interview were currently experiencing symptoms that could affect their work and their well-being. This report of symptomatology should be considered in the context of very high incidence of exposure to trauma. The fact that the rates of PTSD symptomatology are not higher suggests important resilience factors at work. However, the extent of distress reported in this interview indicates that staff need support for continued development of resilience as well as amelioration of current emotional distress.

Positive adjustment

The Satisfaction with Life Scale (SWLS) measures general subjective well-being with five items rated on a seven-point scale (1 = strongly disagree, 7 = strongly agree). In research for development of the scale, the SWLS correlated with other measures of subjective well-being, such as self-esteem.[51] The scale includes items such as:

- I would change nothing about my current life.
- The current conditions of my life are excellent.
- I have the important things I want right now.

Staff participants did not report strong agreement with the life satisfaction items. In fact, the average total score for five items was 21.8, indicating a score between ambivalence and slight agreement. These results may represent context and culture issues. First, the nature of any field context includes limitations of resource and compromised living conditions. Second, the items ask an individual to judge his or her personal satisfaction. In many non-Western cultures, the perspective of family or community is considered primary, rather than the perspectives of the individual. Finally, humanitarian aid workers might view satisfaction as synonymous with complacency. Specifically, given their desire to make a positive difference in very stressful situations, their life satisfaction scores might reflect strong motivation to make an even more positive impact on their surroundings than they are currently making.

Summary and Recommendations

These results of the assessment support the claim that the experience of humanitarian aid workers is complex and multifaceted. Participants reported a strikingly high level of exposure to both direct and indirect trauma events. Twenty-five percent of staff reported that they had experienced an event where they felt their life was in danger while working on their current assignment, and 86 per cent were exposed to specific incidents of witnessing or hearing about traumatic events in their current post. In addition to trauma exposure related to their work, one-third of participants reported a history of family or relational abuse. This prior trauma experience may contribute to sensitivity toward the suffering of others and a keen sense of compassion. However, unresolved childhood trauma can also contribute low self-esteem and emotional distress. Earlier trauma exposure has also been identified as a risk factor for development of PTSD symptoms for those later exposed to additional trauma.[52] In light of the extensive report of both work-related and personal / historical trauma in this sample, research in the humanitarian aid field should continue to assess current direct and indirect, as well as historical, exposure to trauma that may lead to emotional and social difficulties in the field.

In addition to traumatic incidents, attention must be paid to the enduring stresses in the field. The "high magnitude" impact of a traumatic event can trigger an acute crisis or period of distress, but handling day-to-day strains of work in a humanitarian environment can seriously challenge emotional and physical resources. In fact, one staff member wrote:

> Lots of the stresses in my job/life are continual, low-impact. . . . The ongoing stresses, such as being targeted by traffic police for traffic offenses (anything they can find wrong, so that you'll pay them) . . . general administrative chaos in[side] and outside the organisation, technological problems, no e-mail, etc. – these are the things that will wear me down, if anything.

Organisations and aid agencies need to take such environmental and organisational factors into account. Staff who have high levels of day-to-day stress and limited resources to respond effectively to that stress may be more at risk to develop health problems, burnout, or other severe adjustment problems in the field. Future research may help identify key areas of organisational, environmental and social stress that can be reduced through policy change and organisational intervention.

Regarding personal resilience, the World Vision staff participating in this survey demonstrate a strong commitment to a positive lifestyle, including healthy physical habits, strong spirituality, adaptive coping, and a strong sense of support from God, family and friends. These factors create a network of personal resources for individual staff and families. However, managers and administrators must remember that this resilience is a *required* element of life on a humanitarian aid field! Staff face decisions, hardships and lack of physical resources that affect hundreds of lives or more in the communities where they work. Staff need to have healthy personal resilience in order to survive and in order to continue contributing to the critical work of their organisations.

Survival leads us to a final key area for future research and organisational response. All staff who responded to the World Vision assessment were currently employed by the organisation. They were doing their jobs in more than thirty countries of the world. Yet for each of the mental health risk adjustment measures (depression, PTSD and burnout) 30–50 per cent of staff scored in the moderate to high risk range. This is a significant number of people in the field who are working and "surviving" while experiencing considerable emotional distress. These staff may not be incapacitated by symptoms presently, but we cannot deny the effects that depression, burnout and PTSD can have on relationships, work and personal health. An NGO's commitment to people includes the welfare of beneficiaries around the world, but it also includes the well-being of staff who commit their lives to serving and saving others.

Notes

[1] The Headington Program in Fuller Theological Seminary's Graduate School of Psychology is an endowed programme established to extend the knowledge of traumatic and chronic stress in international ministry settings through research and scholarly training.

2 To maintain confidentiality, this story is a composite of experiences of staff participants. Names and details do not represent one living person.

3 C. B. Eriksson et al., "Trauma Exposure and PTSD Symptoms in International Relief and Development Personnel," *Journal of Traumatic Stress* 14 (2001), 208.

4 Ibid., 209–10.

5 B. L. Cardozo and P. Salama, "Mental Health of Humanitarian Aid Workers in Complex Emergencies," in *Sharing the Front Lines and the Back Hills*, ed. Y. Danieli (Amityville, N.Y.: Baywood Publishing Co., 2002), 245.

6 Ibid., 248–49.

7 This sample represents a response rate of approximately 31 per cent. The rate is approximate due to the uncertainty of the receipt of the e-mail request. Several staff involved in the second phase of the research indicated that they did not receive the stress survey e-mail.

8 B. De Haan, "Humanitarian Action in Conflict Zones: Coping with Stress," *International Red Cross Guidelines* (Geneva: IRCR Publications, 1994); M J. Friedman, P. G. Warfe and G. K. Mwiti, "Mission-Related Stress and Its Consequences Among UN Peacekeepers and Civilian Field Personnel," in *Trauma in War and Peace: Prevention, Practice and Policy*, edited by B. Green et al. (New York: Kluwer Academic/Plenum Publishers, 2000).

9 Eriksson et al., "Trauma Exposure and PTSD Symptoms in International Relief and Development Personnel."

10 J. E. Richters and W. Saltzman, *Survey of Children's Exposure to Community Violence* (Washington, D.C.: National Institute of Mental Health, 1990); M. Macksoud, "Assessing War Trauma in Children: A Case Study of Lebanese Children," *Journal of Refugee Studies* 5 (1992), 1–15.

11 P. Salama, "The Psychological Health of Relief Workers: Some Practical Suggestions," *Relief and Rehabilitation Network Newsletter* (November 1999); B. Smith, I. Agger, Y. Danieli and L. Weisaeth, "Emotional Responses of International Humanitarian Aid Workers: The Contribution of Non-Governmental Organizations, in *International Responses to Traumatic Stress: Humanitarian, Human Rights, Justice, Peace and Development Contributions, Collaborative Actions, and Future Initiatives*, edited by Y. Danieli, N. Rodley and L. Weisaeth (Amityville, N.Y.: Baywood Publishing Company, 1996); Friedman, Warfe and Mwiti, "Mission-Related Stress and Its Consequences Among UN Peacekeepers and Civilian Field Personnel."

12 H. S. Resnick, "Psychometric Review of Trauma Assessment for Adults (TAA)," in *Measurement of Stress, Trauma and Adaptation*, edited by B. H. Stamm (Lutherville, Md.: Sidran Press, 1996),

[13] M. A. Straus, "Measuring Intrafamily Conflict and Violence: The Conflict Tactics Scale," *Journal of Marriage and the Family* 41 (1979), 75–88.

[14] J. Knutson, "Physical and Sexual Abuse in Children," in *Handbook of Pediatric Psychology*, edited by D. Routh (New York: Guilford, 1988).

[15] J. E. Ware and C. D. Sherbourne, "The MOS 36–Item Short-Form Health Survey (SF-36): I. Conceptual Framework and Item Selection," *Medical Care* 30 (1992), 473–83.

[16] N. B. Belloc, L. Breslow and J. R. Hochstim, "Measurement of Physical Health in a General Population Survey," *American Journal of Epidemiology* 93 (1971), 328–36; J. W. Meltzer and J. R. Hochstim, "Reliability and Validity of Survey Data on Physical Health," *Public Health Reports* 85 (1970), 1075–86.

[17] For example, S. Cohen et al., "Social Ties and Susceptibility to the Common Cold," *Journal of the American Medical Association* 277 (1997): 1940–44.

[18] For example, S. Cohen and T. A. Wills, "Stress, Social Support, and the Buffering Hypothesis," *Psychological Bulletin* 98 (1985): 310–57.

[19] For example, M. E. P. Seligman, *Learned Optimism* (New York: Random House, 1991). For a review, see D. R. Wienmiller et al., "Measurement Strategies in Social Support: A Descriptive Review of the Literature," *Journal of Clinical Psychology* 49 (1993): 638–48.

[20] Eriksson et al., "Trauma Exposure and PTSD Symptoms in International Relief and Development Personnel."

[21] C. E. Cutrona and D. W. Russell, "The Provisions of Social Relationships and Adaptation to Stress," *Advances in Personal Relationships* 1 (1987), 37–67; C. E. Cutrona, "Ratings of Social Support by Adolescents and Adult Informants: Degree of Correspondence and Prediction of Depressive Symptoms," *Journal of Personality and Social Psychology* 57 (1989), 723–30.

[22] Behavioral Risk Factor Surveillance System Questionnaire 2000 (Atlanta, Ga.: National Center for Chronic Disease Prevention and Health Promotion, 2000). The questionnaire is also available online.

[23] R. S. Lazarus and S. Folkman, *Stress, Appraisal and Coping* (New York: Springer, 1984); and K. I. Pargament, "God Help Me: Toward a Theoretical Framework of Coping for the Psychology of Religion," *Research in the Social Scientific Study of Religion* 2 (1990), 195–224.

[24] C. S. Carver, M. F. Scheier and J. K. Weintraub, "Assessing Coping Strategies: A Theoretically Based Approach," *Journal of Personality and Social Psychology* 56 (1989), 267–83.

[25] R. Walsh, *Essential Spirituality* (New York: Wiley, 2000).

26 H. G. Koenig et al., "Modeling the Cross-Sectional Relationships Between Religion, Physical Health, Social Support and Depressive Symptoms," *American Journal of Geriatric Psychiatry* 5(2) (1997): 131–44; J. Levin, L. Chatters and R. Taylor, "Religious Effects on Health Status and Life Satisfaction Among Black Americans," *Journal of Gerontology: Social Science* 50(B) (1995), S154–63.

27 J. S. Levin and P. L. Schiller, "Is There a Religious Factor in Health?" *Journal of Religion and Health* 26 (1987), 9–36.

28 L. Seidlitz et al., "Development of the Spiritual Transcendence Index," *Journal For the Scientific Study of Religion* 41 (2002), 439–53.

29 Ibid.

30 W. E. Fiala, J. P. Bjorck and R. L. Gorsuch, "The Religious Support Scale: Construction, Validation and Cross-Validation," *American Journal of Community Psychology* 30/6 (2002), 761–86.

31 K. I. Pargament et al., "The Congregation Development Program: Data-based Consultation with Churches and Synagogues," *Professional Psychology: Research and Practice* 5 (1991): 393–404.

32 K. I. Maton, "The Stress-Buffering Role of Spiritual Support: Cross-Sectional and Prospective Investigations," *Journal For the Scientific Study of Religion* 28 (1989), 310–23.

33 Fiala, Bjorck and Gorsuch, "The Religious Support Scale."

34 J. C. Jolley and S. J. Taulbee, "Assessing Perceptions of Self and God: Comparison of Prisoners and Normals," *Psychological Reports* 59 (1986), 1139–46; L. A. Kirkpatrick, D. J. Shillito and S. L. Kellas, "Loneliness, Social Support and Perceived Relationships with God," *Journal of Social and Personal Relationships* 16/4 (1999), 513–22.

35 H. G. Koenig et al., "Religious Coping and Depression Among Elderly, Hospitalized Medically Ill Men," *American Journal of Psychiatry* 149/12 (1992), 1693–1700; C. L. Park and L. H. Cohen, "Religious and Nonreligious Coping with the Death of a Friend," *Cognitive Therapy and Research* 17 (1993), 561–77.

36 J. P. Bjorck and W. E. Fiala, "God Concept, Appraisal, Religious Coping and Adjustment." Poster presented at the Fifty-first annual convention of the California Psychological Association, Pasadena, California, 1998,

37 J. P. Bjorck and L. H. Cohen, "Coping with Threats, Losses and Challenges," *Journal of Social and Clinical Psychology* 12 (1993), 56–72.

38 R. R. McCrae, "Situational Determinants of Coping Responses: Loss, Threat and Challenge," *Journal of Personality and Social Psychology* 46 (1984), 9l9–28; R. R. McCrae and P. T. Costa, "Personality, Coping and Coping Effectiveness in an Adult Sample," *Journal of Personality* 54/2 (1986), 385–405.

[39] K. I. Pargament et al., "God Help Me: (I): Religious Coping Efforts as Predictors of the Outcomes to Significant Negative Life Events," *American Journal of Community Psychology* 18 (1990): 793–824.

[40] Lazarus and Folkman, *Stress, Appraisal and Coping*.

[41] For a review, see K. I. Pargament, *The Psychology of Religion and Coping: Theory, Research and Practice* (New York: The Guilford Press, 1997).

[42] K. I. Pargament, B. W. Smith, H. G. Koenig and L. Perez, "Patterns of Positive and Negative Religious Coping with Major Life Stressors," *Journal for the Scientific Study of Religion* 37/4 (1998), 710–24.

[43] C. Maslach and S. E. Jackson, *MBI Manual*, 3d ed., edited by C. Maslach, S. E. Jackson and M. P. Leiter (Palo Alto, Calif.: Consulting Psychologists Press, 1996).

[44] Ibid.

[45] Ibid.

[46] Cardozo and Salama, "Mental Health of Humanitarian Aid Workers in Complex Emergencies."

[47] L. S. Radloff, "The CES-D Scale: A Self-Report Depression Scale for Research in the General Population," *Applied Psychological Measurement* 1 (1977), 385–401.

[48] Cardozo and Salama, "Mental Health of Humanitarian Aid Workers in Complex Emergencies."

[49] American Psychiatric Association, *Diagnostic and Statistical Manual of Mental Disorders*, 4th ed. (Washington, D.C.: American Psychiatric Association, 1994).

[50] L. King, D. King, G. Leskin and D. Foy, "The Los Angeles Symptom Checklist: A Self-Report Measure of Posttraumatic Stress Disorder," *Assessment* 2 (1995), 1–17.

[51] E. Diener et al., "The Satisfaction with Life Scale," *Journal of Personality Assessment* 49 (1985), 71–75.

[52] B. T. Litz et al., "Early Interventions for Trauma: Current Status and Future Directions," *Clinical Psychology: Science and Practice* 9 (2002), 112–34.

The content of this chapter is based on material originally presented in the Final Report of the WVI – Headington Program Occupational Stress and Trauma Assessment. The authors would like to acknowledge colleagues and students who made this work possible: Mr. John Fawcett, the WVI co-investigator, and Dr. David Foy, the co-primary investigator for the assessment project, were invaluable colleagues; Gary Trice, Elizabeth Adams Nelson,

John Johnson, Linnea Larson, Corinne Green, Tina Houston, Barron Hung, Gladys Mwiti, Elizabeth Rupp Barton, Daryl Schrock, Erin Smith, Danielle Speakman and Valla Penrose Walker.

chapter 5

Assessing front-line staff for stress, trauma and social support: theory, practice and implications

GRAHAM FAWCETT

F-16's circled high in the clear blue sky above my vehicle and then suddenly swooped, afterburners glowing red. Moments later my radio crackled. The colleague I was on my way to meet reported crisply, "We're being shelled. I'll be a bit delayed meeting up with you." Two hours later I sat in his office, drinking coffee, wondering if I had the courage to ask this gracious front-line staff worker about his stress levels.[1]

Introduction

Overview

Models of how folk are protected from stress and trauma falter if they cannot be applied in stressful and traumatic situations. Practical ways of measuring stress and the mitigating factors are required, and staff need to have the confidence that the assessments and consequent training are worth crossing roadblocks for, and that those involved as assessors are prepared to put their own safety on the line. Questionnaires sent out from a distant HQ coupled with some theoretical modules on stress management will not meet the perceived need of front-line staff.

The approach outlined in this chapter takes assessment and mitigation of stress and trauma to front-line staff, in the places where they are encountering the realities, sometimes horrors, of everyday life. In the course of designing and developing this assessment process, staff and consultants involved learnt that practical implications of trauma assessment and mitigation went far beyond mechanics of administering questionnaires and focus groups.

This framework developed as part of a human-resource initiative by World Vision (Middle East and Europe) to identify levels of exposure to stress and trauma amongst more than 1,000 staff and to establish the nature of the relationship between exposure to stress or trauma and mediating effects of social support, particularly team cohesion and leadership style. The work reported here began as a series of meetings and discussions within World Vision to determine valid ways of supporting staff working in stressful and/or traumatic situations. The theoretical underpinning for the approach used is reported in Chapter 3 of this book. Initial application of the approach has been a two-year process across eight nations, from which results for the first two nations are summarised below. Details regarding the nations involved have been kept anonymous to preserve the confidentiality under which these results were obtained.

Results and implications of this study appear transferable and applicable across different cultures and types of aid organisations. Critically, social support was confirmed as a significant mitigating factor in stress and trauma prevention, as would be anticipated from the literature in the area. Not anticipated were the serious implications for mental health of very low levels of social support. Broadly high levels of social support were protective of stress when it occurred, but low levels of social support were toxic to mental health irrespective of stress exposure.[2]

The results strongly suggest that focusing scarce human-resource capacity in team building and social support capacity enhancement will be more productive than, for example, individual or group stress management education.

These different approaches are not mutually exclusive and do provide some grid for deciding how to allocate proportions of HR capacity.

Theological and Philosophic Rationale

Being a humanitarian aid worker on the front line is hazardous. Visiting one can be equally hazardous.

What makes it worthwhile is the knowledge that, to parrot a well-known advert, the staff are worth it. For World Vision as a diverse and broadly experienced Christian agency, the fundamental source of this worth lies in the deep truth that we are made in the image of God and, as such, have inherent value that accords us a certain status and dignity. Modernist views of humankind have generated the idea that humans are resources to be deployed, and entire new technologies have grown up around the notion of human-resource management.[3] This is, in some measure, to be deplored. Humans are subject to the love and creative grace of a loving God rather than objectively quantifiable and deployable automata.

Even from a secular humanistic perspective, the first principle of the People in Aid Code of Best Practice[4] is that people are important. Aid agencies recognise they have an ethical duty of care to ensure that, as a minimum, the organisation is not inherently toxic to the well-being of individual staff members. Again, this idea of minima is a modernist notion, rooted in the Hippocratic Oath – "first, do no harm" – ensuring that interventions in a situation do not leave the situation worse off.

The vision for Christian agencies, however, cannot be purely a minimalist, damage-limitation exercise. The vision needs to incorporate hope for the reign of God – creative spaces where colleagues may flourish, where the hope for the communities that are established is Shalom, and where people, whether staff or beneficiaries, Christians or otherwise, are recognised as image bearers of the living God.

Assessments and models Christian agencies generate need to reflect that hope and aspiration. The assessment outlined in Chapter 4 is one such model. It is rooted in the notion that we live in a fallen world (life is stressful), but that we can prevail (live healthy and productive lives). The intervening variable enabling this centres on functioning communities within which people are free and enabled to flourish in their relationships with God, with one another and with creation (the environment). The idea of flourishing is encapsulated operationally in the recently described phenomena of Post Traumatic Growth (PTG), where survivors of trauma emerge enhanced psychologically from their experience.[5]

World Vision faces the challenge of applying this set of values across a wide range of beliefs and spiritualities among its staff and beneficiary communities, ranging from atheism or agnosticism to a variety of deistic beliefs. Not all believe or adhere to the theological claims above. The People in Aid code states that people are important as a core value and thus can be adopted freely by faith organisations. Theology gives an account of why people are important, but in practical terms, it is the People in Aid code that codifies minimum expectations for both faith and non-faith agencies.

The challenge for secular organisations is dealing with the strong theme of heightened spiritual awareness that emerges continuously through the secular PTG literature and throughout many of the focus groups of this study. As was said in the trenches of the First World War, "There are no agnostics here". Chaplains of all faiths are provided for the militaries of the world. They are rare in the humanitarian aid world.

Walking across the border was hard. The automatic weapons pointed at my back were held by nervous 19 year olds trained to shoot first and then make enquiries. The automatic weapons pointed at my front were held by nervous 19 year olds who were barely trained at all. I walked in a straight line, keeping my hands very visible and willing neither set of 19 year olds to sense anything that could be misinterpreted. I reached the other side keenly conscious that I had to do this all over again in the other direction some hours later and that many did it daily simply to earn enough to eat.

Field Assessment

Implications of the beliefs outlined above imply that aid agencies, and Christian aid agencies in particular, must uphold the highest possible human standards of caring for staff and, consequently, the beneficiary communities they serve.

Assessing stress among staff on the front lines can never be the same as straightforward assessment of stress in organisations generally. Getting the consultant and the staff together for necessary meetings may be hazardous for both parties, so much so that individuals may be unwilling to risk their life to participate. For other front-line workers, day-to-day logistical challenges of meeting up can be formidable. In the midst of that, the necessary rigour and professionalism assessments require have to be maintained.

Yet staff should never feel that they are the objects of some intervention; that they are only resources being audited; that their feelings and thoughts are merely being collected according to some preset programme or schedule. In addition, academic literature demonstrates clearly that debriefers and stress managers need to be credible in the eyes of those they are debriefing or whose stress they are managing. Credibility is defined straightforwardly – to have been in the same battle; failing that, to have been in a similar battle; failing that, to at least have been in a battle. The latter two are poor substitutes for being in the same battle however.

The stress front-line staff experience may not map directly onto readily available assessment tools. Somehow aware of this, one staff member eyed me keenly as he chain-lit another cigarette. "In the last N years I have been in prison X times and held without trial for Y years. I have been tortured for Z months. . . . Does that count as stress?" He said this partly to draw attention to his history and partly to see my reaction. Was I able to accommodate and contain his evident pain and frustration, or was I simply interested in gathering data for some obscure project?

The principles, then, of credibility and containment seem crucial in any front-line assessment. Implications of this are straightforward: Those conducting assessments must visit the field locations and demonstrate at least a willingness to share the same privations as the front-line staff; and those conducting the assessments must be able to empathise in some measure with the stress staff are facing. These credentials lie neither in the professionalism of the assessors nor, particularly, in their knowledge base, but rather in their own personal history of suffering and grief, dynamics they can draw on to comprehend the enormity of what staff are encountering. Above all, in a Christian organisation, can assessors nurture among staff a deeper knowledge and understanding that Christ really did take all our suffering upon himself and understands exactly what those who suffer are encountering? This understanding needs to be coupled with an ability to mediate that compassion in some tangible way.

Given that, the techniques reported in this chapter to assess stress in front-line staff may seem surprisingly modernist, to support the aim of eliciting both numerical and statistically analyzable data in a reasonable time frame. At the same time, staff are given a reasonable sense of being heard, of solidarity and of opportunities for future input. The latter dynamic is not so much a function of the assessment tools themselves but rather of the credibility of those using the tools.

I reflected my heavy heart to my boss some hours later. Out a window I could see the smoke from further shell fire only a few kilometres distant. I was deeply aware that coming out had been the wrong choice, despite the protocols, but that the deed was done. Was I anything more than a voyeur of the pain of others? My boss and I resolved there and then that some situations simply had to be visited with due regard to the overall support that could be offered through demonstrating solidarity by staying longer than absolutely necessary. Grimly we recognised that there would be times where HR managers would have to at least consider compromising their own safety when visiting field staff.

Questionnaire Assessments

Seven assessments were used to measure the three dimensions of the underlying model. All were translated into the local language of the nation being assessed. English versions of all assessments were also available.

Stress

Prevailing stress was measured using a life-events schedule, which measures the amount of stress defined as life change, both positive and negative, an individual has experienced during the preceding twelve months. A cutoff score was established to indicate whether an individual was under severe stress.

In addition, participants were invited to agree or disagree with the DSM-IV condition for traumatisation – that they had encountered a life-threatening situation which had invoked intense feelings. Those who agreed with the statement were considered to have experienced a traumatic episode in their life.

Social support

Individual and organisational resilience was measured using two social support questionnaires. These measured social support experienced by an individual within a team (Social Support - WV, Team Cohesion Questionnaire - cohesion) and social support experienced by an individual outside of the team (Social Support - "outside" social support). They also measured the extent to which individuals felt their leader was consultative (Social Support - Leadership and Team Cohesion - Leadership). Scores in the bottom one-third of the possible range were set as an indicator of compromised social support.

COPE, a measure of coping styles, was used to assess whether participants use approach or avoidance coping styles when faced with stressful situations. Cutoffs were established to indicate compromised approach and avoid-ance coping styles.

Assessing symptomatology

Two questionnaires were used to assess symptomatology. The PENN Inventory measures the extent of psychological traumatisation. A wide range of possible scores measure response to a set of statements, which participants agree or disagree with on a five-point Likert scale. A threshold of 35 was set to indicate significant traumatisation.

The "General Health Questionnaire - 28 item" (GHQ) was used to assess general symptomatology and prevalence of "casedness", that is, those sufficiently symptomatic to attract a psychiatric diagnosis. A threshold for casedness was set to indicate a significant level of symptomatology. Subscales cannot strictly be used diagnostically, but thresholds were set for three of the subscales - physical health, anxiety and depression – as a way of identifying factors involved in the GHQ results.

The sense of welcome in another nation was clear. There were no wars nearby, streets were safe, and people went about their daily affairs broadly untroubled by anything except the rank injustice of being on the wrong side of the Iron Curtain for fifty years. The HR manager greeted me warmly, and the next few days passed in a blur of activity as I was shown the beauty of the nation and met one highly competent aid worker after another. "Thank you for taking the trouble to find out if we were OK," they said, as I departed with gifts and greetings for my family.

Results from HR Perspective

Participants

A total of 215 people participated in the questionnaire assessment from ten locations in two countries. One nation was on a low level of security alert at the time of the assessment (193 staff); the other nation was on a high level security alert (22 staff).

Each site was visited by one consultant who met with the staff group, explained the model, administered the questionnaire battery and then facilitated the requisite number of focus groups.

On average the questionnaires took less than an hour to complete and seemed well received. The focus groups, using a modified carousel approach, took up to a further two hours.

Overall Results from the Questionnaire Study

Forty-five per cent of staff in the high security alert nation (HSAN) were experiencing very stressful personal circumstances, compared with 14 per cent in the low security alert nation (LSAN).

In the HSAN there was a significant split between those in comparative safety in the regional capital and those in the area development projects (ADPs) in the conflict zone. For those in the ADPs, levels of extreme stress were universal with individuals scoring very high on the life-events schedule. Three individuals scored at the 3,000 mark which, given the threshold for extreme stress set at 1,000, is indicative of incredible stress. It needs to be noted that the stress scores do not reflect other daily realities of life, including hostile checkpoints with the threat of arbitrary detention, imprisonment and torture.

In the national office, of 11 staff who completed the questionnaire, only two were currently experiencing stressful personal life events.

In the HSAN, 14 of the 22 respondents had experienced at least one traumatic incident. Again, distribution in the ADPs compared to the national office was disparate. In the ADPs 9 of the 11 respondents (82 per cent) had experienced at least one traumatic incident; in the national office, 5 of the 11 respondents (45 per cent) had experienced at least one traumatic incident.

By contrast only 14 per cent of staff in the LSAN were experiencing significant stress levels. No measures were taken of the experience of trauma in this nation.

The two principal measures of symptoms in the HSAN yielded extraordinary results. No World Vision staff in the HSAN was traumatised. There were individuals who were distressed. However, none was experiencing full-blown PTSD as measured by PENN. This was certainly true in the national office, where the PENN scores were, broadly, consistent with what would be expected in a benign urban setting.

In the LSAN some 6 per cent of staff registered as traumatised on the PENN assessment.

The GHQ results for the HSAN indicated that four staff (18 per cent) were broadly symptomatic of stress, with ten staff (45 per cent) reporting symptoms of a physical nature. Six of these were in the ADPs and four in the national office. Five staff (21 per cent) scored at or beyond the threshold for anxiety, all in the ADPs. Considering the ADP staff alone, 45 per cent scored at or beyond the threshold for anxiety. One staff member scored at the threshold for depression in the national office.

The GHQ results for the LSAN indicated that 13 per cent of staff were symptomatic of stress on the GHQ.

Social support for all staff in the HSAN was high, with the exception of one person in the national office who indicated a lack of support from management. This was in complete contrast to the general scores within the office and indicated an issue for an individual rather than a general problem. Social support in the ADPs was universally high, both from within World Vision and from the wider community.

Social support for the staff in the LSAN varied, with 11 per cent experiencing compromised levels of social support. The results indicated clearly that this was an individual-by-individual phenomenon. Compromised social support for individuals was not clustered in any one particular team.

The COPE scale for the staff in the HSAN indicated that all staff, with one exception, were very competent at using approach styles to problem solving and stress management. Coping by avoiding the issue is seen as toxic to mental health, and four staff yielded scores suggesting they were attempting to ignore issues they were facing. These scores were at or just above the threshold. All of these individuals were in ADPs.

Overall Results from the Focus Groups

Results from the focus groups in the LSAN were categorised according to dimensions of the underlying model: prevailing stress, individual/organisational prophylaxis and expression of stress.

Prevailing Stress

In the LSAN some 70 per cent of participants felt mistrustful of apparent political stability within the nation, and most did not believe that the state would be able to respond to a catastrophe such as an earthquake. 70 per cent of HSAN participants also mistrusted the political system. Against this background of general uncertainty in both settings, there was a strong sense of personal insecurity due to limited-term employment contracts with WV.

Individual/Organisational Prophylaxis

Within the LSAN the majority of staff believed that WV encouraged them to act according to their beliefs, a factor understood to be protective against trauma. Intriguingly, however, many believed that WV should not "interfere" in their religion as this was a personal matter. Thus, although WV is an ostensibly Christian organisation which, in this situation, is employing Christians, the local understanding that faith is a private matter inhibits WV from being perceived as an actor in the process of enhancing and encouraging the faith of staff.

Among HSAN participants, 80 per cent felt that WV encouraged them to act according to their values, beliefs and practices. Many staff here came from faiths other than Christian, and so the faith question was critical for them. Given that, the staff felt broadly supported, although they felt that WV was too evangelical in its outlook and maybe did not understand other Christian spiritualities or faiths.

In terms of social support, participants from the LSAN were content to maintain their existing relationships that were already present independent of WV; they believed that the most valid form of social support is that received from (preexisting) friendship networks. Generally participants did not perceive their social support as coming from within WV.

In the context of a high workload, the HSAN staff were broadly able to spend time with their family and friends and had energy to pursue those relationships. Staff felt the organisation could ensure a reasonable workload to enable them to have quality time off. Overall responses indicated that colleagues were seen as friends or team and as a valid source of support. For about half the group, this social support was sought in the context of work; the other half were open to the idea of pursuing friendships outside the work setting. Some were willing to pursue social support outside of work, but realities of the security situation meant this was not practical.

Results from asking the LSAN staff about ideal ways to cope with stress as a team fell into four categories:

1. *Communication and education concerning the event and advance preparation on how to handle stress.* It was seen as essential that the organisation prepared staff for stressful events and demonstrated that it collectively understood the stress staff were under.
2. *Team unity and collaboration.* Team unity, expressed as collaboration among team members, was seen as key to team cohesion. In other words, structural social support was seen as supportive rather than the anticipated "giving and receiving of affection" (functional social support).
3. *Positive attitude.* Echoes of professionalism and keeping going are heard in the notion of positive attitude – somehow that the work setting would provide a place

where staff can work in a positive atmosphere, probably in contrast to the atmosphere in the nation as a whole, which was felt to be generally negative towards the possibility of change.

4. *Consultative leadership.* Consultative leadership means being involved in necessary decision-making processes during a crisis and being involved in open dialogue with the leader. Transparency in decision-making was seen as key to this process.

For the HSAN staff, two categories of response were reported:

1. Open communication and information-sharing, leading to better coordination and team work.
2. Individual responses reflecting a calm response and taking time to gain perspective.

The HSAN responses had a flavour of carrying on and getting the job done rather than seeking emotional support. Both sets of responses demonstrated the common desire to see improved communication flow during a crisis and some desire to have individuals respond calmly.

Enhancing team cohesion was seen as very valuable. Ninety per cent of participants in the LSAN wanted social events organised in which everyone could participate. This particular culture sets great store on social events and has numerous protocols and traditions which guide the process of, for example, an all-night "celebration" which WV could easily encourage and facilitate to enhance team or national bonding. It was seen as essential that WV staff participate in such events freely, not by obligation. The HSAN group also indicated a desire for more social gatherings, though this was not universal.

Having a common set of values was also seen as important in the LSAN. Particular values included giving to and receiving emotional support from to one another, sincerity in speech and consideration for one another, knowing the common values expected by WV, and being able to admit one's own mistakes.

Clear structural issues emerged in the LSAN, particularly flexibility in approaching various responsibilities whilst at the same time placing limits on tasks and roles and identifying different ways to motivate the staff.

Consultative leadership qualities were identified as needing improvement in the LSAN, particularly enhancement of mutual respect between team leaders and members, and more open, transparent communication. Generally, in this particular LSAN, the decision-making process is inclusive, but staff felt this could be enhanced. In particular, it was suggested that all opinions be considered and that participatory decision-making be realistic and objective, explained adequately, and representative of consensus rather than just the decision of one person. Preferred emotions involved were identified idiomatically – "should be made with a smile".

For the HSAN, suggested improvements to team cohesion broadly centred on improved communication within the organisational structure and a desire for leadership to promote team cohesion. Given the extreme nature of the stressors the teams in the HSAN were facing, this is consistent with the literature suggesting that, in a major crisis, social support from management and peers is actually derived from perceived competence rather than directly given emotional support.

The desiderata for ideal characteristics of a leader mapped extraordinarily onto the biblical notion of a godly character and of Agape love (Gal. 5: fruit of the spirit; 1 Cor. 13: "Love is . . . ") in both groups and included characteristics such as transparency, kindness, caring, wisdom, dignity, perseverance, desire to listen and understand, morale, interest, ambition, initiative, optimism, trust and enthusiasm.

Results with Respect to Underlying Model

Rationale for Statistical Analysis

The model makes two strong sets of predictions:

Hypothesis 1. There would be some significant relationship between life events/trauma (where relevant) and stress-related behaviour, but there would be evidence of an intervening set of variables.

Hypothesis 2. The intervening variable that mediated the effect of life events on an individual would be social support as measured by team cohesion, social support outside the team, and the consultative leadership style of the individual's manager.

Statistical analysis has been kept to a minimum, since the effects being looked for need to be clearly obvious at a management level rather than needing to be teased out statistically. That is to say, the model needs to be powerful enough to operate with a minimum of analysis to be sustainable in a busy HR environment with limited resources. The statistical tests are therefore geared to confirming that any large effects noted are, in fact, statistically significant and not artefact.

Chi-square tests are used as a measure of the differences between the frequency counts of staff appearing in different categories as a result of the questionnaire studies.

It is only possible to report on the effects of social support from the LSAN. The HSAN results yielded no staff that felt they were experiencing very low levels of social support.

Results

Is There a Direct Link Between Stress and Trauma and Being Stressed or Traumatised?

A statistically significant correlation was found between life events and trauma, and between life events and measures on the GHQ. This would be anticipated from the literature; however, it was also clear from the results that the correlation only accounted for some of the variance. In other words, another variable was involved in the association.

This was confirmed by using statistical tests measuring association between stress and symptoms for both the HSAN and the LSAN. These were nonsignificant, indicating that there was not a significant association between the stress individuals were under and becoming symptomatic of stress.

In the population of aid workers assessed there was an overall correlation between stressors and stress symptoms. However, it was clear that another set of variables was involved and, with that in mind, attention was given to the associations between social support and stress symptoms.

Does Being Poorly Socially Supported Compromise Mental Heath?

Given that, we are now able to test the second hypothesis, that those who have their social support system compromised in some way will be more at risk of stress-related behaviour than those whose social support systems are intact. Here it was predicted that low levels of social support are a more potent predictor of stress levels than high levels of social support predicting "wellness". It was also predicted that compromised social support would yield a higher prevalence rate of "un-wellness". This analysis was only possible using data from the LSAN nation because the HSAN nation reported no toxic levels of social support.

The first step was to examine the correlational data; here, the data was very robust. The correlational data seemed to suggest that social support within the World Vision teams and also outside the World Vision teams was critical, though in subtly different ways. As would be expected, trauma symptoms were less likely if social support was high. However, the effect was stronger for social support outside the team. The reverse was true for symptoms of anxiety and depression. Social support within World Vision was protective, but social support outside World Vision did not correlate significantly with levels of anxiety and depression.

These are very preliminary results and have to be treated cautiously. As a minimum, however, it is possible to say that social support networks within an agency and outside an agency are both protective of mental health. Intriguingly, social support outside the agency may protect mental health in different ways than social support inside the agency.

A further speculation is that the social support may be more structural in nature inside an agency and more functional outside the agency. Several people within one office were clear about this. Coming to work gave them purpose and hope, a sense of control and camaraderie that they could not get in the effective war zone outside the office. They did not appear to be crossing potentially lethal checkpoints to engage in reciprocal, close, confiding, supportive relationships, but rather had crossed checkpoints for the camaraderie of engaging, with others, in a meaningful job and of taking their minds off the other realities of life around them.

The second step was to look at how mental health varied with social support. It was assumed that very low levels of social support were harmful and so results from that group, labelled the "compromised social support group", were contrasted with those experiencing medium to high levels of social support.

Results, in summary, indicate the following: Compared with those with medium to high levels of social support, those with compromised social support are:

- 4 times as likely to be experiencing traumatisation;
- 3 times as likely to be experiencing some form of unwellness;
- 2.4 times as likely to be experiencing some form of acute anxiety; and

- 2.5 times as likely to be experiencing some form of physical illness.

All these results were also statistically significant.

Conclusions

The questionnaire study shows unequivocally that if social support is compromised, then front-line aid workers are not only statistically more likely to be symptomatic of stress and trauma, but that the differences are huge (up to four times the likelihood of being traumatised, for example).

Intervention is mandated on a number of different foundations: the sanctity and dignity of these individuals as bearers of the image of God, as outlined in the introduction; the implications of the People in Aid Code; and desire to enhance performance of the team for the sake of beneficiaries.

The questionnaire study alone cannot answer all the ensuing questions. Here we turn to the focus group results, which, in turn, cannot provide the sort of statistical data above but do fill in some blanks regarding praxis.

The data show that poor social support, lack of consultative leadership and poor vertical cohesion are toxic to mental health in the presence of stress and trauma – the focus groups in the LSAN guide us to what to do about that, in a culturally specific way. From the focus groups we can see what social support, team cohesion and consultative leadership look like in each culture and how team members desire to see them improved. There is some evidence that interventions will vary according to the overall stress levels within a nation or team; that is, those in low stress nations will desire to see opportunities for functional social support dynamics enhanced and those in high-stress nations will desire to see structural social-support mechanisms enhanced.

It is therefore possible to build culturally specific and time/event specific interventions based on the information gathered from the focus groups, predicated on the knowledge that the intervention is worthwhile because of the questionnaire study and its confirmation of the underlying model.

Using the methodology above, an "at risk" profile for teams in potentially difficult circumstances may be created. If teams are socially well supported and led in a consultative style pre-incident, then one form of trauma and emergency support service may be required, focusing on practical concerns and ensuring that the psychological and social resources of the teams are recruited for the necessary defusing and debriefing. However, if the team is broadly toxic in its social support structures, then even a mild critical incident may require a full and rapid trauma and emergency support service intervention involving both practical support and outside psycho-social intervention. It seems that the use of trauma and emergency support service may not be predicated simply on the intensity of the critical incident, but also on the vulnerability of the team to the psychological effects of a critical incident.

In HR terms, before any critical incident, the interventions required are to enhance the social support structures of the teams through selection, induction, maintenance, corrective action, training and education of team members and of team leaders using known and culturally specific inputs generated by the teams themselves.

Generally this study lends credence to the growing awareness that social support structures and dynamics in an aid worker's life are key in protecting workers against the effects of stress and trauma. HR initiatives to encourage and ensure team cohesion and consultative leadership during selection, team formation and team maintenance phases are a critical and practical response to the challenges they are expected to face daily and the traumas we all hope they will never encounter.

Upon returning from Southern Sudan in 1995, an aid worker told me: "We were laughing and joking. It was a dreadful time with so many people dying of starvation and cholera all around us. Yet the sense of team was incredible and we were able to support one another. If we hadn't had one another, a sense of being in the right place and clarity on what we were there for, I really think I would have gone mad."

Notes

[1] Eyewitness accounts are from the author's personal experience unless indicated otherwise. Details have been changed to maintain confidentiality.

[2] Toxic organisations are ones which, by their very structure or internal dynamics, tend to produce high levels of stress symptoms such as illness, burnout, and so forth in their staff irrespective of the nature of work they are engaged with.

[3] M. Heidegger, *The Question Concerning Technology* (1953).

[4] S. Davidson, *The People in Aid Code of Best Practice in the Management and Support of Aid Personnel*, Network Paper 20, Relief and Rehabilitation Network (London: Overseas Development Institute, 1997).

[5] R. G. Tedeschi, C. L. Park, L. G. Calhoun, *Posttraumatic Growth* (Mahwah, N.J.: Laurence Erlbaum, 1998).

Part III

Recommendations:
creating work environments that renew life and hope

chapter 6

Strengthening relationships for health

Sometimes I just wish I could be alone. I mean, all this living together in one house is all very well, but after a couple of months it can get on your nerves. But really, you know, I wouldn't be without it. These guys are my life. We laugh together, we eat together, we sing together, very badly, and occasionally we cry together. We always keep in touch. After we worked in Liberia in the early '90s we found ourselves being together in Angola and then Sierra Leone. Now we are back in Liberia. Of course we have other friends and most of us are married and have kids. But this team, this group, you know, we know each other. We've seen things, done things that we can't really explain to others, not even our family. We don't often talk about it all, but we all know we know, if that makes sense? Yeah, we get on each other's nerves, it's not all wonderful, and when the pressures get going then we can have some heavy arguments. But we are a team, a unit. We work hard, play hard and look after each other. Couldn't do it without them.

—Serge, from Sweden, working in Liberia in 1999

Traditionally most stress management guides start off with recommendations related to healthy behaviours such as eating the right food or maintaining an exercise regime. While such strategies are obviously effective (and will be discussed in detail later), research has discovered that the most protective strategies have to do with social and group behaviours. As described in the introduction and earlier chapters of this book, it now appears that social support is the greatest part of keeping well while doing international humanitarian work.

If it were possible to assign a value to the various aspects of a potential stress management strategy in international humanitarian work, it is now thought that personal coping abilities and resilience may account for only 20–30 per cent of the factors that protect individuals from negative impacts of stress. The factors carrying the most potential for protection relate to social and organisational relationships and structures in which an individual exists. Team functioning, for instance, in field environments is much more significant in maintaining individual health than an individual repertoire of personal coping strategies.

However, while such strategies may be only a small part of an overall stress management plan, they are important, and people need to make choices about how to develop and maintain coping skills and healthy behaviours. It is very unlikely that any personal strategies detailed in the following pages will cause ill health. Research in many fields supports these activities as promoting health and a sense of well-being. The caution here is that individual coping mechanisms are not sufficient in themselves. Social and organisational practices will be a component of any comprehensive stress management strategy.

Social support both inside an agency (and a team) as well as outside the workplace can be measured using validated social-psychological instruments. Many such instruments are available throughout the world, most readily accessed through psychologists and organisational-development specialists. The following section contains open-ended and specific questions that individuals and employers might wish to consider as a method of either opening up a dialogue or beginning a process of self-assessment. Utilised in an agency or team setting, the formal instruments can be quite powerful ways to assist team-building processes.

Social Support

Support Networks

Everybody has a list of acquaintances and friends. Most humanitarian workers have many colleagues. But a telephone directory or an e-mail list does not equate to an active social support network. To be health-promoting and protective, a social network needs to comprise people who know each other very well and remain in close communication. It is not sufficient for an individual to know a number of people very well. It is much more protective for the people that form this social network to know one another very well. The most protective social networks need not be very large, but they must be very interconnected.

What does *interconnected* mean? Protective relationships of this kind of social network provide much more than exchange of information. Attributes of social support to look for include:

- personal commitments to one another
- ability to offer and receive advice and criticism
- affirmations of worth shared openly
- access to nurturing or caring for one another
- perceptions of the group by its members as being a group
- opportunities to meet and engage in social activities

Family Connections

Family networks often (but not always) provide natural social support networks for humanitarian workers. Such networks include family of origin and new families created through marriage or intimate relationships. The protective factors of family networks are often undermined by the nature of humanitarian work, however. In the past twenty years international humanitarian work has become extremely mobile and global, and most aid workers find themselves moving frequently from field location to field location, often spending only a few years, or even months, at any one place. Younger or new aid workers initially may find separation from family obligations liberating. Even otherwise happily married workers speak positively about separations from spouses and children. Of course, family therapists and counsellors have long acknowledged that too much of even a good thing can be disadvantageous. So it would not be correct to assume that family separation is always a bad thing. However, the literature confirms that generally close family relationships are protective, and workers are encouraged to build and keep affirming and supportive relationships with family members.

Checklist for Individuals

Know your own social support capacities:

- Name the people who form this network.
- How extensive is the network?
- Where do they live?
- Do they know one another? How well?
- How do you communicate? e-mail? telephone? in person?
- How often do you physically meet?
- Do you both give and receive support in this network?
- Do the members of this group know what you are facing right now in your work?
- How would they receive your gripes or complaints? Would they want to hear?
- What are the limits of support you could call on from them? How would you know?
- Do you have close friends of both genders? Why? Why not?

If you find that you do not have a very strong social support network, then make an effort to create one. There is some evidence to suggest that humanitarian workers manage to cope with the strain of the first three to four field assignments quite well, but as the number climbs, there appears to be increasing distress. It may be that weakening (or unattended to) social support networks contribute to the higher prevalence of ill health in more experienced aid workers. As prevention is always much easier than treatment, it is strongly recommended that social support networks be established well before they are needed. Distressed, depressed and burned-out people have very little capacity for creating healthy interpersonal relationships. Lack of such resources for someone experiencing severe distress could result in a deeper decline into ASR or other conditions.

Know your family support capacities:

- Define your supportive family network. Name the individuals who make up this network.
- Where do they live? Are they easy to access?
- How often do you communicate? By what means?
- If you are married, how long in terms of days or weeks are you separated from your spouse each year?
- When you are away, how often do you communicate? Measure this in hours or minutes.
- What is the nature of this communication? Is it mainly information sharing? Or does it include affective communications (the difference between listing the bills to be paid and how you feel about being apart)?
- Do you receive as well as give emotional support during this communication?
- After you have talked, do you feel relieved to have ended the conversation? Or do you wish for more?
- When you return home, do you feel positive or negative?
- How long is it before you feel the desire to depart again?
- If you have children, how old are they?
- Do you know the day-to-day issues being faced by your children?
- How do you provide support for your children? phone? e-mail? letter?
- Does your spouse share the same enthusiasm for the work that you do?

- Does the rest of your family share this passion?
- How well does your family know what you actually do?
- Do you want your family to know what you do? Or do you prefer the privacy or even mystery created when you depart?
- What extended family responsibilities do you have?
- Do you have family members who are ill or disabled or aged? Are you expected to support them in some way?
- Are you able to perform these duties?
- What about the future? How will your present family roles alter in the next 12 months? the next five years? ten years? How have you prepared yourself for these changes?

Many younger aid workers take family support for granted, assuming family members will be there if and when required. However, family relationships require as much nurturing and maintenance as other kinds of social support. It is not unusual for humanitarian workers, like all human beings, to find great relief in being away from the demands of parents, siblings, aged relatives, spouse, children and all the aspects of family responsibilities. This feeling is a natural part of life, and the career of an international aid worker provides one of the best avenues for maximising such separation. Not only is it an itinerant career, but the work is intrinsically valuable.

The aid worker brings life to the dying and hope to the hopeless, and as such has social permission to be separated from family and community for lengthy periods of time. Indeed, many cultures and subcultures (such as faith-based communities) actively seek recruits for such careers, lavishing status and honour as well as, in some cases, substantial financial rewards. This is not restricted to international workers from first-world countries. Increasingly, employees recruited from developing or very poor countries find that a career in aid work carries with it many positive aspects, not the least being the potential to open up opportunities for family members to access better health, education and careers themselves. It is not uncommon today to find international and even national aid workers recruited from developing-world countries who spend months and even years without seeing spouses and children.

To understand the extent and nature of a family support network, it is suggested that humanitarian workers know why they have chosen to be separated from family members. This is not to suggest any sinister reason for choosing a career as an aid worker. Rather, when distress is experienced (and in this line of work, nothing is more certain) it is better to know just how supportive a family network really will be. Trying to create that support at the moment of need may prove difficult. As in the case of a strong and dense social network, preparation is much more likely to succeed than relationship-mending after a traumatic incident.

Other Forms of Social Support

While close social networks and family provide the best protection against distress, other forms of social support are useful to build into an aid worker's health strategy.

- Do you belong to any professional associations?
- How often can you meet professionally with such colleagues?
- Do you contribute to professional discussions? conferences? newsletters? capacity-building events?
- Do you belong to a group such as a church or other faith-based community? (Remember that a dynamic and flexible faith is very protective.)
- How often do you meet with other members?
- Does the church (or the group you belong to) know what it is you do? Do the members want to know?

- Think of a time when you might need support from the church or this group. What could they give? How far could they go in supporting you or your family?
- Do you contribute to as well as receive from this group? (Remember that there is a direct relationship between the extent of support available and the depth of the relationship between the person needing support and the providers.)
- Do you belong to any group not related to your career as an aid worker?
- How often do you meet with members of that group?
- What level of skill do you have with regard to the purpose of that group?
- Are you able to continue to develop that skill or interest when you are working? (For example, you may have musical skill and be a member of a musical interest group. How much time are you able to devote to developing that interest?)
- Before you commenced this career, did you have a wider range of activities and interests than you do now?
- Are there activities or interests you would have liked to have become involved in but haven't?
- How would you go about creating opportunities to get involved?
- Is your career at the centre of your life? How long will this continue? What would bring about the end of this focus? Would that be a good thing or a bad thing?

It is not uncommon for international aid workers to find after a few years in the job that the job has become everything. This is especially true for emergency and relief workers, whose lives often consist of extremely long hours in very dangerous and demanding environments. When the "down time" does arrive, many such workers find that their priorities are getting physical rest, recovering from health issues, and dealing with personal matters such as taxes, property or family issues. Very little time or energy is left over for other seemingly less valuable activities. Yet without personal balance, especially in relationships, it is likely that over time the pressures of chronic and cumulative stresses will be harder to deal with. Long-term humanitarian workers know that having active interests apart from the primary focus of the job is essential to maintaining health and a flourishing life.

Interests provide protection and preparation for the time that inevitably comes when active front-line fieldwork is no longer possible or offered. Careers with high demands and fulfilment are known to be the most challenging to retire from successfully. Yet retirement must occur at some stage. If not prepared for early on, then the impact of separation from the career is likely to be much more brutal and potentially damaging than if some distance has been maintained throughout the length of a career.

Checklist for Employers

These recommendations are directed at senior management in humanitarian agencies. It is recommended that the divisions or groups responsible for programme design, staffing, recruitment and staff support be concerned with addressing these matters.

- Does the organisation consider the nature and extent of an applicant's social support network at interview?
- How would you go about assessing the presence, absence or strength of such a network?
- Are there organisational policies or guidelines relating to staff access to support networks?
- Does the organisation place value on social support networks?

- What documents support that value? In other words, where is the proof?
- Is this value operationalised in any way? How?
- How much time can a staff person take to be in contact with a social support network?
- Is the employee permitted to make use of agency communications systems to keep in contact with support networks?
- Does the organisation encourage staff members to keep in contact with spouses, children or immediate family?
- Does the organisation provide access to agency equipment to make this possible?
- What restrictions are placed on the availability of such equipment for "personal" use? Why?
- How does the agency know if there are difficulties in a staff member's family or marriage?
- Are managers trained in skills required to assist staff in maintaining positive support relationships? Why? Why not?
- Does the organisation either overtly or covertly reward staff for spending excessive time away from family?
- Does the organisation restrict staff who spend too much time away from family? Why not?
- Does the organisation have clearly documented policies relating to cultural differences in defining family and community?
- Are provisions designed around the needs of one cultural group or flexible enough to meet all cultures' requirements? Why or why not?
- Which unit or department in the agency would be responsible to investigate the above issue?
- Do staff know this unit has this authority?
- Are all staff encouraged or required to maintain relationships with appropriate professional groups?

- Do staff have opportunities at agency expense, to be part of professional conferences, meetings or training outside the agency's own programme of events?
- How does the agency ensure that staff have opportunity to take part in activities that are not part of the work environment, such as hobbies or interests?
- What provisions does the agency have to support staff as individual responsibilities change with time? Or does the agency leave all that to the individual to deal with?
- Does the organisation have systems to assist staff working in remote locations to manage personal matters such as taxes, house payments and other personal matters?
- In an emergency, is it possible for an employee to be with family members? How does the organisation assist with this? What are the limitations?
- How does the organisation define "close family"? Does it use a Western model of two parents and children, or broader and more globally prevalent concepts?
- What access do family and support networks have to the staff person or the agency management structure?
- Do staff and family members know the agency limits? Have these been clearly explained, and are they generally understood?

The above questions do not imply that an employing agency is solely responsible for the maintenance of individual social and family support systems. However, evidence is very clear that individuals who have access to good social support, and who have sound family relationships, are more productive, less likely to suffer from ill health, more likely to be loyal to the employing agency, and less likely to complain about their employer – either covertly or more expensively through the courts.

Organisations that invest in policies, guidelines, training and systems that assist employees to develop and maintain healthy and strong social relationships will benefit in many ways. Shortsighted agencies will view such suggestions as luxuries or overhead expenses to be reduced or to be provided only during economically flush times. But to the contrary, investment in these provisions will over time reduce agency costs and significantly advance field objectives and programmes. Individuals seeking employment in humanitarian work should carefully assess prospective employers for their ability and willingness to provide social support and access to such support once in a field role. Individuals are strongly advised to avoid employment offers with agencies unable to describe clearly how they would provide such support and assistance.

Team Dynamics

This section may appear out of place in a book about stress management in humanitarian work. But the available evidence clearly demonstrates that aid workers assign most causes of stress to organisational factors such as team relationships, leadership, clarity of mission objectives, and agency structure. The most effective strategy for stress management in international aid work is preventative. Addressing matters of social support, team cohesion and quality of leadership will show the most return on investment. The sections that follow discuss ways in which individuals can assist in protecting themselves from stress injury. However, the research is clear that, all things being equal, the strongest and most careful individual will still be at very high risk of stress injury if organisational and social factors remain unattended to.

Teamwork is now at the core of humanitarian work. It was not always this way. At the beginning of the development of emergency relief work, resources were severely limited and many agencies could only afford to send one or two people to the front line. It was expected that these people would be very skilled in a wide range of abilities, would be able to function well in locations isolated from the main decision-making offices of the agency, would be able to survive hostile environments for long periods of time, and would be able to take actions to alleviate pain and suffering in the target populations. As the extent of humanitarian work boomed in the last two decades, these forerunners became indispensable to agencies competing for funds and marketing opportunities. But relief and development work in the 2000s is quite different from that of the 1980s or even the early 1990s. Many larger global NGOs maintain extensive emergency relief capacity, with mobile teams of experts able to relocate to a disaster zone in a very short time. Relief work today is a team operation, not one for the lone operator. Two aspects of this transition still have to be understood fully by NGOs and many of their staff.

First, as agency funds increased, it became possible to create expert teams. Naturally, membership of these teams consisted of successful veterans of earlier relief work. But the very success of these individuals can threaten the viability of the new relief teams. Many veterans came into the work as strong and independent individuals; they very quickly found that the best way to survive was to strengthen their independence and individualism. Many appeared to believe that their worst enemy in keeping well was not the extreme environment of the disaster site, but rather the strange and varied ways in which their employing agency operated. Headquarters managers might often make decisions or demand actions that, in the reality of a front-line operation, would appear illogical or even dangerous. So the veterans learned ways to avoid "crazy" agency requirements while at the same time delivering the care and retaining employment. The energy and skill required to achieve these often competing needs are considerable, and only a few have managed to do so for a full lifetime career. A large number have not managed without significant impact to either personal physical health or close family relationships. When it came time for a fieldworker to choose between the victims of a disaster, agency requirements, and personal or family well-being, most chose to sacrifice themselves and even family relationships rather than lose the opportunity to provide care.

It is time for employing organisations to recognise publicly and honour the cost that front-line emergency relief and development workers and their families have bourne over the years. This is the very least that is owed them.

The second change that came, when it became possible to fund teams of relief workers. These teams were often pulled together on the basis of specific skills, knowledge or experience. These collaborations were not created on the basis of assessment as to how well the individuals would function as members of a team. Even today, advertisements for relief team members focus on individual technical skills rather than proof of ability to act as a member of a team. Where an agency does specify teamwork skills in a recruitment process, in the face of very high competition for the best, final selection will often be decided on technical skill level alone. The reasons are twofold. First, there is a belief that anyone is better than no one, and having staff on the ground is a prerequisite for grant and donor funds. Second, most agencies do not yet know how to assess for teamwork skills. Where teamwork is valued and efforts are made to create and manage teams, it is often the case that, despite growth in numbers of staff, there are still too few available to allow employers the opportunity to shuffle staff around to create the most effective teams.

Despite this, as detailed by Graham Fawcett earlier in this book, team dynamics remain a key element in stress and trauma prevention. As such, it is imperative that both individuals and agencies deliberately pay more attention to these factors in the future.

Team Cohesion

Team cohesion is not about how well a team meets organisational objectives. Performance outcomes may be a result of sound team cohesion, but are not a measure that can be used to grade the quality of team cohesion. Cohesion in a team is more about the capacities of team members to "give and receive affection," as Graham Fawcett describes. This concept of shared affection is difficult to define and to measure. Yet the presence of cohesion is seen by many psychologists as a primary factor in protecting individuals against the dangers of both chronic stress and major critical incidents.

A team with high cohesion will be seen to work more closely together as stress levels increase. A team with poor cohesion will tend to fracture into groups or individuals as pressure rises. Cohesion has a lot do with how individuals view their personal commitment both to other team members and to the mission objective. If mission objectives are shared, and this sharing is clear, then individual commitment becomes a group commitment, creating a bond among the individuals. This bond increases the depth of relationship between members and appears to set up a kind of feedback effect whereby individual team members both give and receive affirmation and support during and after a mission.

Cohesion can be enhanced in a variety of methods. Invitation to become a team member is the place to begin. A common social background among team members will facilitate the process. Does this mean that members all have to come from a common cultural or ethnic background? Probably not. Social forms are common across cultures, and it is possible to find most social grouping types in most cultures. A university graduate from Thailand will have a similar social background to one from Brazil and another from the Netherlands. They will share some similar experiences but not an identical history. On the other hand, a person who grew up on Smokey Mountain in Manila may have a markedly different social background and worldview from an individual born and educated in Beverly Hills, California. This is not to say that these two people could not work together well, but recognising the differences in social background and assumptions will enable organisations to prepare team members to work effectively together.

Shared experiences become the tie that binds teams together. In many ways this can overcome differences in social background. The shared experience, however, has to be a positive one or it will destroy relationships and may prevent objectives from being obtained. A bad experience increases the potential for future stress damage. This is intuitively understood by most experienced humanitarian workers and is extensively referred to in the literature of military psychologists. Hence the uncanny, almost mystical abilities of veterans to be able to spot a dysfunctional team very quickly and to be able to make judgements on risks associated with particular individuals. All of us in humanitarian work have two lists of names in our heads. One is of those with whom we would never go to a major relief site, because of the danger they pose to us, and the other is the list of those we would feel quite safe with. These two lists often do not match organisational charts or assigned management status.

Because shared experience is such a powerful factor in team cohesion and subsequent stress protection, it must not be left to chance in creating field assignments. Team experiences can be designed, and teams can be built prior to assignment. A wealth of team-building opportunities are currently available to humanitarian agencies, most of which have been under-utilised by NGOs. Admittedly, in the corporate business world team-building courses have become something of a joke, treated somewhat cynically by many staff. This is often because reasons for building teams have been misunderstood by both employers and staff. Where organisations use team building as a method to increase productivity alone or as a reward for individuals who have outperformed others, it is likely that the team-building exercise will not be effective. A key component for team cohesion is the presence of a clear and meaningful team mission objective. If the group brought together for team building is there for the organisational reasons mentioned above and if members do not have a clear organisational mission, then it is unlikely that the experience will be shared positively.

This is not a book about team building; many excellent texts are available resources for those wishing to build quality teams. It is important, however, to be aware that team building involves change, and that change can sometimes provoke resistance and criticism. Even team building in a small segment of an organisation can have implications for the wider structure. Three essential elements of any successful team-building activity are participatory decision-making, excellent communication, and shared commitment to collaboration.[1] Team building must include a climate and culture of trust within an agency. Otherwise, individuals will be reluctant to open themselves to potential actions while exploring options for improvement.

Humanitarian agencies generally have very clear mission goals. The organisation's reason for existence is not share-holder profit, personal advancement or financial reward. Because humanitarian missions are value based, it should be relatively easy for agencies to bring together participants of teams to team-building exercises. As an example of how this is possible, World Vision has found its six-day, intensive, field-based security training workshops run for front-line teams to be a fruitful team-building process. This was not the original objective, but it is now apparent that the group experiences during the intense exercises, in pursuit of a stated and clear common objective (improved field security), have had a significant impact on team cohesion. Many other opportunities for such experiences remain.

Team cohesion must include attention to a clear and meaningful team mission or objective. For those who had the mixed fortunes to be involved in the early days of the Rwanda disaster in the early 1990s, the lack of mission objective was profoundly stressful and possibly traumatising. Humanitarian workers from around the world were summoned or sent to Rwanda in 1993 to "help". But in those first terrible weeks and months, separating victims from perpetrators was rarely straightforward. Strategies designed in other locations to be protective of victims, such as refugee camps, became prisons of violence and massacre as perpetrators were locked in with victims at night as aid workers departed. Donors demanded unrealistic results, and agency leaders in Europe and North America floundered as individual aid workers struggled to stay alive and relatively sane. Lack of a clear mission objective overall, and then the failure of mission leaders to identify a shared mission objective on the ground, created a nightmare, one still playing out in many dreams and dark moments.

Teams were both destroyed and created in Rwanda. The brotherhood and sisterhood of Rwanda aid workers may not be registered in any telephone book, but survivors of Rwanda will recognise and acknowledge each other as close colleagues, even if they never shared the same employer.

Lack of mission clarity contributed to a failure to protect staff from stress and trauma. Those who responded to the call to come to Rwanda were in immediate psychological danger from their own organisations' mismanagement even before they saw the mass graves or walked on the bodies in the churches.

Consultative Leadership Style

Many current humanitarian teams are led by the person believed to have the most skills or experience. Often this equates to length of time in the job and the grade of the position occupied. This generally has very little to do with how good a leader a person is. Up until very recently, humanitarian organisations focused on appointing managers, not leaders. This is true even when the language of leadership is used in recruitment processes. Skill sets identified with desired leaders are more often those associated with excellent management capacity. As any experienced field person knows, a great manager does not mean a great team field leader. Indeed, it is possible that some qualities of successful management are counter to those required by a good leader.

Of course, many leadership styles exist, and some would argue that management is a style of leadership. This may be accurate. Research both in military and humanitarian environments has shown that the most effective style of leadership in providing protection from stress injury for team members is that style called *consultative*.

A consultative leader will engender trust in members. To achieve this, the leader demonstrates competency and skills, recognised as such by the members. It is essential, then, for agencies recruiting team leaders to involve team members in the process of assessing candidates' competency. The team leader will be the one in charge, where "the buck stops". The team leader will lead by example; be present at the location where the team is acting out its mission objective; and demonstrate through personal behaviour the kind of actual responses and actions that will safeguard mental, spiritual and physical health. The consultative leader will not demand team members take risks that the leader would not take. Nor would the leader take risks that could be potentially damaging and then expect the team to follow. The team leader will not only be physically present with the rest of the team but will also share the same living and working conditions as the team. This is not to say that the leader might not have a personal satellite phone while team members have access to only VHF radios – the leader will have responsibilities requiring specialist equipment. But a consultative leader will not be sleeping in the hotel in town while the team spends night after night in small tents in the middle of an earthquake zone. The team leader will share the same risks the team members face. If the team leader requires an armed escort in the war zone for safety, then everyone does.

Team leaders will know their teams quite well. They need to know them personally, not just their specialist skill sets but also aspects of their family and social life. This does not have to be an exhaustive exercise, but it needs to move beyond sharing of work-related information. At the same time, the team leader cannot afford to play favourites or treat members differently. Some distance and objectivity must be retained. All the team members need to feel they are being treated fairly and with justice. Most of all, a team needs to know that its leader is prepared to provide for members' needs ahead of his or her own.

It is possible to measure both team cohesion and assess leadership style. It is also possible to find out how much those components are contributing to stress levels within a team or field operation. The psychological instruments used for this purpose are generally relatively easy to both use and score. A range of such instruments is available through most organisational psychology services.

Checklist for Individuals

Recruitment practices are changing, but it is still the case that most humanitarian agencies hire primarily on the basis of individual skills and experiences, rather than on an assessment of potential "fit" within a new or existing team. Individuals are therefore encouraged to review both their own team capacities, as well as that of the team they are considering entering.

Team Cohesion

- How do you work as a member of a team?
- What is your team member style? Are you a leader, compromiser, peacemaker, challenger, silent partner, outsider?
- What has been your previous experience of front-line aid teamwork?
- Are you really a team person? Or do you function better as a highly mobile individual? Again, one or the other is neither right nor wrong. But if you are most suited to working alone, then being placed on a team may be dysfunctional for the team and stressful for you.
- What characteristics of other people most irritate you in teamwork? How do you cope with that?
- What attributes of others do you find most supportive in teamwork? How do you encourage that?
- Is your present team really a team? Or is *team* merely a term used by your organisation to describe a group of staff working in a similar area of responsibility? Many times the word *team* is used to describe a work group, or unit, that does not function, nor need to function, as a team in the true sense of the word.
- If your present team is supposed to be a team, does it function as one? Why? Why not?
- What makes this work group a team? Name the individuals or activities or experiences that prove this is a team.
- Are there weak links in your team? What or who are they?
- If there are poor components of the team, what is the process for dealing with them? Is there one?
- Do you feel supported by team members? How is this support demonstrated?
- Could you describe your team as providing affection as described above? (Affection does not have to be explicitly stated, of course.)

- Do you share a similar social background with other team members?
- Does your team share personal information without being overly familiar? If so, is this supportive for you?

Leadership Style

- As a leader, what is your style? Do you lead from the front, issue commands, expect compliance, wait on others? None of these is wrong in itself, but knowing your style will help you adjust and fit in.
- What is the style of your present team leader?
- Does this style promote or hinder the team's objectives?
- Is the leader present with team members during operations?
- Does the leader share the same living and working conditions as the team?
- Is the leader competent in a professional capacity?
- Does the leader see to team members' needs before seeing to his or her own?
- Does the leader know you well enough to know when you are tired or stressed? Does the leader appear to want to know you?
- Does the leader inspire confidence during difficult times? Does the leader remain calm when all hell is breaking loose?

Mission Objective

- Does the team have a clear operational objective?
- Is this objective an overall one or one specific for the present task?
- If there are two objectives, are they congruent? Or do they conflict?
- Is the objective attainable?
- Are there sufficient resources provided to enable the objective to be attained?

- Is the organisational reporting structure clear?
- Does the team (or team leader) report to more than one superior? How does this help or hinder?

Checklist for Employers

These recommendations are directed at senior management in humanitarian agencies. It is recommended that divisions or groups responsible for programme design, staffing, recruitment and staff support be concerned with addressing these matters.

Team Cohesion

- Does the agency have a process to assess team skills at recruitment?
- Has the organisation clearly identified required team skills when advertising positions?
- How would an NGO determine a good team player from a poor one at interview?
- Is there a process of team building?
- Does this process involve regular, ongoing team-building exercises?
- If a team member leaves, what criteria does the organisation use for replacement? primarily skills and experience? team fit?
- Does the remainder of the team have any input into the replacement/recruitment process?
- Does the organisation have a clear definition of what makes a team? Are work units teams? Do they need to be?
- Is what makes a team and what makes a work group universally understood throughout the agency? Whose responsibility is it to ensure that this distinction is shared?
- If a team member is performing well in terms of skill set but poorly as a team player, how does the organisation address this?

- Does the regular performance assessment review team functioning? How might this be included in future?

Leadership Style
- Does the organisation have a clearly defined set of criteria for team leaders?
- How does the agency assess qualifications of the team leader?
- Are professional skills and experience the primary criteria for selection as a team leader? Where does leadership style fit into these criteria?
- Is there training for leadership of teams? Is this ongoing?
- When a team leader is in place, what process does the agency have to assess ongoing leadership practice? Are team members involved in that process? Is there a process for removing a team leader without having to terminate employment?
- Is being a team leader a requirement for promotion to other, higher status positions within the organisation? If the only way to senior management positions is through team leadership roles, then it is highly likely that all teams will, at some time, have leaders who may be skilled and competent employees but who are not good team leaders. Is it possible to create an alternate promotion path that would preserve leadership quality and professional skills?
- Is a team leader expected to be with the team during operations? Does the leader share similar living and working conditions during deployment?

Mission Objective
- Does each team in the organisation have a clear, attainable objective? Is this in the form of a global statement only? Or does each mission/deployment have clearly articulated objectives?

- How are objectives shared in the organisation? Does the wider agency structure share the same objectives as the front-line team? In the case of multiple objectives, do these complement or conflict?
- In the case of conflicting objectives, how is the conflict resolved? Specifically, who in the agency is responsible for clarifying conflicts in objective?
- Does the team have input in identifying operational or organisational objectives? Can the team veto an objective designed by others in the organisation? Why? Why not?
- Once deployed, who in the agency provides direct support to the team leader?
- How is this support provided?
- Does a team leader (or team) report to more than one person? If so, why?
- Is the team leader the same in every circumstance? Do different workplace requirements require different leadership styles? How would such a decision be made?
- Is there a process of reviewing leadership when team membership changes? Consultative leadership should be a transferable skill, but the makeup of specialist teams, such as emergency relief teams, may benefit from a leadership review if there are changes in the rest of the team.

Note

[1] J. C. Quick, J. D. Quick, D. Nelson and J. Hurrell, *Preventative Stress Management in Organizations* (Washington, D.C.: American Psychological Association, 1998), 202–3.

chapter 7

Spirituality as the foundation for growth

---

*I came into this work partly as a consequence of a deep, personal
belief in the power of God to heal. I was taught as a child that God
works through people, and that many of the problems we face in the
world today could be sorted out if people would only work together and
listen to God. My understanding of God has changed so much in the
past ten years. Everything was so black and white when I was younger.
Evil versus good, and all that stuff. It's a whole lot different for me now.
I still believe in God, but not in the judgmental God I grew up with. I
think God is a whole lot more forgiving than I was told. At least I hope
so, for my sake. (Laughs.) For me, God is all about life, and life is good.
It's possible to see God almost everywhere, even in the camps. Sure
they are miserable places, but if you look carefully you can see life and
love, people genuinely trying to help each other. This is a very good work
to be doing.*

—GRACE, FROM KENYA, WORKING IN SOMALIA IN 2000

Research documented in this book confirms and further
expands on findings in recent studies that spirituality
underpins all of the most successful stress and trauma
management strategies. This is in contrast to earlier, more
traditional recommendations. Many otherwise excellent
strategies ignore or avoid the issue of spirituality completely,
relying on behavioural changes to manage stress. This is a
mistake. An action, a thought, a behaviour or a plan arises
not out of thin air but out of a person's worldview, a theory
of why things are the way they are, and what right and proper
actions are required to influence the present to change.

In international humanitarian work, as with any kind of
social service, concepts of right and wrong are central.

Ethics, morals and responsibility form the underpinning reasons for performing aid work. Such principles, whether articulated as religious doctrine or encapsulated in United Nations agreements, arise out of a profound spiritual basis, not a vacuum.

Individual aid workers, when questioned, will describe their motivations for being in the work using spiritual descriptions, even if phrased as moral or ethical statements. Even the statement "because it is wrong that people should suffer in this way," is a deeply spiritual assessment leading to very practical actions and plans.

It is important to distinguish between spirituality and religious behaviour, however, especially within faith-based organisations. At least as far as existing stress management research is concerned, religious behaviour has been shown to be either neutral or negatively correlated to stress experiences. This is particularly so where the religious behaviour is rigid and religious concepts are held strongly with no possibility of modification. *Religiosity*, that is, the way in which religious belief is practised, is not a predictor of health. Rather, the more rigidly a religious behaviour is held to, the greater the prevalence of ill health in highly stressful environments. This is not to say that religious behaviour is unhealthy. But reliance on a set of religious activities alone as a protective function against increased stress is unlikely to prove successful. Of much more utility in stress management is a dynamic and flexible worldview or spirituality.

Why is this? Recalling that change is the cause of stress and strain the consequence, it is apparent that maintaining good health in the area of spirituality has its challenges. On the one hand, faith-oriented aid workers may intuitively assume that having a strong foundation of belief (or faith) will help them cope with difficult circumstances. So it may appear that this book recommends adopting a belief structure that alters with every new day. Rather, current research seems to imply that knowing what one believes in and holding to this belief generally promotes overall health. But the research also shows that individuals who are unable to integrate new learning and information into their system of thought or belief will eventually find that system collapsing or becoming unworkable. The key component of a belief structure that seems to provide the most resilience is faith, rather than particular behaviours or habits. In terms of measurable statistics, faith appears useful even if held in fairly general terms, such as faith in the goodness of human-kind, or faith in the goodness of God, or faith in the future, as well as faith in oneself. Where rigid religious behaviour is used in an attempt to bolster a faltering faith, especially in front-line field environments, it appears that both faith and overall healthy behaviour suffer.

A mistake made by some humanitarian workers from religious traditions is to attempt to rebut or reject or avoid conclusions of new experiences (exposure to evil) or infor-mation (this place is cursed and abandoned by God) by increasing the intensity or number of previous religious behaviours. Faced with extreme examples of evil or incidents where the presence of God can be easily doubted, one common response is to seek refuge in previously protective behaviours. For example, a person who attended a religious service once a week may increase this frequency to three or four times per week. Justification for this is often couched in religious terms, consigning the new information to catego-ries of heresy or secularism or, in worst case scenarios, as a deliberate attempt by someone to destroy his or her faith. While this approach does protect the individual for a period of time, it is ultimately unsustainable in the face of increas-ing evidence to the contrary (whatever the contrary view would be). Workers who adopt this approach will often take one of three courses, or a combination of all three: (1) They may retreat from the field, returning to a more familiar (and "safer") environment; (2) they may pull around them others who share their rigidity in an attempt to create group sustenance; or (3) they may begin to exhibit signs of emotional or physical distress.

Alteration of a worldview, another term for describing a spirituality, will be one of the most important challenges that all humanitarian workers face during their careers.

There isn't a worldview rooted in any location, culture or country that will not be significantly challenged upon exposure to front-line humanitarian work. Yet very few aid organisations specifically prepare their staff for this stress. Because it remains one of the hidden components of doing front-line humanitarian work, very few opportunities exist for discussion to promote spiritual growth in the face of worldview changes. When staff do become aware of the issue, they are often concerned about their position in the agency (particularly in religious or faith-based organisations) and may not raise questions in public. Organisations that have no mechanism to address these concerns will find themselves with employees who appear to have lost confidence in the agency values and mission and who face accusations of having "lost their faith" or "gone rogue". If individuals are struggling to integrate their own experiences and new knowledge at the same time they face real or imagined threat from their employer, then stress and distress levels will increase rapidly.

Most humanitarian organisations, including faith-based agencies, have not addressed in sufficient depth spirituality as a protective or destructive factor in humanitarian environments. Yet history shows that some of the most effective human endeavours have grown out of a spirituality or values base. The International Red Cross, for example, is based clearly on values reflecting a worldview requiring that all nations and people care for those in pain and suffering. Articulated clearly, these values are the basis for significant humanitarian assistance throughout the world. The United Nations is another, somewhat different example of an institution established according to very clear values and beliefs. Continued articulation of these values continues to provide assistance and protection to many people around the world. Unfortunately, it has gone without saying that individuals who aspire to work within such agencies and institutions also hold to values and a spirituality that motivate them to be where the pain is being felt. It has become essential for employing agencies to consider how to dialogue with their own employees regarding spirituality and values issues. Such dialogue created these organisations in the first place, and it is imperative that places be created for the dialogue to continue, to flourish, and to expand the humanitarian work that has historically grown out of such conversations. Fruitful dialogue will inherently involve questioning of the status quo.

The following checklists are intended as tools to assist in personal and organisational assessments. They are not proscriptive, nor are they intended for diagnosis. They are more accurately a series of questions that deserve to be attended to at some stage in the life of a humanitarian worker, and in the strategic directions of organisations seeking to provide care and assistance.

Checklist for Individuals

- Know and understand your own theology, spirituality or values basis. Try to articulate this either to yourself or, preferably, to a close friend or colleague before you enter humanitarian work.
- What do you have faith in? Aim for clear understanding of precisely where you place your faith. On examination, will this faith be sufficient to withstand challenges? How do you know this? Can this faith grow or expand with challenges, or is it set in stone?

- Ask yourself, Why do I want to go into this work? What drives me?
- Consider your religious behaviour. This will include any behaviour or actions that connect directly to your spirituality or set of personal values. Be comprehensive. Simple questions might be, Why do I go to church? But other, more complex questions might be, Why do I not drink alcohol? Why do I think that smoking is bad? Do I think smokers are likewise bad? Why do I feel energised by close proximity to the sea, the mountains, the sky? Where does the spirit of life/truth/hope really lie?
- Ask yourself which religious behaviours you would be prepared to alter. Why? Which would you insist on holding onto no matter what? Why?
- What in your spirituality or religion permits change and allows variance? Or, to put it differently, what would give you permission to make changes in what you believe or in your religious behaviours?
- When you are faced with a spiritual or religious dilemma or question, to whom do you turn? Do you have friends, family and colleagues who could hear your dilemma without harming you with their response? If you can't identify anyone, then consider a very strong recommendation that before entering this work, you take the time to create a pool of such people. You will need them in due course.
- Are you able to allow the statement *I don't know why* to be larger in your life than the statement *I know for certain the reasons for this, and the solutions?* There will come a time, if you pursue this career for long, when a profound lack of understanding will threaten to sweep away your actions, beliefs, achievements and even reason for being. Knowing that this challenge will come, and ensuring there are close friends who can hear your questions without harming you, is an essential component to preventative stress management.

- Should a workplace environment become potentially too spiritually stressful in itself, are you able to depart that place for somewhere more supportive? Why? Why not?

Checklist for Employers

These recommendations are directed to senior management in humanitarian agencies. It is recommended that divisions or groups responsible for programme design, staffing, recruitment and staff support be concerned with addressing these matters.

- Does the organisation clearly articulate basic values to which the organisation aspires? Is this statement available to all employees? Value statements are also faith statements, even if worded as values.
- Are these values clearly connected to a worldview or spirituality? If so, does everyone know this? What mechanism ensures that all employees understand this connection? What unit or department is responsible to ensure this occurs?
- Are these values clearly connected to a set of behaviours that are expected or required of employees?
- How do staff know this? Are the behaviours clearly related to the core values, or more strongly related to particular cultures? (For example, an organisation might argue that its practices are a specific component of a particular religion, but closer examination may reveal that such behaviours are relevant only for specific cultures. People of the same religion in another culture might behave in different, even contradictory, ways.)
- Is the connection between values and behaviour overt (policies, guidelines) or covert (lack of appreciation, snide comments, no promotions)?
- What is the process by which the organisation could discuss or alter its value statements? Does such a

process need to be created or realigned? Which unit or division is responsible for this process? How would employees be a part of this process?

- Is the organisational spirituality or values base dynamic and growing, or rigid and fixed in a particular time and place (era)? If there is no room for change, then it is likely that individual staff will exhibit increasing signs of distress and pain. Morale will decrease, turnover increase, and productivity reduce. Which unit or division in the organisation is responsible for assessing this process?

chapter 8

Personal strategies for wellness and hope

I have found it quite difficult to understand Europeans. I have worked with many of them for over ten years, and I am still trying to under-stand. For me, my family is everything. Without my husband and chil-dren I could not keep on doing this. I know I spend a long time away from them, but they are always where my heart and spirit lie. My parents, my brothers and sisters, all my aunts and uncles, all those people that European people call cousins. These are my family, my community, my life. When I am there I am truly, totally there. It's hard to describe to Europeans. I don't want a holiday. I don't want to go on "vacation". I'm not sure I really understand what a vacation is. Why do Europeans try to get away from their family so much? They come to my country to help, and I admire them for that, but they most often come here alone; they have no children, they don't go back to their parents often. Then they take their leave on some beach for two weeks and then go back to work. Can they really live so far apart from their home? Are they so strong as individuals that they don't need people? Maybe I have not grown strong enough yet, because I can't live like that. I need to be with my family, and I mean all my family, not just one or two. Maybe Europeans don't have families, so that is why they need special services like counseling and psychiatrists? Being alone is very hard. Maybe they should find their families again.

—HUYEN, FROM VIETNAM, WORKING IN VIETNAM IN 2001

Individuals come to humanitarian work with unique genetic makeup, distinctive life experiences, a range of abilities to cope with and manage stress, and differing goals and objectives. Studies indicate that, as one would expect, some factors are common to aid workers globally, but these are more in the area of trends rather than specifics. Individuals need to identify their own particular strengths and weaknesses, their coping and adaptation capacities, and where they are most likely to find themselves experiencing stress, strain and potential trauma. While the research detailed in this book shows that the most protection for fieldworkers is to be found in social and organisational factors, individuals can do much to bolster their defences. Even the best-equipped aid worker will find the relentless pressure of fieldwork over a lifetime career wearing away at personal coping abilities. Because the most likely stress exposure is chronic, rather than traumatic, it is not always easy to assess the state of one's own health or present capacity to withstand more stress.

For this reason, and for other reasons that will become clearer in this chapter, it is strongly recommended that international aid workers conduct regular personal inventories. This type of review should be done at least on an annual basis for all aid and development workers. For emergency and relief personnel who spend more than 65 per cent of a year on front-line deployment, personal reviews should be conducted more frequently, at least once every six months. The process of review need not be arduous and need not necessarily involve agency management. It is probably best to keep this type of assessment separate from performance processes, and more akin to regular medical checkups. Certainly information obtained through this process should remain confidential to the employee whether performed as a self-assessment or by referral to an external professional.

A number of self-assessment tools are available for quick and easy personal stress measures. This type of measure does not constitute a clinical or medical diagnosis. Use of self-scoring instruments is recommended, but in the wider context of appropriate professional guidance and advice. Most self-scoring tools provide indicators to the extent of stress being experienced and highlight some potential sources of stress. But these must not be taken as definitive clinical measures. Any person who uses these measures and obtains scores in the high levels is strongly advised to seek the assistance of a qualified professional. Only with such advice and expertise should any conclusions be drawn about mental or physical health.

Genetics and Personality

Many recruiters and senior managers have expressed a need for a simple tool that could predict stress-related behaviour on the basis of examination of an individual's genetic makeup or personality type. Unfortunately, such predictions are generally about as effective as an intuitive guess by an experienced interviewer. The problem is that the mixtures of life experiences individuals accumulate by the time they enter humanitarian work is so varied and unique that comparison with any degree of certainty on the basis of either genetics or personality is not possible. Also, most personality testing has been performed on first-world Europeans or North Americans, and the majority of aid workers today are neither. Therefore, the efficacy of such testing is doubtful.

One of the clearest conclusions that can be reached concerning genetics and stress relates to outcomes. Stress will most likely be experienced first in parts of the body where there is already a genetic weakness. So, if there is a genetic tendency towards cardiac problems, then heart illness is likely to be related to stress and strain. A family history of diabetes may indicate a propensity for an individual to develop diabetes following exposure to high levels of stress. Similarly in mental conditions with a connection to heredity, such as depression or schizophrenia, it is possible that high stress could affect mental functioning. Another area of genetic tendency that should be considered is potential chemical dependency. Considerable debate continues in the professional literature as to whether, say, alcoholism is essentially genetic or behavioural. Enough evidence exists, however, to advise individuals to be aware of any previous history of chemical dependency (alcohol, prescription or illegal drugs, etc.) in their family of origin. Drug-taking amongst aid workers may be quite common (if one includes smoking and caffeine use, over-the-counter medication, as well as alcohol and cannabis), and, especially in high stress environments, an individual with a predisposition to dependency would be wise to be informed prior to exposure to stress.

It would seem prudent for any person entering a high-stress career such as humanitarian aid work to be fully aware of any inherited physical conditions. Very few inherited predispositions would automatically exclude a person from fieldwork. There are always, of course, extreme cases, but by the time heightened risks become obvious, individuals are likely already aware of these and so do not seek to enter this career. Many physical conditions can be managed with due care and it would be up to the individual, in consultation with the employer, to determine what kind of field restrictions might be imposed, depending on the level of support required.

Much has been written in recent years about different personality types. The most common distinction is between so-called Type A and Type B personalities. Type A people are seen as go-getters, active, high-energy individuals, while Type B persons are said to be more laid back and less concerned about deadlines. Many assume Type A's will experience more distress and illness because they are constantly butting up against the realities of the world and human limitations. One discussion in the professional literature concerns the distinction itself, between types, with some arguing that the two types do not exist. Another component of the discussion regards the ability to alter a personality type. Those who accept the initial distinction are now more inclined to believe that some severe manifestations of Type A personality (aggression and violence) could be altered through insight and, in some cases, with the assistance of prescription drugs. In the professional literature, extreme Type A individuals are often termed "adrenaline junkies"; interestingly, this term is also commonly associated with emergency relief personnel.

The proportion of each type in society (North American and European) is said to be about 60 to 40, with Type A being the larger. It is also believed that the proportion in urban environments is more like 80 to 20, again favouring Type A personalities. The author is not aware of research findings dealing with proportions of these types among humanitarian aid workers, but it might not be surprising to find a predominance of Type A, particularly among emergency relief workers. Of course, such analysis would need to be considered in the light of the huge cultural and ethnic ranges in humanitarian work.

Do these distinctions really matter? Some indicators suggest that Type A personalities may have higher rates of heart problems, high blood pressure and strokes. Given that environmental stress factors in humanitarian work are generally high, and predicting that Type A personalities may choose such work in higher numbers than Type B, it could be that higher rates of physical ill health could be found in this group. A recent study of international humanitarian workers, however, did not reveal any significant health problems among workers employed in high-risk front-line positions when compared to those working in headquarters locations.[1]

One factor that may contribute to this result is that it appears personality type may be modifiable, if not completely changed. Research has shown that through counselling, group work and behaviour management, Type A individuals can quite significantly reduce the extremes identified with this group. Others suggest that it is not the Type A personality that is being altered, but that Type A behaviours can be treated in a similar fashion as a chronic disease, that is, reducing symptoms of the condition without altering the basic personality type. Whatever is actually occurring may be of little importance to fieldworkers. Type A individuals are an advantage to front-line relief work, and if the extreme impact of such personalities can be modified through a specifically designed programme, then agency objectives and individual health may be achievable.

Another predisposition of significant concern is mental health. Very clear evidence shows that distress and ASRs (including PTSD) are highly correlated to previous psychiatric illness. As Graham Fawcett has articulated earlier in this book, some agencies recommend that an individual with a previous psychiatric history should be fully evaluated prior to receiving a field assignment. Youth with a Mission UK goes so far as to exclude any person from fieldwork who has a previous history of PTSD or ASR. The list of psychiatric conditions requiring further investigation includes psychotic episodes, eating disorders, or recent depressive or anxiety-related disorders. Some organisations require a full psychiatric history and even include history of the immediate family, as well, in order to reduce risks in a field environment. Such levels of investigation may be beyond many agencies and may be illegal in some countries. However, evidence of the relationship between prior psychiatric ill health and subsequent serious distress, even years or decades later, is now well established and should be considered by employing agencies.

Lifestyle

Stress has a way of spilling over between work and home, sometimes creating a feedback loop that increases distress in both environments. At the same time, differences between specific stress factors in the two environments can have a moderating effect on both. It is possible for employers to assist this process by including a focus on family support systems as a preventative strategy. Organisations will have more direct influence over breaks from work and assisting an employee to maintain a balanced lifestyle.

Vacations as well as rest and relaxation (R&R) are long-standing components of humanitarian work. On paper and in policy, at least, most agencies offer apparently reasonable periods of time for staff to take real breaks from work. Most Northern NGOs provide a basic annual vacation allocation of four weeks, with some exceeding this. Virtually all organisations have a system of additional R&R breaks. Most often this allocation is tied to specific jobs or locations. Front-line relief programmes will have varying amounts of allocated R&R, depending on a variety of factors. The objective of these programmes is to enable workers to get away from the high stress levels of the front line for a period of time in order to maintain health and promote resilience. The objective is excellent, but in many cases the application falls short.

When asked, a disturbing number of aid workers, especially those in emergency relief, report not taking either vacation entitlements or R&R. Many reasons and excuses are often advanced for this, but all really sift down to one: poor management practices by both the staff and the agency. Whatever the causes for not taking leave, the fact is that this action (or inaction) would not be possible without a covert agreement between employer and employee. Because such an agreement has to exist (even if unspoken), it is within the organisation's area of influence to effect change. Managers with staff who have leave accruals at the end of a leave period could be audited and even penalised. Teams that allow members to accumulate large amounts of leave could be "grounded". Individuals who ask to have vacation leave added to the next year's entitlement could have this noted as an indicator of poor performance in annual reviews, so long as it was the individual who had sole control over the taking of the leave. Relief teams are often provided with R&R in cycles, such as six weeks on and one week off. Many times, however, teams or individuals will decline to take the first R&R when it is due, citing extreme pressure of work at a critical time of the operation.

Time off, in emergency contexts, is costly. Even in the case of longer-term development projects, chronic under-staffing may make time off costly both to the agency and to the individual whose workload accumulates while he or she is "off". However, deferring rest, recuperation and invest-ment in social or family support is a dangerous gamble and should be resisted strenuously by agency officials. Chronic stress has an extreme effect on productivity. A task that may have taken only an hour during the first week of deployment may take three or four times as long by the sixth week. This is not because the task is more complex. Rather, chronic stress levels have reached the point where every task takes longer to achieve conclusion. Relief workers find themselves with an increasing number of incomplete tasks and appar-ently less time in each day to bring closure to them. Staff take to working later and later at night, getting less sleep, less rest, with the consequent lessening of functioning the following day. If the decision to allow a worker to remain on site rather than take R&R is left solely to the team leader who is also at the crisis location, then the leader's own chronic stress levels may well negatively influence the decision.

The cost of burnout is considerable. Every agency has horror stories of key staff who burned out at critical times during an emergency response. The time, cost and com-plexities of attempting to remove a burned-out staff person during management of a major critical event are staggering. The financial and strategic price is much higher, when properly accounted for, than the managed cost of insisting that each and every front-line individual take allocated R&R when it is due. These cost-benefit ratios become especially stark when accounting for the fact that a burned-out worker may not be able to return to a front-line role for many months, if at all. What conceivable service can be so vital that it is deemed more effective to allow a highly skilled employee to become disabled when the alternative was simply ensuring they spent a week away from the front line? In the heat of the moment, of course, everyone appears indispensable. But in the cold light of day, a few years down the track, would a few days off in the middle have made a significant difference to the final outcome of the overall emergency response?

An aspect of R&R or vacation that could bear further examination relates to how the entitlement is taken. Some evidence suggests that following a period of intense activity (six to eight weeks) it might be more refreshing to take a series of three-day weekends, say five to equate to five days R&R. Five three-day weekends with well-planned activities have been shown to enhance recovery, sometimes better than a full week immediately following the intense period.[2] It is important to note that this plan is recommended for the end of the intense activity, not the middle of it, and is subject to the individual having returned to a more stable work location. For mobile relief teams, this might be similar to the end of assignment and return to the regional or global base environment where more regular hours of work are standard.

It also appears important that the activities opted for during the three-day period be specifically designed as refreshing and restoring. Selecting the right thing to do during the vacation is essential, whether for a three-week period or a three-day period.

There is no reason most humanitarian workers could not, with the agreement of their employers, adopt this kind of vacation cycle. Many employers may welcome the three-day weekend, as it ensures that the individual is present at the workplace for at least a part of the week the vacation is taken.

Another type of leave becoming popular, at least in discussion, is the sabbatical leave. Universities have long provided this kind of long-term, paid leave as a way to allow faculty members to take up learning opportunities, review research findings, spend time at other educational facilities, and generally provide respite from regular duties. Although employers are generally reluctant to implement such programmes on a wide scale, sabbaticals have been used with success. The purposes of such leave need to be very clearly defined. A sabbatical may be primarily for research or book writing, activities that bring direct benefit to the agency. As such, sabbaticals should not be viewed as "stress leave". But in terms of stress relief and protection, the positive outcomes could be manifold, with the organisation achieving some larger objective and the employee being refreshed and re-energised by the time away.

Sound team building prior to deployment and sound management practices, along with personal education and insight into stress factors and tendencies, would result in all involved taking full advantage of all vacation and R&R leave entitlements. Without compromising the objectives of the mission, these strategies would almost certainly reduce the risks of ASR, PTSD or burnout.

Stressful Life Events

Humanitarian workers face their biggest stress challenge not from traumatic events but from cumulative chronic stress factors. (Although when they occur, traumatic events are significantly disabling.) Because chronic and cumulative stresses are so insidious, it is easy to miss the point where pressure turns to strain and strain to distress. The best way to avoid this is to maintain a kind of running inventory of stress factors. This kind of assessment is relatively easy to do and can be performed at regular intervals. Such an assessment should be performed on an annual basis. For those in front-line relief work, a six-month basis may be better.

One instrument for humanitarian workers is the well-validated Holmes and Rahe Social Adjustment Scale.[3] This measure, along with others, can be found in Appendix 1. The principle behind the instrument is that even though an event may have occurred twelve months previously, an individual may still be experiencing strain as a result. Life events will have different magnitudes of impact and have been assigned weighting in order to address this. An individual completes the measure by creating a list of life events during the previous year and adding up scores assigned for each event (some events may occur more than once). The resulting total score indicates the cumulative life-event stress being presently experienced as a result of the last twelve months. The test is self-administered and gives an individual immediate feedback as to present stress levels.

Caution is required. Virtually all humanitarian workers who have used the Holmes and Rahe Social Adjustment Scale complain that significantly stressful life events are not included in the list of possible items. Military or quasi-military checkpoints, for instance, are intrinsically stressful but are not listed. The work-related items beg for adjustment in the humanitarian context. How many times does "change in responsibilities at work" occur in the life of a relief worker? daily? hourly? Some items are clearly related to an American, Christian environment – Christmas is not an event experienced universally, for instance. What does "marital separation" mean in the context of a work environment where couples may be separated for work reasons for months, if not years? How do you define "family" when the Western nuclear family concept is not applicable?

Additionally, this scale does not adequately measure chronic stress. It measures, for instance, a change in sleeping habits. But what if a good night's sleep is not possible for weeks on end, as often occurs in emergency relief situations? Or what if adequate nutrition is not available for months? These obviously significant chronic events occur on a day-to-day basis in humanitarian work. When the extent of "stress" is measured with reference to how many change events have occurred, it could appear that regularly not getting sufficient sleep or proper nutrition is not change (stress) but normal. Many humanitarian workers live and work in environments where the classification of "normality" would surprise many who live in first-world locations.

Obviously what is required is an adjustment scale for international aid workers, one applicable to all cultural and ethnic groups. At present, such a tool does not exist, although discussions are under way amongst specialists about the design of one. In the meantime we have found that alterations to some items in the existing scale (replacing "Christmas" with "religious celebration" or "social holiday") is acceptable. This is because stress is defined as change, and special days such as these constitute a change.

Other more sophisticated measures examine workplace stress, quality of employment and job stress. Most of these instruments require some kind of statistical analysis and some supervision in application. Many have copyright restrictions as well. For field offices or teams that wish to conduct more in-depth assessments of work-related stress, the involvement of specialist assistance is recommended.

Another tool that can be applied fairly easily across cultures is the General Health Questionnaire (GHQ - 28). The GHQ consists of twenty-eight items that indicate levels of physical health, anxiety and depression, although, as with all the instruments referred to in this book, this cannot be used for individual clinical diagnosis. The GHQ is best used to assess the relative health of a team or a unit.

Prevalence of Physical Symptoms

As we have already seen, distress is often associated with physical symptoms. Some people find that making an assessment of their physical condition can assist in determining the level of strain they may be presently experiencing. One list of symptoms some fieldworkers have found useful is the Stress Signal Inventory developed by Tubsing and

Tubsing.[4] This checklist is divided into various categories: physical, emotional, spiritual, cognitive, behavioural. While not a scaled instrument, an individual who identifies a large number of symptoms in the various categories is advised to seek further advice.

Of course, it isn't always apparent whether symptoms are related solely to stress or whether there may be some kind of underlying physical condition. This is particularly the case when applied to front-line aid workers. Many individuals working in extreme conditions may have physical conditions as a result of disease, poor food quality, or excessive heat or cold. If a symptom is actually caused by a serious physical condition and yet assumed to be a result of chronic stress, not addressing this with a medical specialist may result in serious harm.

The best advice for the fieldworker is to assess changes in physical symptoms. Any change noticed should be treated seriously and medical advice sought. Only when disease or other causes are eliminated should it be assumed that stress is the sole reason for the symptom. All humanitarian workers should have a full medical examination at least every twelve months, and preferably also after medium-term emergency relief assignments.

Behavioural Measures

As with physical symptoms, assessing changes in behaviour can be of some value, as long as other factors are taken into account. The easiest method to use is self-assessments. However, these do have the disadvantage of being easily influenced. Considering that changes in behaviour are the indicators being measured, it is useful for individuals to examine changes in body weight, sleeping patterns, numbers of cigarettes smoked, amount of caffeine consumed, other drug use, types of food being consumed, and so forth. While these are obviously subjective, substantial evidence appears in the literature that most adults tend to stay within a fairly limited weight range throughout their lives and tend to have a markedly regular sleep pattern. Aside from short-term alterations, these measures do not generally alter significantly with time.

Emergency relief workers will notice the obvious flaw in the above analysis. Eating habits, sleep patterns, and so on are often governed not by choice but by circumstances in humanitarian environments. In Herat, Afghanistan, circa 2002, the range of food types available was very limited and facilities of any sort in which to obtain a sound eight hours of sleep each night were well-nigh nonexistent. Some front-line workers claim that the number of cigarettes consumed during the first phases of an emergency response does not represent average consumption over, say, a twelve-month period. Likewise, many aid workers noted that personal alcohol consumption in Sarajevo during the siege of the city was time limited; once the need to travel the dangerous snipers' alley that was the road to the airport was over and a more secure home base had been attained, consumption dropped. This may, in fact, be the case. However, it is also possible that across the span of a career in front-line work (and recall that five years comprises a career in humanitarian fieldwork) there has been an average and steady increase in alcohol and cigarette consumption, or a slow but steady weight gain.

The usefulness of behavioural measurement increases if a baseline can be established early in the career, allowing an aid worker to identify and monitor change at a later date. Behavioural measures recorded during an adult's mid-20s are generally a sound indicator. As with all of these self-assessments, behavioural scoring may be affected by a wide variety of conditions, and where alterations give rise to concern, individuals are strongly advised to seek professional assistance.

Resilience

In some respects, resilience is the sought-after treasure of international aid work. Intuitively, individuals and managers believe there must be some clear way to measure resilience. Once this method has been identified, it should be easy to determine who will survive great stress and who will not. Unfortunately, this treasure hunt has not hit gold. Basically, the variables that make up individual lives are so numerous that exactly how one individual got to be resilient and the next one did not may remain unknowable in many cases.

A better term may be *hardiness.* Hardy personalities appear able to cope with higher levels of strain than those who are not hardy. A hardy personality demonstrates commitment, control and challenge. Commitment is engagement with the surrounding environment that leads to activities being experienced as enjoyable and interesting. It includes the ability to believe in the importance and value of one's self and, because of this, becoming fully involved in all aspects of life – social, work and family. Control is the perception that one can influence outcomes and the processes of events in a positive manner. The opposite of this would be the feeling that one is a passive recipient of whatever life presents. Challenge is the belief that change is normal and antici-pated. In other words, things do not stay the same, and change is to be expected. Further, rather than viewing change as a threat to personal security, a hardy personality accepts change as bringing opportunities for growth and development. Change allows individuals the opportunity to exert influence in situations.[5]

One of the more interesting findings in the last few years has been the indication that length of experience may not be a positive factor in developing either resilience or hardiness. The Centers for Disease Control mental health survey in Kosovo in 1999 found that workers who had more than five previous assignments were at significantly higher risk for developing ASR than those with only two or three career assignments.[6] Rates of ASR among veterans appeared higher than for individuals in their very first assignment. While much investigation needs to follow, one wonders whether the hardiness factors identified above may be influenced over a period of exposure to significantly stressful environments. Should hardiness factors be negated, or even worse, turned in on themselves, an individual's ability to cope with distress and strain might be compromised. In relief work this could be significant. As a career develops, and as success is noted, it is likely that both the organisation and the individual could anticipate being able to cope with even more challenging and stressful assignments. If changes in hardiness factors occur incrementally, it may be a long time before an individual is able to identify such change in an accurate self-assessment and take appropriate steps to return to health.

This finding, if confirmed in further research, has significant implications for both agency management and individuals. If, for some reason or set of reasons, ability to cope with strain and reduce distress is eroded over periods of exposure to stressful field conditions, then more senior practitioners may be at high levels of risk. Given that experience is also a major factor in operational success, organisations would be wise to consider ways in which experience can be retained in the organisation, especially in delivering relief services appropriately.

Exercise

Physiological responses to stress referred to earlier prepare the body for activity, whether fight-or-flight or tend-or-befriend. In the present world, much stress occurs in environments where activity is not an appropriate reaction. Chronic or even traumatic stress occasioned through a stressful e-mail does not allow much opportunity for physical activity. Nor, generally, does finding oneself suddenly in the middle of an uncleared minefield. Yet the chemicals and hormones released with the onset of stress urge one to do something. Exercise, even moderate exercise, will greatly help the body process these hormones and restore body chemistry to a more normal state. A build-up of hormones in muscle tissue is not healthy and has been connected to heart conditions. Following the onset of stress, and after the stressful situation has been stabilised, it may be useful to take some brief moderate exercise to assist in coping with the distress. Exercise can also be a useful preventative activity. Regular moderate exercise – twenty minutes per day four or five times a week – helps regulate hormone release while at the same time improving muscle tone and significantly reducing incidence of heart conditions.

When aid workers are asked about exercise, responses fall into two broad categories. The first has to do with opportunity. Many field locations do not appear to offer exercise options that do not include increased personal risk. This is often true, but in the author's experience, it is more often a case of not identifying options rather than an absolute lack of options. Walking is one of the most effective forms of exercise, and most field assignments will have locations where 20 minutes of walking is possible, even if this means walking the perimeter of the local market a couple of times. Rather than leaving full responsibility for this to individuals, managers can assist in providing or pointing out options. While space may be limited in a few locations, generally it would be possible to provide access to equipment such as hand weights, which are proven to be very effective aerobic tools as well as promoting muscle tone and bone density.

At the other extreme, a number of emergency relief workers always find both time and opportunity to exercise. Several acquaintances regularly run quite long distances even in locations where being outside secure areas may be questionable. When their behaviour causes concern, they may report that they find exercise an essential component of stress management and if they "give in" to environmental restraints in one location, they fear giving in to most. The risk is deemed acceptable. Given the ability of experienced fieldworkers to assess security risks, they may well be accurate. However, for less experienced individuals, the advice is to think very carefully before running or walking in high-risk environments. Running itself could be a risky activity in many contexts where people who run in public may be assumed to be engaged in suspicious behaviour.

Nutrition and Diet

Maintaining a regular eating pattern is difficult for emergency relief workers but should not prove a challenge to most humanitarian workers. Diet is not neutral in managing stress. Rather, diet can moderate stress response, helping to reduce the impact of stressors and thus reduce distress. The key is balance.

It is well established that foods high in fat contribute to heart disease. But when under stress, many people find high-fat foods contribute a sense of well-being, providing extra energy to deal with the immediate situation. In the immediate onset of a crisis, this may be acceptable. But when the most common form of stress is chronic or cumulative, such a response could result in consumption of high levels of fat. Another related response is to increase intake of sugar during times of pressure. While sugar does give an immediate burst of energy, it can also stimulate the body's stress reaction, thus increasing subsequent distress. Also, the effects of sugar wear off quite dramatically, sometimes resulting in depression-like moods and physical lethargy. Continued intake of sugar during chronic stress will alter the body's chemical responses, to the detriment of good health.

Fresh vegetables, fruit, cereals and nuts are the food types recommended by most dietary experts to avoid negative physical conditions. Naturally, these are also the food types that are hardest to obtain in many humanitarian locations and, when uncooked, carry a relatively high risk of food poisoning. The general rule for keeping healthy is to eat only those fruits that can be peeled, to eat cooked vegetables when possible, and to avoid salads (in particular lettuce) or cold fruits and vegetables washed in local water. Cooked vegetables need to be boiled, not just heated, as only a vigorous boiling will kill most parasites. Many veteran relief workers, and those who travel frequently, carry their own supplies of nuts, dried fruit and cereals. These foods contain much of the required daily vitamin and caloric intake and can sustain health for considerable periods of time. Agencies could even create travel packs of such items for frequent field visitors needing to avoid local foods.

A comment on adaptation may be helpful. Most locations contain varieties of parasites and diseases that local people have developed some internal protection against. Newcomers who do not have this protection may be significantly impaired by eating as the locals do. However, after working in the location for a period of time, it is possible to develop some resistance. Sometimes such resistance is transferable to other places, but not always. It is also vital to note that appearances can be deceptive. Apparently active and fit locals may be affected by internal parasites or other diseases, accepting some of the distressing consequences. This is one of the reasons for shorter life expectancies in poor regions. Parasites can be extremely difficult to rid the body of once they have taken up residence, and symptoms of their presence should always be treated professionally. Such conditions fall into the category of chronic illness, and any form of chronic illness will lower a person's ability to cope with stress. Physical ill health likely contributes to the frequent background of chronic stress experienced by aid workers.

Caffeine, as already mentioned, is often the drug of choice among humanitarian workers, consumed in coffee, tea and soft drinks. Caffeine is a stimulant. The body fairly quickly habituates to its effects. In moderation (about three drinks per day) it is probably one of the safer drugs to consume. However, studies have shown that people who drink no caffeine at all and substitute fresh water in relatively large quantities (two to three litres per day) are actually mentally alert for longer periods of time than those who start the day with a high caffeine "fix". The problem many of us face, however, is that the local water supply may be much more dangerous than any kind of boiled or processed drink. First-world suburban supermarkets stocked with pure spring water are not often found in locations visited by most aid workers.

As a consequence, many aid workers opt for either soft drinks or beer, both of which go through a process of purification which sterilises the water. A lot of discussion is occurring in the aid community about consumption of alcohol along with some tales, largely mythical, of huge alcohol consumption. Obviously at times, in certain circumstances, as in all professions, alcohol abuse occurs. But levels of alcoholism or alcohol abuse do not appear to be high amongst humanitarian workers. Certainly it is hard to be accurate, as alcohol consumption is generally self-reported and long-standing evidence indicates that, in any group, alcohol consumption is almost always under-reported. Any NGO that finds survey results indicating next to zero alcohol use among its staff should treat those findings with a degree of suspicion, even in faith-based agencies.

Alcohol, contrary to marketing claims, is a depressant drug. While personal inhibitions may be relaxed under the influence of alcohol, its major chemical effect is to depress mood rather than elevate it. Alcohol is high in calories and has a tendency to deplete B vitamins, which are useful in dealing with stress. Alcohol also reduces the available supply of water inside the body. Because of this dehydration effect, while it may appear that large amounts of water are being consumed, much of this water is expelled fairly quickly as a result of alcohol's diuretic effects. Frequency of urination removes not only the water contained in the beer but also takes water from other organs in the body.

There appears to be no escaping the fact that pure water intake is probably the best approach to adopt. Avoiding caffeine and sugar is possible in some locations where diet soft drinks are available; where they are not, appropriately treated water may be an alternative. Organisations should provide staff with water purification systems, large ones for offices and individual portable systems (or tablets) for those travelling alone.

Salt is often a hidden enemy of good health. Many countries add large quantities of salt to food, often for cultural or dietary reasons. Salt contributes to high blood pressure, which has many potential negative consequences. While it is true that some ethnic groups benefit from additional salt in food, others do not, so aid workers need to control how much salt is consumed, depending on individual needs. People who may be predisposed to high blood pressure may be able to cope with high stress levels and maintain normal blood pressures until they consume excess salt, which often triggers very high blood pressure.

Moderation and balance are key. Diet suppression (either through not eating or through lacking desire) or overeating (or eating the wrong foods in large amounts) may well be a sign of distress. If continued, these behaviours will almost certainly become a stress factor themselves, leading to a higher level of distress.

Sleep

Sleep research is extensive, and the present knowledge about requirements and needs for sleep is relatively standard. On average, individuals need eight hours sleep each night to maintain good health. Some researchers claim that nine hours is the minimum required. Other experts talk of a "sleep bank" where "deposits" constitute the amount of sleep contributed by an individual and "debits" represent the difference between hours actually slept and the target of eight hours. Thus, a person getting six hours sleep has "spent" two hours; to put "credit" back into the account, the two hours need to be recovered at some time. The central point of this argument is that cumulative sleep loss will contribute to a general deterioration in physical health over time. Sleep experts acknowledge that people can live for many years with sleep deprivation, and may even be able to adapt their bodies to a point where it is difficult to sleep beyond, say, six hours per night. However, researchers argue that this sleep deprivation affects health in the long term by reducing the body's ability to fight off infection, contributing to raised blood pressure, affecting hormone production, and interfering with cognitive ability.

Anecdotally, many humanitarian workers comment that their major predicted activity for R&R or vacation is "to sleep for a week". Others report beginning a vacation with a heavy cold, flu or other respiratory condition requiring substantial bed rest or sleep. There seems to be a connection between sleep deprivation and lowered immunity to disease.

Certainly lack of sleep can significantly impair cognitive ability in the short term. Humanitarian workers in locations where only limited sleep is possible will find their basic cognitive functions compromised. This effect may not be immediately noticed by them or even by team colleagues; however, comments by others away from the field site are fairly common. Lowered cognitive ability means that tasks take longer to complete, mistakes are more likely, coping mechanisms are reduced, and relationships strained. Often the response from a team or individual is to try to do more work the next day to compensate for lowered functioning the day before. Unfortunately, problems tend to compound if this pattern continues for long periods.

Despite the difficult realities of many field locations, more work of higher quality will be found where staff receive adequate sleep and rest. This is a key activity for quality leaders to model for their teams. Many things can, in fact, be put off until tomorrow (or left undone completely). Many complex and urgent tasks turn out to have achievable solutions or lowered priority following a good night's sleep.

Of course, there will be times when lives are at stake and there is no time for sleep. But most emergencies of that nature do not last much beyond a week, so it should be possible to create opportunities for team members to sleep, even if a form of shift work is required.

During the designated rest period, workers should be protected from other responsibilities, especially agency ones. Fieldworkers should not be telephoned in the middle of their night by agency staff sitting in headquarters offices or elsewhere. Telephones, even satellite ones, can be turned off or handed over to a designated team member on duty. Headquarters staff who insist on making calls during their working day at the expense of staff at the field location should be subject to discipline or at least awareness-raising. Field personnel need to remind themselves, and their colleagues, that urgent matters from headquarters are very rarely issues of life or death; as such, they can fall into the category of messages to be returned in due course. Because this practice is so widespread, and field staff have allowed themselves to be influenced by the schedules of headquarters staff, everyone needs to be reminded that huge relief and development programmes worked extremely well only ten years ago when the only instant communication available was either telex or the occasional fax. Cell phones are wonderful tools, but they can, and should, be turned off during sleep or handed over to someone else with firm instructions to "take a message".

Most of all, team leaders need to ensure that they rest. Their objectivity and leadership is essential.

Relaxation Techniques

Relaxation involves a wide range of individual preferences. It may be that the element of choice itself plays a key role in successful relaxation. A basic definition of relaxation includes getting away from whatever stress is being experienced. Because stress can be external (environmental, relationship, etc.) or intra-psychic (worry, anxiety, repetitive thinking, etc.) actions to step away will vary considerably. It is likely that many relaxation methods are learned and intimately connected to culture. Perhaps one of the most striking examples of this is how the presence or absence of other individuals is viewed. In the European West, high value is placed on the opportunity to be alone, which can lead to relaxation. In many other cultures, being alone is itself stressful, and relaxation methods will often be group activities, especially family ones.

Whole books have been well written on relaxation methods, and the range will not be detailed here. In humanitarian work it is often the lack of or restriction in time available to relax that can be most stressful. Also, because much aid and development work does involve groups of workers, relaxation needs of those who find social activities relaxing are somewhat easier to meet than the needs of those who find solitude relaxing. In Myers-Brigg terms, an introvert is likely to find fieldwork, especially where bedrooms need to be shared, to be highly stressful, whereas extroverts may describe the whole experience rather like a very long party. Individuals should have a good idea as to their personality type before heading out on field missions. Assessment tools, such as those developed by Myers and Brigg have been used extensively by NGOs and should form part of any individual and team preparation.

Although basic personality type tends to remain fairly constant, situational influences at the time of testing may alter test results. Some evidence exists that over time, quite significant changes in personality type can be observed. Discussion about how life experience influences type is increasing. If this proves to be the case, then it could be that years in humanitarian work might bring about changes in type. Knowing what type of relaxation works best for you is the significant point here. Finding this out is essential.

Research pioneered by a team at Harvard Medical School in the 1970s may be helpful in determining what constitutes relaxation for an individual. Benson and his colleagues found that there appears to be a common physiological mechanism in relaxation methods ranging from religious group activities to individual relaxation techniques.[7] Benson and Stark termed this response the relaxation response, and it has the characteristics of being essentially the reverse of the stress response. Essentially metabolism, blood pressure, heart rate and so on decrease during relaxation, instead of increasing as during stress. They reported that there are only two basic steps required to attain the relaxation response. The first is repetition of a word or phrase or muscular activity. The second is to passively ignore thoughts that come to mind and go back to the repetition.[8]

Evidence that regular relaxation utilising these two steps actually improves health is overwhelming. Everything from psychosomatic complaints to work absences and productivity increases have been associated with use of relaxation techniques. The basic structure of a relaxation method such as this is fairly well established.

1. Find a location where you won't be disturbed for about 30 minutes.
2. Sit comfortably, allowing muscles to relax.
3. Choose a word, phrase or saying that has meaning for you.
4. Close your eyes.
5. Breathe in and out slowly and naturally.
6. Silently repeat the word or phrase as you breathe in and out.
7. As random thoughts flit across your mind, dismiss them through a combination of ignoring them or silently "speaking" them away. You may even use a dismissive phrase such as "Let's move on".

8. Do this for 15–20 minutes.
9. When the time is up, do not immediately jump to your feet. Allow a minute after you have opened your eyes before getting up.
10. Practice once a day.

Generally, effects of this type of relaxation take several weeks to be noticeable, so perseverance is necessary. Because the techniques essentially involve slowing bodily processes down, it is probably wise not to extend the sessions much beyond 30 minutes at one time. Becoming too slow for too long a period may induce unwanted lethargy when action is required.

Another form of relaxation now quite popular is progressive relaxation. This is similar to the above approach, except that it involves a process of tensing muscle groups and relaxing them in a sequence. Generally the sequence starts at the head and neck and progressively moves through the body to the feet and ankles. The process takes 30 to 60 minutes to complete, depending on skill level. The advantage of this method is that over time, individuals become aware of the relative tension in various muscle groups. As stress often results in muscle tightening, this awareness can help signal relative stress levels. As control over the various muscle groups increases with practice, individuals are able deliberately to relax muscles during periods of high stress. This can be effective in countering stress responses.

Meditation

In the secularised West meditation has a curious reputation. Yet researchers have shown that various forms of meditation are quite successful in reducing stress responses and improving general physical health. In the Christian West the religious aspects of meditation have sometimes obscured the physical practices, and some faith-based groups (missionary agencies, churches, and so on) are reluctant to include meditation in stress management programmes. For those uncomfortable with the religious overtones of many procedures, a secular version called clinically standardised meditation (CSM) has been developed by Patricia Carrington, a Princeton University psychologist. This form of meditation has been successfully incorporated into a number of organisational stress management programmes.[9]

The various forms of meditation available are innumerable and too diverse to cover in this book. While a preponderance of models arise out of Eastern religious traditions, there are a number of Judeo-Christian forms that have excellent provenance. Meditation in the Christian tradition, for instance, has an unbroken history of nearly 2,000 years and is undergoing a recent upsurge in interest in the West. Because of the intensely personal nature of meditation, each individual will need to find the form that fits his or her physical and spiritual requirements.

Relaxation techniques and meditation methods are extremely useful for international aid workers because they are portable and require virtually no resources other than a small amount of time each day and a relatively private place. As stress management techniques, because they do alter metabolic rate and physical and mental activity, these two activities are available to virtually all aid workers all the time. There seems to be no good reason for agency management not to introduce such methods into the life and culture of any humanitarian organisation. Training is simple and very cheap, and the outcomes are overwhelmingly positive.

Checklist for Individuals

Your genetic predisposition:

- Is there any history of physical or mental illness among your blood relations? Especially note such conditions as cardiac problems, diabetes, stomach ulcers, migraines

or other headaches, high blood pressure, backaches, schizophrenia, depression, anxiety disorders, and the like.
- Do you know your personality type? Do you know how your personality profile (such as a Myers-Brigg profile) interacts with other personality profiles? especially at times of high stress? Are you aware of your team members' profiles or preferred working styles?

Present life balance:
- How many vacation days do you actually take each year? Do you take them in blocks or spread out? Do you take work with you on vacation? Do you check e-mails or make business calls regularly on vacation? Do you take R&R allowances when they are due? Do you work during R&R?
- Do you take sick days, or do you work through sick-ness?
- What patterns of life stressors can you see over the past year?
- Can you predict how things will be during the next 12 months? the next three months? More stressful? Less?
- What is the state of your general health? Have you looked at assessment measures such as the GHQ?
- How many hours per day do you sleep on average? How well do you sleep? Do you take any kind of sleeping aid on a regular basis? Why?
- Are you at or near your ideal body weight?
- Has your weight altered much since your career in humanitarian work started? If so, does this concern you?
- What does your usual diet consist of? What is the fat content of the food you eat?
- Has your diet changed during your career? If so, does this concern you?

- What quantities of mood-enhancing drugs do you regularly consume? (Include caffeine, alcohol, smoking, prescription and non-prescription drugs.)
- Has this amount altered during your career as an aid worker? If so, does this concern you?

Life Resilience
- Are you "hardy"? When you consider your present commitment, control and challenge, what do you find?
- Have any of these changed during your career?
- What kind of regular exercise do you take? How often do you exercise?
- Is your exercise portable? Or only possible at home base?
- Do you do both aerobic and anaerobic exercise?
- What relaxation techniques do you practice? Are you able to do this on a regular basis?
- Do you have any meditative skills? Are these useful?

Checklist for Employers
- Does your recruitment process include health assessments? Does it assess psychological health?
- Do you consider preexisting conditions (physical or mental) when assigning duties?
- Does your organisation have a stress education programme?
- Do managers understand the relationship between productivity and health?
- How do you assess the health of front-line staff? Is there a regular health-check process?
- How many vacation days per year are employees entitled to?
- Do they use their entitlement?
- What are the organisational consequences of not taking leave?

- Are there R&R provisions?
- Is it mandatory for staff to take R&R?
- Is there a process that encourages or enables a balance between work and leave?
- Does your organisation provide advice or information on nutrition, diet, exercise, sleep and relaxation?
- If yours is a faith-based agency, how does belief or practice inform stress management practices?
- Is this intentional or merely expected to be a result of recruitment?

Notes

1 C. Eriksson et al., "WVI and Headington Program Occupational Stress and Trauma Assessment," paper to WVI (October 2001) (Fuller Theological Seminary and WVI).

2 R. S. Eliot and D. L. Breo, *Is It Worth Dying For?* (New York: Bantam Books, 1984).

3 T. H. Holmes and R. H. Rahe, "The Social Adjustment Rating Scale," *Journal of Psychosomatic Research* 11 (1976), 218.

4 N. Tubsing and D. Tubsing, eds., *Structured Exercises in Stress Management* (Duluth, Minn.: Whole Person Associates, 1983).

5 J. C. Quick, J. D. Quick, D. L. Nelson and J. J. Hurrell, *Preventative Stress Management in Organizations* (Washington, D.C.: American Psychological Association, 1997), 52.

6 B. Lopes Cardoza and P. Salama, "Mental Health of Humanitarian Aid Workers in Complex Emergencies," in *Sharing the Front Lines and the Back Hills*, ed. Y. Daneli (New York: Baywood Publishers, 2002).

7 H. Benson, J. Beary and M. Carol, in Quick et al., *Preventative Stress Management in Organizations*.

8 Benson and Stark, in Quick et al., *Preventative Stress Management in Organizations*.

9 P. Carrington et al., "The Use of Meditation-Relaxation Techniques for the Management of Stress in a Working Population, *Journal of Occupational Medicine* 22 (1980), 221–31.

chapter 9

Strengthening organisational factors that promote flourishing

Getting out of Freetown (Sierra Leone) in 1997 was like running through hell and back again. We were trapped in our homes and lost contact with each other. We tried to make our way to the assembly points for evacuation, but the rebels had the run of the streets. It was very dangerous. When we finally got together, there was still no way out. The airport was cut off and we were on the coast, trapped between the sea and the guns. The organisation worked really hard to help us, and it succeeded in hiring a couple of ancient ex-Soviet helicopters to fly us out of the country. It was a bit hairy at times. When we finally landed in Dakar (Senegal), the sub-regional director came out to the aircraft to meet us. He didn't have to do that; all the arrangements had been taken care of. But he came out to welcome us and to assure us that we would be taken care of. All of us, staff, spouses and children, were very touched that he had come to see us. It meant a lot to us that the organisation cared so much.

—Andrew, from the United States, working in Dakar in 1997

International aid workers appear to experience the most stress as a result of organisational and management factors, not external, environmental ones. Living and working in the environment of a complex humanitarian emergency is stressful and tiring, but the onset of ASR appears to be most linked to failures in the organisational environment. Further,

---

Parts of this chapter are modified from John Fawcett, "Preventing Broken Hearts, Healing Broken Minds," in *Sharing The Front Lines and the Back Hills*, ed. Y. Danieli (New York: Baywood Publications, 2002).

it seems that the factors that protect humanitarian workers from developing acute stress and trauma responses are most likely to be social, relationship and leadership factors rather than individual factors. If stress protection is best obtained through sound relationships, good team cohesion and quality leadership, then organisations become the best vehicle to provide management of stress and trauma for fieldworkers.

Organisational success in stress management requires making employee well-being core to agency objectives and operating plans. There are many very good reasons to do this. First, naturally, is the reality that emergency aid and development work cannot be performed other than by human beings. This is not the kind of job that can be done more efficiently by machines, nor can it be done at a distance through electronic means. Second, it is cost effective to have a healthy staff with high morale. Third, disabled people often seek legal remedies to recover costs and gain compensation from employers they believe have contributed to their disability. Court cases and settlements relating to stress disability in the last five years have resulted in substantial expenses for employers, and these can be avoided. Finally, because research indicates that the cause of much stress in aid work lies within the organisational environment, substantial opportunity exists to effect positive changes.

Organisational culture needs to affirm in practice any values ascribed to human beings and human community. Discrepancies between agency mission statements relating to communities being assisted and employment practices for staff will be very clear and are often a cause of staff distress. This becomes even more apparent for agencies that adopt policy and value statements such as the People in Aid Code, the Red Cross Code of Practice, the Sphere Standards, and various UN charters. If the values contained in these documents are applied to operational programmes but not to staff, then a protective mechanism against distress has been removed.

This means that agencies must have clear and specific employment policies ensuring internal as well as external compliance to the values held by the organisation. Unfortunately there are still some NGOs that claim to perform programme operations according to specific donor requirements while having only limited human resource or employment policies or guidelines. This practice has to end. In the same way that donors are becoming very reluctant (and rightly so) to advance funds to NGOs unable to articulate objectives, outcomes, time lines and operational plans clearly, neither should such donors fund agencies that cannot clearly demonstrate adherence to professional employment and staff management standards. Moves towards this practice are already occurring and should be welcomed by international aid agencies.

Practical steps agencies could take to reduce stress on staff significantly include (1) reducing the risk of distress during recruitment; (2) building capacity to manage stress during employment; and (3) creating (and maintaining) organisational support systems.

Reducing the Risk of Distress During Recruitment

Clear task description and expectations. Too many jobs in humanitarian work consist solely of a title. Written job descriptions should contain statements of both outcome goals and limitations. Limitations protect the employee from being exposed to increasing job loads after employment begins. While job descriptions can rarely be 100 per cent accurate, especially in relief contexts, clear guidelines should outline the extent of responsibility for each staff member. There also needs to be a clearly detailed process that can be undertaken when it becomes necessary to expand responsibilities of employees. This process should not be based on an assumption that staff will automatically take on extra or increased duties merely because they are being paid by the agency. It follows that each employee must have an employment agreement in written form.

People employed for jobs must have the *skills and expertise* to achieve expected outcomes. This may appear obvious, but field managers recount experiences of being caught between a donor with funds to allocate and the requirement that there be an employee to run the new programme. When deadlines press hard, the temptation to hire almost anyone to ensure that donor funds become available is very hard to resist, especially if HQ is also pressuring the field manager to commence the new programme. Evidence reveals that considerable stress is being experienced by staff who know they do not have the skills or expertise to perform the requirements of their present assignments. Organisational (and personal) consequences of mismatching individual skills and operational objectives are considerable.

Employ all staff according to *recognised employment law*. This is especially true for local staff. Even in countries where there is no law, the international community (the International Labour Organization, for instance) has access to agreed standards. These should be applied universally. This is not to say that all staff should have the same salary and benefit packages. However, any payment system needs to be based on accepted employment standards rather than on availability of funds. Where there are discrepancies among groups of employees, these should be addressed. One example is in personal taxation payment. Many NGOs have fairly sophisticated methods to ensure that international staff do not experience double taxation, that is, paying taxes in both their home and the host locations. This has led to the practice of not paying income taxes for local employees in countries with poor taxation-enforcement practices. Often this practice results from attempts to reduce expenditure in the field location. However, the consequences could be disadvantageous to local staff. Apart from the inherent message that taxes are something to be avoided, it is likely that development practices will result in improved enforcement procedures in due course. NGO employees who have not filed tax returns may find themselves in breach of local laws at a later date. Would an agency see itself as responsible for defending staff in these circumstances and/or meeting any costs ascribed? Better to avoid the situation in the first place.

Staff selection processes should include assessments of the extent and nature of stress-protection capacity. This can be done for all staff regardless of position. It should be mandatory for all front-line relief staff, all management or supervisory staff, and any staff who travel to field locations in the course of their duties. Assessment must include all local staff as well. All staff employed for international duties (and especially emergency relief locations) should have a full psychiatric history taken. Indications of previous psychotic episodes, previous mental health problems, ASR or PTSD should be taken seriously. While not an automatic exclusion from employment, incidences of previous mental health issues should result in referral to a specialist for more in-depth assessment. Applicants need to be assessed for resilience or hardiness (see Chapter 8). Such an assessment would include examination of individuals' worldview and faith – not a religious assessment, but a process of determining the relative rigidity and flexibility with which beliefs are held. Research shows that the more rigidly a belief is held, the greater the risk for "shattering" in the face of extreme experiences. Evidence of coping skills should be apparent.

Social support networks need to be assessed. Much protection against harm is found in the maintenance of sound social relationships both inside and outside the work setting. It is possible to determine the nature and strength of individuals' social support using valid psychological processes.

Previous field experience and *prior life events* must be assessed. While the number and nature of life events is certainly important, of more interest to employers is an applicant's demonstrated ability to manage the transitions of these life events. People who are unable to cope with change are poor risks for front-line deployment. Caution needs to be exercised with regard to experienced humanitarian workers with a number of previous front-line assignments. This is, unfortunately, the other side of the recommendation regarding evidence of coping. Some evidence suggests that fieldworkers who have had a number of assignments may be at a high risk of developing ASR, despite evidence of having handled prior assignments well. This is possibly due to cumulative effects of doing this work and may be an extreme form of burnout. Individuals who have a history of consecutive assignments with little time to refresh or regroup may be at greater risk than those who demonstrate balance over a period of years.

Experience as a member of a team should be assessed at interview. If team cohesion is critical to protection from ASR and PTSD, then it is essential that candidates demonstrate significant team skills. This is especially true for emergency relief environments. Many NGOs blame poor interpersonal relationship skills on the working environment. While conditions do affect behaviour, it is still possible to create good team cohesion if team members are selected appropriately. A history of poor team relationships should be further investigated during the recruitment process.

During recruitment, *leadership style* should be assessed. Consultative leadership style is an effective protective mechanism against ASR. Competency (including the perceived competency) of the team leader is paramount, especially in relief situations. Competency is measured by professional expertise, but also by the manner in which leaders relate to team members. A team's ability to place trust in the leader is significantly related to its ability to cope with high stress levels.

Building Capacity to Manage Stress During Employment

Every staff member should be provided with personal and organisational stress management training. This would include strengthening social networks, improving personal skills such as relaxation techniques and habits such as sleep and diet, strategies for improving team cohesion and the importance of consultative leadership. This training should be provided at induction and as part of a regular staff training process. Local staff should be included in the training. Where possible, spouses and/or immediate family would be invited to participate, as this would assist in increasing social support. Stress management training should include explanation of health policies and provision of services, as well as how to access counselling or therapy if required.

Security training should be provided for each staff person and should be designed appropriately for each working location. Personal security education must be given to each individual, and every field office team should design a security plan that is regularly updated. Stress and security are intimately related. Poor security, and perceptions of poor security, increase distress, adding to cumulative stress. Distress, in turn, affects the maintenance of good security. Most deaths and injuries related to lapses in security occur in the first three months of assignment. This means that staff at highest risk will be those who travel frequently, such as donor agency programme officers, communications staff and senior managers. Yet these groups are often left out of both security training and security plans.

Team building should be a key component of all staff training and development strategies. For emergency relief teams, such training should be mandatory. The building of teams should not be left to circumstances. The notion that adversity builds relationships should be abandoned. Adversity will only be coped with where relationships already exist. Where relationships are poor, adversity will almost always result in increased distress. It is essential that team leaders participate fully in team-building exercises. The presence and involvement of the team leader are critical to the success of team building and are of the utmost importance in ensuring team cohesion in a field environment. Absence of the team leader will significantly reduce the ability of the team to cope with high stress. In some situations the combination of a strong team coupled with absence of the leader can result in major dysfunction. (An extreme example of this occurred in some military units in Vietnam, in which troops killed their own officers when cohesive teams perceived the leader as being more of a danger to their lives than the enemy.)

Leadership training must be mandatory for all staff required to lead teams. Such training has to include focus on interpersonal skills, group dynamics and team functioning. Training should also include practical experience under the supervision and guidance of a training specialist. Assessments should be made to judge real as well as theoretical understanding of leadership expertise. Leaders need to be able to assess basic psychological states and to judge with a degree of accuracy how stress levels are affecting team members. The ability to assess both individual and team distress regularly is critical. Leaders need to be able to demonstrate that they are competent in these areas.

Social support networks need to be promoted and assessed. Individuals who have passed recruitment checks need to be able to demonstrate that social networks continue to be supportive during assignments. Access to support networks needs to be provided. Agencies need to ensure that individuals have access to systems (e-mail, telephone, radio, etc.) to maintain close relationships with their support base. Such access should be increased during high-stress assignments.

Unfortunately, most agencies actually decrease availability of communications systems at the time when support networks would provide their most effective protection. While it may appear to be costly, open access to telephone communications by front-line staff separated from their support networks will reduce costs in the medium to long term. Individuals who have ready access to close supporters during times of high stress will experience less distress, will develop less chronic stress and will avoid burnout for much longer periods of time. They will also require less "down time" between assignments, because they have been able to take care of family or group responsibilities during the field assignment. Front-line staff should never have communications time restricted because of monetary considerations alone. Virtually all humanitarian workers are extremely aware of financial realities and behave in highly ethical ways with agency funds and equipment. An open access policy will result in minimal abuse and will almost certainly result in significant reduction in distress levels.

Organisations should regularly assess the quality of workers' support networks, preferably on an annual basis. Reductions in the size of a network should be investigated. Individuals should be asked to describe the extent and, in general terms that respect privacy, the nature of communications with the members of the support network over the previous period of time. Long-term humanitarian workers may have very small networks, but the depth of relationship among members may be considerable. Depth is more important than size, but a network of only one or two is probably insufficient to fully protect an individual against distress.

As with personal support networks, agencies should promote membership in other social groups such as churches and professional bodies. Most humanitarian workers are specialists, and many are experts. As such, organisational policies should make it possible for individuals to be part of professional and academic groups. Such membership could be funded by the agency. Properly planned, there are many advantages to employers for workers to be part of wider networks. Churches, interest groups, social organisations and peer academic networks all provide excellent protective factors for individuals, and involvement should be encouraged. While the highly mobile nature of much relief work sometimes poses challenges to membership, it is possible for employing organisations to provide training and education for individuals in how to manage part-time or transitory membership of groups. Some societies, groups and churches even cater to people employed in highly mobile occupations. Employers could assist staff by identifying groups or churches that have skills in this area.

Creating (and Maintaining) Organisational Support Systems

Agency structure must be simple and clear. Evidence shows that lack of clarity in organisational structure and confusing reporting responsibilities create stress, reducing potential protective factors inherent in group dynamics. The tendency to require front-line leaders to report to more than one manager must be avoided. Agencies should never permit more than one manager to have authority over an individual staff member. Despite the complexity of fieldwork, particularly emergency relief work, team members and team leaders should only be required to report to (and obey) one superior only. Where there is a requirement for more than one superior to be issuing instructions, it should be extremely clear which superior outranks the other and in which specific areas. Organisational structure should never be created after the deployment. Structure should be designed and clearly understood by all parties prior to any agency activity. Deviations from the agreed structure should be avoided and, if required at all, reasons should be communicated to all parties. Leaders must have the authority to decline an instruction from anyone other than their designated superior without fear of negative consequences, unless the giving of such an instruction falls under previously agreed-to and understood policies. Lest this advice be interpreted as a means to avoid the principle of one supervisor for each staff, it is strongly recommended that the ability of other managers to issue instructions be restricted to those of an emergency or crisis nature, and only when the authorised supervisor is for some reason unable to issue the instruction.

Programme objectives must not exceed programme resources. Too many field programmes are designed with a primary emphasis on access to donor funds, rather than provision of appropriate services to local communities. The pressure on NGOs to continue to receive donor funds sometimes results in programme objectives that are unattainable, given the resources provided or expertise of the staff on the ground. Many programme managers find themselves being criticised by their own agency as a result of this failure. Yet often programme objectives are designed by people away from the field location. Many of these off-site staff are also required to meet funding targets set by senior management and thus experience pressure to create programmes that will attract the funds. Humanitarian workers find such circumstances stressful, adding to distress already inherent in the local environment. When distress is perceived as being caused by one's own employer, reduced morale occurs, leading to increased staff turnover and often inability of the agency to meet its own objectives.

Another component of adequate resources relates to security. Communications equipment such as VHF and UHF radios do not always appear directly related to programme outcomes. Because such equipment is expensive, some agencies are reluctant to invest funds in this area. However, there are virtually no safe places in the world today to do humanitarian work. Effective operational security requires adequate communications. Radios and satellite phones can be replaced; experts in humanitarian relief are virtually irreplaceable.

All staff must have access to adequate time away from work. Annual vacation entitlements must be clearly identified. Four weeks (20 working days) per 12–month period is the minimum standard for virtually all fieldwork. For workers located in dangerous or complex environments, entitlement should be increased. War-zone assignments, such as Afghanistan 2002, Palestine 2002 and Iraq 2003, and places where civil violence is occurring, such as Gujurat 2002, North East India 2002 and Colombia 2002, should come with six to eight weeks' paid vacation time every 12 months. This entitlement must be available to all staff in the zone, not just internationals, and should be in addition to any R&R leave provided. While these recommendations may sound extreme, especially in a North American context, it is essential to humanitarian workers' health that they have adequate time to refresh from extreme circumstances. Many workers use the first week of vacation to catch up on lost sleep, the second to begin to reconnect with social networks and if there is a third, to prepare for return. This is not sufficient time to properly enhance stress protective mechanisms. Many Western economies provide minimum annual vacation entitlements of six or more weeks in employment categories that are not nearly as inherently stressful as humanitarian aid work.

The most extreme humanitarian locations must have provisions for regular R&R on top of any vacation entitlement. R&R should be defined in policy and designed to assist in the process of stress management. Provision of R&R leave, therefore, could include components of physical health assessment and requirements to attend counselling or a mental-health assessment process. Many agencies, and aid workers, view R&R as additional vacation allocation. However, if vacation allocation issues were adequately addressed as suggested above, it should be possible for organisations to redefine R&R leave as time more focused on organisational and operational matters. A seven-day R&R, for instance, could occur at a pleasant location. Spouse and family, or close support network, could join staff at the location. Time for recreational activities should be included. Physical and mental health assessments could be performed on site and, if required, brief counselling entered into. Operational debriefings could also occur, with time put aside to prepare reports or complete other agency requirements. If R&R were framed as work time rather than vacation time, it would be possible to provide both the recuperation allowed by a break from the front line and opportunity for professional review and assessment.

All staff must have access to comprehensive health services. Most international humanitarian workers are covered by insurance and health policies that provide emergency evacuation services and extensive health care. Such provisions are not yet generally available to local staff. While there are obvious challenges in this process, agencies should intentionally move to provide appropriate and adequate health services to local aid workers. Services should be comprehensive and must be designed with full regard to cultural norms and practices. The importation of external values and expertise should be avoided unless a sound assessment has revealed that alternative local services do not exist.

Agencies must develop and implement policies that provide for access to appropriate mental health services for all staff. Policies should include assessment of candidates for advertised positions and both pre- and post-assignment assessments for staff. Psychological services should be available close to, if not actually in the field assignment country. Psychological assessments should be the norm rather than the exception. They should form part of the assignment processes and should not be used to punish or set an employee at a disadvantage. As with other health information, psychological assessments must be confidential.

Organisations must create a comprehensive emergency mental-health strategy. Such a strategy should include provision of crisis response staff support teams that are able to relocate to the site of a major critical event within a very short time frame. Obviously many NGOs will not have the internal capacity to provide such resources themselves. Therefore the use of contracted crisis teams is recommended. Such teams need to be created or employed well before a crisis erupts. It is already too late to begin this process once a crisis has occurred. World Vision has, over the past five years, trained a pool of existing staff from which a crisis response team can be drawn. There has to be a clear understanding with field management that people in this pool will be made available when required. The pool needs to be quite large, as not all members will be available at all times (see Chapter 11).

Priority must be given to retaining stable and long-term teams. Humanitarian work, especially emergency relief work, is highly mobile with rapid career changes, even within a single agency. However, if team cohesion is a significant factor in providing protection and enhancing productivity, then investment in team functioning will pay dividends.

Organisations must create career development opportunities that will limit exposure to the most intense stress environments. Presently, most career planning is left to the individual and agencies rarely plan careers for staff. Even if it is not possible to engage with staff in designing individualised career plans, it is essential that NGOs have policies regarding field assignments and other duties. Employers can, and must, protect staff from continuous exposure to extreme front-line assignments. There needs to be a balance between types of assignment to allow workers to refresh and recover. Substantial and increasing evidence suggests there is not a lot of difference with regard to exposure to traumatic events between relief and development locations. The traumatic events may differ, but the severity of stress reaction appears similar. Rotation among assignments therefore needs to be planned carefully and may need to include some headquarters time or other assignment. This could be an excellent opportunity to implement a sabbatical policy, whereby staff could be paid to take further study or to contribute their learnings to the organisations' knowledge base.

Checklist for Both Individuals and Employers

Every humanitarian organisation should have policies and guidelines for the following:

- Clear job descriptions with attainable objectives
- Simple and effective organisational system with clear reporting relationships
- A selection process that will assess previous field experience with a focus on stress and trauma responses
- Criteria for selection of team leaders and supervisors based on team dynamics as well as sectoral skills
- Consultative leadership training
- Comprehensive security management, including security training
- Stress management training for all staff
- Strengthening of individual social support networks
- Team functioning and team dynamics
- Health and welfare provisions, including R&R and vacation
- Access to appropriate health services, including mental health
- Emergency response services for all staff, including evacuation procedures
- Sabbatical leave or other types of learning assignments
- Career development, including job rotation

chapter 10

Partners in development: strategies for local staff

When the foreign teachers first came to my country they put us in a room with rows of chairs and desks. They made us sit quietly and listen while they told us many, many facts with numbers and names and words. There were bells that rang when the hands of the clock reached certain positions. When that happened, we had to close one book and open another. Later, after the war, special doctors called psychologists came and told us we were suffering mental health problems. They made us sit in chairs and listen to facts, and tell them of events that happened to us. This was very uncomfortable. In my village, when we think of such things, we sing or dance or tell stories of our ancestors or of the animals in the forest. We learn by doing, not by sitting in chairs. We do not need clocks or bells to tell us when our learning is over. Sometimes a story could take all night. Sometimes the singing and dancing might last a whole day. How can we pray to God just using spoken words? How can we hear God's Spirit without music and dance and stories? How can we be healed without the village being part of the process?

—AKIBA, FROM TANZANIA, 2000

One of the most divisive issues in humanitarian work today relates to perceived employment differences between staff hired internationally and staff hired from and within the country where the work is being performed. Aid personnel are strongly egalitarian in philosophical outlook, and apparent structural differences sometimes rankle. Discussions seem to revolve around pay and conditions but are actually deeply philosophical. International staff receive substantially higher salaries than local staff, and international employment contracts appear more stable and less prone to sudden termination as a result of funding pressures. Differences in staff support are most often apparent in extreme situations where field evacuations are required. When international staff and dependents flee advancing violence by whatever means possible, local staff and family members appear to be left behind to guard agency assets and, in their spare time, themselves and their dependents.

Reality, of course, differs somewhat, and most organisations are working hard to bring equity to employment conditions. However, the truth is that such disparity will not be resolved merely by bringing local staff employment conditions "up to" international levels or by "reducing" international employment conditions to local levels. The conflict, in fact, is about *practices* and *principles*.

Much of the argument arises because of lack of clarity concerning practices and principles. All staff support should be guided by principles, first of all, before comparing practices. This would bring staff support into line with the manner in which modern humanitarian work is largely performed. A principle is agreed to, and then practices can be developed around the guiding principles. For instance, a principle relating to provision of shelter for refugees can be quite broad. A statement of the principle could be: All refugees should be provided with adequate shelter as a core component of emergency relief operations. In practice, the nature of that shelter will be determined by a wide number of variables including prevailing weather, health of the refugee population, presence or absence of intentional violence, and availability of funds. International humanitarian work has become much more consistent and efficient in recent years as principles have developed through thorough analysis of practical components involved in ensuring that these principles are achieved and maintained. The Sphere Project, for example, is a comprehensive effort to provide practical guidelines to support agreed-upon principles in humanitarian work.[1]

Creating a principle that cannot be realised in practice is of little use, and it is also essential to understand that failure to achieve in practice does not mean that no principles are at work. For instance, a principle stating that in the event of an evacuation being required, all staff and dependents must be evacuated is not realisable, nor is it, in fact, truly a principle. It is a guiding practice, and one that will almost surely fail. A statement of principle with more usefulness to humanitarian work might be: All agency personnel and immediate family members will be supported as appropriate by the agency structure. Principles and policies are closely related, but are not the same. In *principle*, we will help all people in need. Policy documents will define how, in *practice*, achievable assistance will be provided.

A mistake made by some commentators has been to observe agency behaviour at times when assistance is required by staff and then to decide, as a result of what they have seen, that the organisation does not really "care" about its local staff. It can appear that a wealth of resources is made available to international staff while local staff make do as best they can. In practice, this may indeed occur at times, but it would be a mistake to deduce that this behaviour is a result of a lack of caring or a lack of principle. The failure, where it exists, is not in agreement to a principle to provide support to all staff but in the inability to determine properly precisely what actions would effectively provide support for local staff. This failure to assess needs adequately can be compounded when an organisation that cares about all staff decides to ensure that all staff have access to the same kinds of support at the same levels across the whole organisation. This is a compounded failure because it does not address the reality that different individuals and different groups can often require significantly different types of practical support.

A stark indicator of the failure to analyse such situations appropriately is found in provision of mental health services.

In the early days of the study of psychological trauma, widespread belief suggested that exposure to a critical event (a major crisis such as a bomb attack) would almost certainly affect all people in much the same way. This belief resulted in the development of a CISD, a structured group process of talking about the incident with a trained facilitator.[2] Partly because the CISD model was quite contained and portable, its use spread rapidly across the First World, becoming the response of choice for many emergency organisations and most critical response units. As the notion of psychological trauma became of importance in international humanitarian work, the practice of CISD was adopted by many relief agencies for use with affected communities and, eventually, staff.

Unlike physical deprivations such as lack of water, nutrition and shelter, however, psychological well-being is tightly linked to both individual personality and ethnic/cultural processes. In short, practices such as CISD do not work for everyone, even in a Western context, and definitions of mental health do not easily transfer across cultural lines.[3] In recent times resistance to CISD processes has grown to unfortunately include organisational and donor resistance to many mental health proposals, a result that has not improved the effectiveness of integrated humanitarian aid.

Part of this reluctance has been due to poorly thought out actions in places of extreme violence, such as Rwanda and the Balkans. In Kosovo in the late 1990s some fairly rash assessments were made without adequate recourse to professional research. Suggestions were seriously circulated that huge numbers of people, up to 700,000 in Bosnia alone, were most likely suffering from PTSD and that very large numbers of psychological personnel would be required to bring healing.[4] While this claim was not credited for long, its consequences included lessening the credibility of war trauma analysis and intervention. A further consequence can result when providers determine that a group of people is indeed psychologically traumatised, and hence disabled, and then determine that resistance to this diagnosis by the group is further proof of the traumatisation. The effect of this process can limit possibilities of working effectively with the group, especially if it is no longer perceived to be competent enough to assist in the healing process. Healing, in this flawed model, is something that must be done *to* people not *with* them.

Part of the problem is that in Western psychological culture, severe psychological trauma is deemed to result in disability. Many first world health insurers concur and cover expenses related to the healing of psychological trauma. This is often supported by local employment laws which prohibit employer actions against disabled employees. Western first-world culture tends to view psychological trauma as individual disability and mental health problems themselves as negative and potentially damaging to individuals and organisations. To reduce risk to staff and organisations, many employers take actions to mitigate the impact of critical events, stress and strain, and burnout.

It is interesting to note that many spiritual constructs, upon which religions are built, do not view trauma as a disability. Even in the post-Christian West, where religious values underpin much of society's structure, Christian tradition holds that weakness is beneficial to salvation. Acknowledgement of individual failure to live up to the higher standards ascribed to God and to one's own standards leads an individual to a realization that spiritual growth, and eventually salvation, is not attainable by one's own actions. Often such understanding is thought to be the result of a crisis or critical event. Many Eastern spiritual systems refer to a process of enlightenment and a path towards understanding that anticipate many crises and opportunities for humility. In the Chinese language the character for the concept *crisis* contains equal components of *danger* and *opportunity.* Many of the world's religions embrace the idea that an individual crisis or challenge will result in an understanding that individual strength is not sufficient to cope with all that life will bring. Gaining this knowledge is not perceived as a disability but a freedom. These crises are also seen as affirmation that all individuals are connected at a significant and powerful level – affirming interdependence and community in place of the illusion of independence. Crisis, then, leads not towards long-term disability but long-term health, where health is maintained in the strengthening of human relationships, relationships among people and the real environments in which they live, not to mention relationships between people and their creator.

This is not merely "putting a positive spin" on psychological trauma. Rather, it challenges assumptions that crisis and critical events will almost always lead to disability and inadequacy of functioning. This view affirms the belief that many cultures hold true – that life is indeed hard, it does indeed cost much, there will indeed be grief and sorrow, and evidence of weakness in oneself or in one's community is not a disability but an acknowledgement. If this is the manner in which many cultures view the world, then the way in which international humanitarian organisations develop support systems for staff and dependents will need to recognise and work with this.

When considering appropriate means of providing support and care for local staff and dependents, a new approach based on old wisdom is needed. Too many organisational responses to disasters affecting staff are focused on the calamity itself and not on the people experiencing it. This is especially important when considering psychological and social support systems. Cultures, communities and individual community members experience crisis in significantly different ways. The "old wisdom" that humanitarian organisations have available to assist them in determining the best manner of providing support is contained in the principles and practices of traditional community development.

It is strongly recommended that humanitarian agencies utilise these principles in developing appropriate support mechanisms for all staff, especially for local staff.

Community Assessment as the Key to Intervention

By definition, local staff are drawn from the local community. They are therefore influenced by cultural realities in the same way as the wider community, despite being employed by international NGOs. While most humanitarian organisations are structured along traditional Western business models, this does not mean that local employees will behave in ways usually associated with Western businesses. Adaptation to externally imposed structures does not, in any real sense, imply a casting off of local culture. If, therefore, an employing agency wishes to provide adequate and appropriate support for local staff and dependents, such support must be designed with due regard for the influences and history of local culture. An understanding of this culture is required before services are designed and implemented.

Assessment of needs within a community is a time-honoured tradition in humanitarian development work. It has the significant advantage of reducing the risk of making unfounded assumptions about either the problem or the solution. But success does require time and expertise. An increasing number of international NGOs are attempting to use community-development principles in designing psycho-social interventions for both agency personnel and communities who may have been affected by trauma. One international NGO which has made significant progress in addressing such complexities in practice is the Transcultural Psychosocial Organization (TPO). The TPO is a World

Health Organization (WHO) collaborating centre supported by the government of the Netherlands and associated with the Free University of Amsterdam.[5] TPO practises a form of ecological psychology – essentially a process of trying to identify exactly how different cultures view mental and physical health and illness. The guiding principle for such processes is that concepts and understanding of what constitute health, particularly mental health, are culture specific. Mental health will not be regarded in the same way in every culture, and psychological interventions should not look the same in every culture. Discovering what mental health looks like in a particular culture requires asking questions of members of the cultural group. A series of assessment queries might include the following:

- *What constitutes stress and trauma in the life of this culture?* Is there a concept of individual stress in this culture? If so, what are the indicators? How do members identify stress in others? What words or phrases (in the local language) are used to describe trauma? How do those phrases translate? Is there a truly psychological component to this culture's definition of stress? Is stress experienced some other way, perhaps physically or spiritually? Is stress experienced primarily by individuals, or is it manifested mainly in family or group processes?
- *Traditionally and historically, what does this culture do to deal with stress and trauma?* What is the role of the individual in managing stress? What is the community role? What role do community institutions such as village elders, councils and government, and religious institutions such as mosques, wats and churches play?
- *In the culture today, what is the nature of stress and trauma?* Have traditional definitions been affected by definitions from other cultures? Are there new definitions or are

they modifications of the old? What today specifically causes stress and trauma? Are these stressors the same as or different from past stressors? What, if anything, has changed during the past twenty years?

- *What mechanisms does this culture use today to cope with stress and trauma?* Are they primarily individual or group? Are they primarily physical or psychological? Are they primarily oral methods or behavioural? Are today's coping methods any different from past techniques? How?

- *Do these present methods provide sufficient power to relieve stress and trauma?* Are the methods presently adopted adequate? Have historical methods been lost to the present generation? Would use of traditional methods provide healing today? Are present circumstances so extreme that they have overpowered past cultural mechanisms?

- *Is there a gap between needs and available resources?* What resources, skills or knowledge does this culture require to address any shortfall between perceived need and identifiable resources? Is a recovery of cultural memory required? Is it a matter of rebuilding social institutions such as churches, temples or monasteries? Is the solution to a resource gap to be found in the training of traditional healers? Or is there a need to create new social institutions to meet completely new situations?

- In what way would this culture benefit from the assistance of an international relief and development agency? Is there a role for an NGO, or is a community response more appropriate? Is it effective to limit organisational responses to local staff, or should provision of services be community wide?

In determining the shape, structure and general conditions of a local staff support service, therefore, it is necessary to consider carefully how the local culture is itself structured, how support is given in that context, and how service can be introduced in such a way as to be welcomed and not condemned. Appropriate care will consider the place of the family in society, the place of the individual in the group, the role of community leaders, how healing is performed and how success is recognised. Healing mechanisms that rely on physical interventions (massage, for example) have sometimes been minimised by Western psychologists, who see psychology as more the realm of the mind than the body. In environments where poverty is extreme and nutrition may be less than balanced, stress and trauma reactions may have more to do with what people are eating than what they are thinking. If a staff members' family is living in a hovel, the staff person may be less able to perform expected duties during the working day.

A full local staff support programme will need to consider the practical conditions of life – food, housing, job security, education, health, insurance, and so on. Psychological support, in its therapeutic form, may be required, but generally not as the foundation of such a programme. Counselling services based on local cultural practices will almost certainly be needed. Spirituality, the need for a person to meet with God, must be central, with an affirmation of past experiences of God being essential. In sum, however, each country, each culture, will need to develop its own unique form of local staff support services if NGOs are to meet the needs of all truly and equitably.[6]

Notes

[1] Sphere Project, *Humanitarian Charter and Minimum Standards in Disaster Response* (Oxford: Oxfam, 2000).

[2] For example, see J. T. Mitchell and G. S. Everly, *Critical Incident Stress Debriefing: An Operations Manual for the Prevention of Traumatic Stress Among Emergency Services and Disaster Workers*, 2d ed., rev. (Ellicott City, Md.: Chevron Publishing Company, 1996).

[3] D. Summerfield, *The Impact of War and Atrocity on Civilian Populations: Basic Principles for NGO Interventions and a Critique of*

Psychological Trauma Projects, Network Paper 14 (London: ODI/RNN, 1996).

[4] I. Agger, S. Vuk and J. Mimica, *Theory and Practice of Psychosocial Projects Under War Conditions in Bosnia-Herzegovina and Croatia* (Zagreb: ECHO/ECTF, 1995).

[5] Transcultural Psychosocial Organization, *Community Mental Health in Cambodia* (1997). The work of TPO is highly recommended to the reader. Further information can be obtained directly from TPO in Cambodia at PO Box 1124, Phnom Penh, Cambodia.

[6] Adapted from John Fawcett, "The Care and Support of Local Staff in Christian Humanitarian Ministry: A Psychological Perspective," in *Doing MemberCare Well*, ed. K. S. O'Donnell (Pasadena, Calif.: William Carey Library, 2002).

chapter 11

Preparing for crisis

Humanitarian workers are more and more likely to be involved in extremely dangerous environments. Many NGOs have developed intentional strategies for assigning teams of front-line staff at the onset of major humanitarian crisis. In recent years (Kosovo 1999, Iraq 2003, for example) NGO personnel actually travelled with advance military units, some of which are still involved in active conflict. Rather than waiting for military actions to be completed, an increasing number of NGO staff are placed in the centre of war zones. A disturbing trend is developing in which military action is planned around the actions of humanitarian organisations. The Iraq conflict of 2003 was largely predicated on the ability (and willingness) of major relief agencies to provide on the ground support to humanitarian activities from the moment the war began. While the politics and strategic limitations of such activities are beyond the scope of this book, this practice necessarily increases exposure of field staff and their families to very high levels of stress, distress and psychological trauma.

Only a few years ago aid agencies could expect extreme stress reactions to be the result of unfortunate accidental exposure to danger. Today organisations deliberately and strategically locate personnel in situations of high risk. Kosovo in the late 1990s was a high-risk environment with concerns about mines, snipers, hostage-taking and the possible presence of depleted uranium. Afghanistan in 2002 held high risks for aid personnel, and in Iraq in 2003, potential risk became certain risk.

In these contexts humanitarian agencies must prepare for psychological casualties amongst their own staff and staff dependents. Trauma is no longer merely a statistical possibility; it is a certainty. Aid workers will die in Iraq and elsewhere in the years to come. Humanitarian workers will be targets of intentional paramilitary and military actions. As the range and type of attack increase and evolve over time, death and injury among aid staff will become even more a part of work-related risk. Unfortunately, most NGOs are not prepared to cope with or support the casualties expected to occur in the first decade of the new millennium. Existing plans are generally not comprehensive, and many smaller NGOs have no plans at all. It is essential when developing extensive plans to meet the needs of war-affected communities that NGOs also develop comprehensive support programmes for their staff and dependents. Such programmes need to be integrated into each and every field initiative and become a full component of the organisation's total human resource management strategy.

For the past five years World Vision International has been developing a model of support based on real and perceived needs of personnel and family members. The model is comprehensive in the sense that it attempts to provide structural methods of protecting staff and dependents from serious impact of traumatic stress. Protection begins before recruitment, before hiring and before deployment. Only by building protection into the whole employment process can risks be brought to acceptable levels. At the core of the model, which continues to evolve and grow, is a process called Trauma and Emergency Support Service (TESS). While the overall objective is to reduce impact, the reality is that stress and trauma will be experienced. Protection is important but is not sufficient on its own. There must be an intervention component to any stress and trauma protection strategy. TESS is not merely an emergency ambulance-type service; rather, it works on a longer-term or ongoing basis to enhance protective factors and to ensure that healing occurs in a timely manner. TESS is therefore based on three beliefs:

- Risk to staff in present-day humanitarian work is increasing each year.
- Some humanitarian staff will die and others will be injured in the course of their employment.
- It is possible to mitigate the impacts of psychological trauma as a result of exposure to major critical events through development of appropriate support services.

This view is not defeatist or submissive. It is based on clear analysis of the trends in humanitarian work and the evidence of all the major NGOs and the United Nations. The world is becoming an increasingly dangerous place for aid personnel.

TESS is not merely a response-focused model. Rather, it endeavours to reduce the likelihood of exposure to traumatic events and, when such exposure cannot be avoided, to maximise the likelihood of survival. Finally, where trauma does result, the model seeks to provide immediate on-site and followup services intended to minimise damage to those affected and to reduce longer-term consequences associated with psychological damage.

The strategy does not rely overly on psychological interventions. Prevention, avoidance, assessment and health maintenance are key components of the strategy. Professional psychological services form a key component of treatment phases when such intervention is required. However, the central principle of the model is that organisational structures and practices can significantly reduce exposure to extreme trauma and reduce the impact of critical events. Keeping staff and dependents safe is the priority.

There are three major phases during which protection for staff and dependents should be provided. All three are critical to providing appropriate support; they need to be considered together as parts of a comprehensive whole. In the past, NGOs have tended to treat each stage separately and without due recognition of the importance of the overlap or connections among the stages. In larger organisations the cause of this may have been a result of separation of functions into departments and divisions that have important obligations in themselves but limited responsibilities for the other phases. The three phases are

- Pre-deployment
- Deployment
- Post-deployment

Pre-deployment

Protection against traumatic stress injury begins prior to employment. The simple truth is that employing the right person for the right job in the right place will substantially reduce the possibility of a traumatic stress reaction at a later date. Recruitment, hiring and selection may not appear to be psychological interventions, but inappropriate employment can be a factor leading to psychological injury at field locations.

The Employment Process

The objectives of the employment process are quite simple. Can the candidate perform the duties expected in this position? Can the organisation provide sufficient assurances of commitment for candidates?

- A clear although not necessarily complex job description.
- Clear and agreed-upon job objectives. What, exactly, is this employee being asked to achieve?
- A clear description of where the job is located – capital city, provincial city, village?

- A clear and obvious match between employee skills and knowledge and the job requirements.
- A clear understanding of the candidate's previous experiences in similar roles.
- A clear appreciation of the candidate's present and past state of health, both physical and psychological.
- A clear and simple employment contract – what is the pay level? for how long? what else will the organisation pay for?
- A clear understanding of the obligations and responsibilities of both employer and employee.

Once individuals are hired, the temptation for NGOs is to deploy them immediately to their intended field location. Indeed, a number of newly hired staff often arrive in their assignment post before the hiring process is complete. Some even live and work in these conditions without pay or other benefits while employment processes are completed elsewhere. This is basically a recipe for disaster. Apart from ethical considerations, there are major legal consequences in not employing someone according to labour-law requirements. While there is always an urgency to get people on the ground, especially in a major relief operation, the risks to individuals and the organisation of premature deployment are too high.

Even when legal processes have been dealt with, an employing organisation should pause before relocating the employee to the field site. Time spent properly preparing staff for deployment will reduce possible stress reactions and improve efficiency and effectiveness on arrival. While many experienced relief workers are quite used to fending for themselves at new work locations, there are an increasing number of new recruits to this type of employment. Nothing causes experienced staff more stress and strain than finding that a new person has not been adequately prepared for an assignment and may even need "babysitting" for a settling-in period. Not only does this create stress for both new and experienced staff, but it also can significantly compromise attainment of programme objectives. In the early stages of a major emergency response, this can quite literally mean the difference between life and death for affected communities.

The Preparation Process

- The organisation must provide clear and up-to-date assessments of living and working conditions before deployment begins.
- Staff need to know what they are going to encounter and what the objectives are. Strategic plans need to be shared with operational staff before deployment.
- Staff need to know how to manage basic field equipment such as communications and vehicles. Training should be provided to ensure skills are appropriate for the location.
- Staff need to know basic stress management skills. Training should be provided to ensure that all staff have stress management understanding.
- Staff need to know how to maintain their own personal security. Training should be provided to ensure security preparedness.
- Field locations need to maintain comprehensive security plans in order to promote safety for staff, dependents and organisational assets.
- Staff need to know the extent and nature of support services and how to access these services if required. Field offices need to have psychological service resources available locally or regionally.

The process of preparation does not end with departure of the staff to the field site. Arrival at the work location needs to be structured as well. A well-planned welcome and orientation process need not be overly burdensome on field staff, and, if performed adequately, can in fact reduce demands on time and energy of already deployed staff.

Deployment

- Staff should be briefed immediately upon arrival at field locations. This briefing will update security information, orient the newcomers to present conditions, introduce them to colleagues and team members, review the reporting relationship and include a geographical orientation.
- Field offices should have updated security and operational guidelines available for all staff.
- Descriptions of available human resource support services and how to access them should be provided upon arrival.
- As teams have been shown to be significant in enhancing resilience, a team environment should be created at the first opportunity and newcomers assigned to teams.
- Team leaders/supervisors should be clearly identified and assigned. Team leaders should have people management skills and be able to monitor well-being of staff and access support services where required. Training should be given to supervisors to ensure they have these skills.

TESS – For When Things Go Wrong

Trauma and emergency support services are designed to minimise the psychological impact of critical events occurring to field staff and dependents. While psycho-social care for community members is a key component of all humanitarian work, this particular activity focuses on personnel and dependents. In effect, it is a specialised employee assistance programme (EAP), similar in many respects to EAP provisions found in most large corporations today. The major differences in practice are that most first-world corporations have ready access to already existing emergency response resources, whilst most field-based NGOs do not.

Essentially a TESS plan comprises a combination of in-house services especially created for this purpose, complemented by existing specialist resources contracted for service provision when required. It is essential that provision of adequate resources is determined before they are required. Globally there are not many professional services able to respond quickly to a crisis at short notice. As it is most likely that a critical event will affect more than one NGO at one time, it is also possible that existing services will be quickly swamped and unavailable to all that need them. The terrorist attack on New York City in September 2001 is an example. After the attacks were over, it was obvious that psychological trauma affected huge numbers of emergency personnel. The high number of lives lost in the fire and police departments, along with those killed in the buildings targeted, almost completely swamped the total psychological trauma response available in the United States. Trauma specialists were called in from Europe and Australia to try to meet the very high needs. If the wealthiest country in the world finds ensuring access to trauma specialists at a time of crisis a challenge, then third-world countries devastated by war or famine are virtually helpless.

Large NGOs with funding abilities should develop some kind of first-response capacity in-house. This will give maximum flexibility to respond to crises involving staff. This resource should be complemented by specialist resources contracted in some fashion to the NGO. If maintaining an in-house resource is not practical, organisations should ensure that service providers have been identified and will be available should the need arise. It is recommended that some type of formal agreement be drawn up with a service provider, if this resource forms the foundation of the emergency activity.

In creating or contracting for specialist trauma resources, ensure that proper accreditation and certification exist. While most first-world countries licence mental health professionals in some fashion, this is not general across the whole world. This is not to say that all service providers must be certified according to European or American criteria. However, when creating a contract or agreement with a service provider, it is an obligation of the organisation to ensure that the service provider does in fact have the skills and expertise to perform as expected.

This works both ways for NGOs. Many first-world mental health specialists are not, in fact, equipped to perform adequately in crisis situations involving NGO staff. This is not a reflection on their competence or training. It is related to the context in which they do their primary work. Humanitarian work is performed in environments staggeringly different from most first-world cities. While this is obvious to relief personnel, it is not always evident to people who have never worked in such conditions. Bringing competent mental health professionals to locations where they themselves become stressed and overwhelmed by the environment will not assist anyone. Further, mental health is much more influenced by culture than physical health. Mental health – and mental distres – is determined by cultural and ethnic parameters in ways in which physical health, education and wealth are not. Mental health draws from a worldview, is influenced by status and hierarchy, has gender components in many cultures, and has religious implications in most.

Treatment of mental health problems is likewise influenced by a cultural view of health and the processes that lead to health. As an example, North American trauma processes are most likely to focus on talking as the road to healing. A major source of healing is in the internal thinking processes of an individual, which is then externalised in verbal conversations with a mental health professional. Healing is an individual achievement gained through this process. By contrast, many African healing processes focus on the group or the community. Talking is not necessarily the preferred activity and can be viewed as unnecessary or even counter-productive. Physical actions such as dance, massage, walking and fasting may underlie many approaches to healing. Healing of an individual is not seen as the primary objective. Healing of the community, family or even the whole people group is what is required.

This book is not the place to detail the rich and varied conversations concerning appropriate mental health provisions across cultures. However, the above discussion should alert organisations that ensuring adequate and appropriate mental health services is not merely a matter of contracting with first-world specialists who will travel to critical events and provide health care to those affected. Psychological trauma services will be most effective when the service provided clearly matches the nature of the need, the culture, the gender and the ethnicity of those affected, and the appropriateness of the methods adopted to enhance healing and reduce the onset of major traumatic reactions. This can only be achieved through a focused plan to provide staff with appropriate services.

TESS is a process designed to meet immediate needs of affected personnel and to continue to ensure that needs are met as long as necessary following the event. We know that severe psychological trauma can require long periods of assistance. Unfortunately, many traumatic event responses are quite time-limited. The popularity of psychological debriefing processes has encouraged the idea that short-term interventions can mitigate most of the impact of psychological trauma. We have seen, as a result, psychological debriefing teams travel to critical event locations, perform a number of group debriefing events, and then return to their home base. The increasing body of literature evaluating such procedures is raising significant concerns about the efficacy and even the safety of psychological debriefing in the absence of other, longer-term psychological support provisions.

The TESS Model

The TESS model is based on adequate provision of services in five specific areas. These are not all mental health interventions but, taken together as a whole process, integrate to provide significant protection against the onset of long-term psychological disability. Integration is the key to success. Research has shown that demonstrations of organisational care and support for staff are a major factor in reducing stress and strain. Existence of an integrated staff support strategy will, in itself, provide some protection to staff. While it is highly likely that many NGOs provide some, if not all, of the services detailed below, combining these into a staff-focused package sends a powerful message of support to staff. Some items detailed will appear simple and common sense, and readers may wonder about the value of including them here. The truth is, however, much support is provided by simple, everyday care actions. It is also true that absence of simple common-sense supports can result in consequences that become very significant later on. Attending, in a planned manner, to these basic needs will maximise staff support and will also lead to increased efficacy of more specialist psychological services when provided later in the process.

Sideline Support Services

When a critical event occurs, the objective of sideline support is to move staff involved safely and quickly away from the event site, providing brief services that will assist this process. A TESS team will be on-site or as close as possible to provide these immediate support services. Interventions may include determining whether someone is injured; providing minor medical assistance; providing water and food; providing emotional, physical and spiritual support; providing transportation away from immediate danger; providing psychological "defusing" services. Psychological defusing services provide brief information on stress reactions and what can be done to promote prevention of severe trauma reactions, or how best to manage such reactions.

The prime objectives of this activity are to reduce risk of further damage, to make an initial assessment of damage caused, and to meet immediate basic needs. This is not always as simple as it may appear. Many critical events occur in remote locations where transport and communications are difficult. Any plan, therefore, to move staff, provide them with food and water, and keep them physically safe, will require consideration of, amongst other things, the following:

- What vehicles will be available at short notice?
- Are there alternatives to road travel?
- How is communication to be maintained?
- Where will essential supplies come from?
- Who is going to deliver them?
- How will immediate psychological defusing services be provided?

Logistic Support Services

For persons affected by a critical event, TESS will organise and provide direct assistance through provision of short-term respite care at a previously designated "retreat-style" location; communication services; emergency personal finances; and local and international travel assistance for those needing to leave the field location or travel to a home destination.

The prime objective of this activity is to provide a safe and secure location for staff and dependents where further psychological assistance can be provided if required. This period of time is also essential for staff and dependents to connect into family and social networks. The sooner people are able to communicate with extended family and social support networks, the more likely that major stress reactions will be minimised. Determination of such a facility should be completed prior to its being required. Such facilities may not be easy to access in some regions of the world, and waiting until they are needed before attempting to reserve them will generally fail.

These types of facilities need to be located in countries with easy access to as many nationalities as possible. The facility needs to be as near as possible to the airport. The facility needs to have transportation and translation services available for arriving staff. The location must be secure and private but with access to a reasonable-size city. Communications systems must be relatively sophisticated, with international telephone and Internet access available.

Staff moved to this facility must have access to cash and shopping. Often critical events involve the loss of personal possessions, clothes and important documents. Staff must be able to purchase replacement items as soon as possible. Assistance must be provided for managing immigration and identity documentation, a process that can require many hours at embassies or other government offices.

International travel for staff being relocated either to such a facility or to another location must be provided. Purchase of air tickets should be done by agency staff and not left to the traumatised persons.

Many staff and dependents will be unable to travel internationally. This does not absolve an NGO from responsibility. Retreat-style facilities should be identified in the host country for staff who cannot leave or for events that don't require relocating to another country. The services listed above should be available whether the facility is in the host country or outside it.

Obviously, provision of such services will cost money. Residential facilities and international air travel are not cheap. However, it is also true that long-term care for severely traumatised people can be extremely expensive. Provision of immediate assistance can mitigate the need for long-term psychological assistance. NGOs have a choice. They can spend their funds on prevention or cure, but they will be spending funds one way or the other.

Trauma Debriefing Services

Group psychological debriefing services are not recommended in the first instance. There is sufficient debate in the professional community at present referring to potential negative effects to recommend caution about procedures such as CISD. However, should an organisation determine to include CISD or equivalent services, it is strongly recommended that this be done in the wider context of an integrated TESS strategy.

A critical event debriefing is a structured, confidential psycho-educational group meeting that emphasises expression of reactions after an acutely stressful event and education on how best to promote prevention or management of any post-traumatic stress reactions. Proponents suggest that such a process is most helpful when provided 24 to 72 hours after the critical event. However, other researchers argue that this time frame is much too close to the event and has the potential to "embed" the trauma more firmly in the minds of participants in such debriefing. Other research suggests that properly performed debriefing can be quite effective when performed as long as some months after the critical event.

Rather than specifically focusing on psychological debriefing at this stage in the TESS process, it may be more helpful to provide psychological assessment services. This would take the form of a professional mental health practitioner making assessments of the impact of a critical event and making recommendations as to what types of psychological services should be provided. This has the advantage of addressing each individual or each family group as unique, with its own specific needs and also its own unique resources. When a specialist determines that a debriefing process could be helpful, then it would be possible to perform that process as required rather than applying the debriefing universally to all affected by the event.

Whatever approach an organisation decides on, it is apparent that locating that service inside or close to the safe facility referred to above makes the most logistic sense. When seeking such facilities, therefore, agencies should look for those that have mental health professionals on staff (preferably) or close by. Specialist psychological services must be able to provide services to individuals, families and children in different languages. This is obviously a very tall order, which is why planning for such interventions must be intentional and done well in advance.

Brief Counselling Services

After the initial crisis psychological debriefing services, especially when individuals and families are still in transit or after arrival at a final destination, brief counselling services should be made available. Brief counselling is not debriefing, but it may contain some of the same components. Brief counselling is not long-term therapy. However, such counselling can be very effective in providing immediate psychological assistance to distressed and traumatised people. Often the person completing the assessment process referred to above will also continue with brief counselling. But when this is not practical, the assessor must ensure that people requiring brief counselling have access to such services as soon as possible.

Whether people are sent to a facility or sent home, or even if they remain in post, it is essential that initial counselling services be provided. Even if staff choose not to take up the offer, the services must be available. Obviously, agencies will need to factor associated costs into planning.

Follow-along Services

After the critical event and with the passage of time TESS team members will continue to track and communicate with individuals and families involved in the critical event. Through tracking it may be seen that certain other types of services are required. These services could include psychological and social support services or referrals; spiritual guidance or support services; health services; employment services; relocation assistance; and insurance claims for personal or property-related matters.

A major challenge for NGOs is followup and evaluation. Yet for critically affected staff, followup and provision of follow-along services is vital. Organisational measures must be designed to ensure that staff and family members affected by a serious critical event continue to have access to services for as long as necessary. While most people tend to recover fairly quickly when they receive adequate assistance early on, others need more structured assistance. Fortunately, many health plans and medical programmes recognise the need for psychological services and cover many expenses in this category of medical care. However, it is incumbent on agency managers to ensure that health plans and provisions do in fact meet the requirements of personnel and dependents.

In summary, it is recommended that humanitarian organisations consider designing assistance strategies similar to the TESS model described above. Structured and intentional support to staff and dependents during and immediately following major critical events results in significantly lowered levels of distress and traumatic stress reactions.

Post-deployment

The nature of humanitarian work is piecemeal. Personnel move from assignment to assignment, from NGO to NGO, from role to role. Discrete employment periods are often compartmentalised and kept separate from those preceding. When people move from agency to agency, there is little continuity and connection. Both agency and individuals tend to view past events as "done and over with," referred to in the past tense. Cambodia was the late 1980s, Rwanda the 1990s, Kosovo the late 1990s, Iraq the early 2000s. Yet each of these events is intricately connected, especially in the lives of those people who worked or lived through more than one of them.

Organisations therefore need to create processes for monitoring the long-term health and well-being of staff. This obviously works best when staff remain with an agency for a long period of time and employment experiences can be tracked. But even when people move among employers or locations, it is possible to take into account previous experiences. This has become more important with recent findings suggesting that cumulative stress may be a major form of disability for NGO personnel. Long-term cumulative stress experiences could lead to conditions closely resembling PTSD or severe depression or other ASR.

Rather than leaving the past to look after itself, individuals and employers need to be constantly aware of the potential for past exposure to traumatic events to emerge in the present. This will require humanitarian workers to take account of themselves, their present stress and distress levels, and how they cope with stress. Organisations need to ensure that personnel understand the impact of cumulative and chronic stress and to assist staff to perform self-assessments. Employers also need to ensure that staff have access to services, should they be required. It is important that agencies make clear to staff that such self-assessment and self-protection behaviour is not only expected but is rewarded. Too often employers penalise staff who have been affected psychologically, reducing their opportunities for career advancement and covertly criticising performance.

Conversely, staff who take good care of themselves will be able to perform services for their employers and the community for a much longer period of time. Agencies should therefore commend and reward staff who intentionally care for their own health.

It should be noted that codes of practice such as the People in Aid Code encourage NGOs to support staff and dependents appropriately. It is likely that in the future agencies that perform well against these type of standards will themselves be "rewarded" by gaining access to donor funds for programme work. NGOs that are unable to demonstrate such care are more and more likely to be cut off from donor funds in the future.

Appendices

Resources for individuals and organisations

Appendix 1

Stress measures for individuals

This section contains a number of measurement scales that individuals can use to evaluate how much stress they are experiencing at a particular time. There are also scales that review an individual's ability to relax and avoid the onset of burnout. Two important provisos apply in using this material:

1. These measures are not clinical diagnosis tools and should not be used as such. They are indicators of well-being only. Any concerns about mental health should immediately be brought to the attention of a mental health professional.

2. These measures should never be used as part of an organisational performance review or to assess suitability for any particular role, task or job. They are not designed to measure ability to cope with stress, nor will they predict performance under pressure.

Scale 1: Life Stressors

The Holmes and Rahe Social Readjustment Rating Scale

Source: T. Holmes and R. Rahe, "Holmes-Rahe Social Readjustment Scale," *Journal of Psychosomatic Research* 11 (1967): 213-318.

This scale should not be used as, or in place of, a clinical instrument. When individuals or supervisors have concerns about the state of health, professional psychological assistance should be sought.

Also, please note that this assessment tool has been designed for persons living in an average first-world environment. Humanitarian workers will note that many everyday experiences in relief environments are not referred to in this scale (see Chapter 8). Work is progressing on such adjustment scales but validation trials will take some time. However, this instrument does indicate stress levels relating to the last twelve months, and its use is recommended.

Instructions: On the line following each event that you have experienced in the last year write the number indicating the events life change units (the number in parenthesis before the event). Add all the numbers you have entered for your total score. This is a personal exercise, so be honest with yourself.

(100) Death of spouse _____
(75) Divorce _____
(65) Marital separation _____
(63) Jail term _____
(63) Death of close family member _____
(53) Personal injury or illness _____
(50) Marriage _____
(47) Fired at work _____
(45) Marital reconciliation _____
(44) Change in health of family member _____
(40) Pregnancy _____
(39) Sex difficulties _____
(39) Gain of a new family member _____
(39) Business readjustment _____
(38) Change in financial status _____
(37) Death of close friend _____

(36)	Change to a different line of work	_____
(35)	Change in number of arguments with spouse	_____
(30)	Major mortgage or loan	_____
(29)	Change in responsibilities at work	_____
(29)	Son or daughter leaving home	_____
(29)	Trouble with in-laws	_____
(28)	Outstanding personal achievement	_____
(26)	Wife or husband begins or stops work	_____
(26)	Begin or end school	_____
(25)	Change in living conditions	_____
(24)	Revision in personal habits	_____
(23)	Trouble with the boss	_____
(20)	Change in work hours or condition	_____
(20)	Change in residence	_____
(20)	Change in school	_____
(19)	Change in recreation	_____
(19)	Change in church activities	_____
(18)	Change in social activities	_____
(17)	Minor mortgage or loan	_____
(15)	Change in sleeping habits	_____
(15)	Change in number of family get-together	_____
(15)	Change in eating habits	_____
(13)	Vacation	_____
(12)	Religious holiday	_____
(11}	Minor violation of the law	_____

TOTAL SCORE _____

Significance of the score: The score suggests the amount of "change stress" you have personally encountered and dealt with over the past twelve months. These stressors could affect the state of your health in the following manner:

150-199	mild risk	suggests minimal "change stress" and probable good health
200-299	medium risk	likelihood of your having had or being about to have a minor illness
300+	high risk	likelihood of your having had or being about to have a major illness

These factors also help to analyse the amount of external stressors faced at a given time, which will influence your ability to cope with additional cumulative stress.

Scale 2: Stress Signal Inventory

Source: Nancy Loving Tubesing and Donald A. Tubesing, eds., *Whole Person Handbook* (Duluth, Minn.: Whole Person Pubications, 1983).

The symptoms below do not constitute clinical diagnosis. There are many reasons for presence or absence of symptoms listed below. If you are concerned about your health as a result of this inventory, you are strongly encouraged to consult with a mental health professional.

Instructions: Check on the lists below the symptoms of stress exhaustion you have noticed lately. Look back for changes to your normal reactions.

Physical
___appetite change
___headaches
___tension
___fatigue
___insomnia
___weight change
___muscle aches
___colds
___crying spells
___digestive upsets
___pounding heart
___accident prone
___teeth grinding
___rash
___restlessness
___foot-tapping
___increased alcohol/ drugs/tobacco use

Emotional
___anxiety
___frustration
___mood swings
___the blues
___bad temper
___nightmares
___irritability
___need to prove self
___"no one cares"
___depression
___nervous laughter
___worrying
___easily discouraged
___little job satisfaction

Spiritual

___emptiness
___loss of meaning
___doubt
___unforgiving
___martyrdom

___looking for magic
___loss of direction
___cynicism
___apathy

Mental/cognitive
___forgetfulness
___dull senses
___poor concentration
___low productivity
___confusion
___lethargy
___whirling mind
___no new ideas
___boredom
___spacing out
___negative self-talk

Behavioural
___isolation
___intolerance
___resentment
___loneliness
___lashing out
___hiding from others
___not talking
___lowered sex drive
___nagging
___distrust
___fewer contacts with friends
___lack of intimacy
___using people

Scale 3: Recognising Signs of Cumulative Stress and Burnout

Source: Sheila Platt and Laurie Sullivan. Response Management International, Inc. (1995).

Stress is experienced in a highly individual manner. The best defence against harmful effects of various stresses is information about common signs and symptoms. Cumulative stress and burnout are a result of prolonged, unrelieved exposure to a variety of work, personal and incident-specific events.

The following is not a comprehensive list, but it provides examples of what those who are suffering from cumulative stress may experience. Cumulative stress and burnout affect us holistically.

Please note that presence of the following symptoms does not infer a clinical diagnosis. Professional assessment is required before any clinical decisions or interventions are made.

Signs of Burnout in the Working Group:
- high job turnover
- increased sick leave
- clique formation
- scapegoating
- frequent conflicts
- lack of initiative
- lowered work output

Signs of Burnout in Individuals:

Physical Reactions
- extended fatigue
- frequent physical complaints
- sleep disturbance
- appetite changes
- ulcers, gastrointestinal disorders
- weight loss/gain
- injuries from high risk behaviours
- increased premenstrual syndrome

Emotional Reactions
- anxiety
- feeling alienated from others
- desire to be alone
- negativism/cynicism/distrust
- suspiciousness/paranoia
- depression/chronic sadness
- feeling pressured/overwhelmed
- diminished pleasure

Cognitive Reactions
- tired of thinking
- obsessive thinking
- difficulty concentrating
- increased distractibility/ inattention
- problems with decision/ priorities
- feeling indispensable/ obsessions
- diminished tolerance for ambiguity
- constricted thought
- rigid, inflexible thinking

Spiritual Reactions
- doubt in value system/ religious beliefs
- questioning of major life areas (professional, employment, lifestyle)
- feeling threatened and victimised
- disillusionment
- self-preoccupation

Behavioural Reactions
- irritability
- anger displacement, blaming others
- reluctance to start/finish projects
- social withdrawal
- absenteeism/tardiness
- unwillingness/refusal to take leave
- substance abuse, self-medication
- disregard for security/ risky behaviour
- shortened or skipped meditation time
- avoiding spiritual leadership role
- decreased quality of service to people most in need

Attitudinal Reactions
- disillusionment
- low morale
- focus on "failures"
- loss of emotional meaning of work
- distrust
- loss of spiritual zeal
- unwillingness to forgive
- hopelessness

Scale 4: How Well Can You Relax?

Source: Sheila Platt and Laurie Sullivan, Response Management International, Inc. (1995)

This scale is a simple way to measure how well you are able to relax in your present circumstances. This is not a clinical diagnosis instrument. If you have concerns about your state of health or have any other questions regarding relaxation, you should consult with a mental health professional.

Instructions: Answer the following questions by placing a number on the line preceding each question. Select the number that best describes your behaviour.

3 = Always
2 = Sometimes
1 = Seldom

_____1. Are you able to shut out your worries when you go to bed at night?

_____2. Are you able to take a nap during the day and awaken refreshed?

_____3. Is your clothing well fitting and comfortable?

_____4. Are you able to concentrate on one problem at a time?

_____5. Do you plan your day's activities?

_____6. Do you find time to relax and stretch during the day?

_____7. Do you take time to prevent tension by relieving sustained positions required in your work?

_____8. Do you know how to relax by doing simple movements when you feel yourself becoming tense because of sustained positions?

_____9. Do you check yourself frequently for habitual tension habits such as scowling, clenched fists, tight jaws, hunched shoulders or pursed lips?

_____10. Do you relax these evidences of tensions at will when you find them?

_____11. Do you find it easy to relax so that you sleep easily and deeply?

_____12. Do you know how to release tensions through simple movements so that you can sleep well?

_____13. Do you play with such interest that you become completely absorbed in what you are doing?
_____14. Do you plan your life so that you can have a change of people, scenery and thoughts?

TOTAL SCORE   _____

Significance of the score:

33 – 42   Indicates a high ability to relax
24 – 32   Indicates an average ability to relax
15 – 23   Indicates a low ability to relax

Scale 5: Relief Worker Burnout Questionnaire

Source: Quoted by Sheila Platt and Laurie Sullivan, Response Management International, Inc. (1995). Reference for this survey is unknown.

This questionnaire is intended to help detect burnout among relief workers. Even relief workers not showing signs of acute distress may develop burnout, with loss of productivity and long-term personal consequences.

Please note that this is not a clinical diagnostic tool. If you have any concerns about your state of health as a result of utilizing this tool, you should consult with a mental health professional.

Instructions: Rate each of the following items in terms of how much the symptom affected you *in the last 30 days.*

> 0 = Never
> 1 = Occasionally
> 2 = Somewhat often
> 3 = Frequently
> 4 = Almost always

_____ 1. Do you tire easily? Do you feel fatigued a lot of the time, even when you have had enough sleep?

_____ 2. Are people annoying you by their demands and stories about their daily activities? Do minor inconveniences make you irritable or impatient?

_____ 3. Do you feel increasingly critical, cynical and disenchanted?

_____ 4. Are you affected by sadness you can't explain? Are you crying more than usual?

_____ 5. Are you forgetting appointments, deadlines, personal possessions? Have you become absent-minded?

_____ 6. Are you seeing close friends and family members less frequently? Do you find yourself wanting to be alone and avoiding even your close friends?

_____ 7. Does doing even routine things seem like an effort?

_____ 8. Are you suffering from physical complaints such as stomachache, headaches, lingering colds, general aches and pains?

_____ 9. Do you feel confused or disorientated when the activity of the day stops?

_____ 10. Have you lost interest in activities that you were previously interested in or even enjoyed?

_____ 11. Do you have little enthusiasm for your work? Do you feel negative, futile or depressed about your work?

_____ 12. Are you less efficient than you think you should be?

_____ 13. Are you eating more or less, smoking more cigarettes, using more alcohol or drugs to cope with your work?

TOTAL SCORE _____

Significance of the score: No formal norms are available for this measure. Based on the content of the items, the following are porbably accurate:

0 – 15   probably coping adequately with the stress of your work

16 – 25   probably suffering from work stress; it would be wise to take preventive action

26 – 35   possible burnout

35+   probable burnout

Scale 6: Burnout Prevention Assessment

Source: Dr. R. John Sturt, Auckland, New Zealand

Please note that this scale is not a clinical diagnostic instrument. It merely measures some of the more effective ways in which burnout may be prevented. If you have any concerns about your state of health, you should consult with a mental health professional.

Instructions: For each question, write the number that fits your reality on the line before the question.

_____1. Do you have a full day off to do what you like?
Weekly (5); Frequently (4); Occasionally (1); Never (0)

_____2. Do you have time out for yourself to be quiet, think, meditate, pray?
Daily (5); Frequently (3); Occasionally (1); Seldom or never (0).

_____3. Do you have good vacations, about three or four weeks in one year?
Every year (5); Occasionally (3); Rarely (1); Almost never (0)

_____4. Do you do some aerobic exercise for at least 20 minutes at a time?
Three to five times a week (5); Occasionally (3); Never (0)

_____5. Do you do something for fun—play a game? go to a movie or concert?
Weekly (4); Monthly (3); Occasionally (1); Never (0)

_____6. Do you practice any muscle relaxation or slow-breathing technique?
Daily (5); Frequently (4); Occasionally (2); Rarely (0)

_____7. Do you listen to your body messages (symptoms, illnesses, etc)?
Always (5); Mostly (3); Occasionally (1); Seldom/never (0)

_____8. If single: Do you have friends with whom you share at a feeling level?
Regularly (5); Frequently (4); Occasionally (3); Seldom/never (0)

_____9   If married (or in relationship): How often do you share intimately?
Daily (5); Occasionally (3); Seldom (2), Not at all (lonely) (0)

_____10. Do you share your stressors, cares, problems and needs with others or God?
Regularly (5); Frequently (3); Occasionally (2); Never (0)

_____11. How would you describe your ability to communicate with others?
Excellent (5); Fair – but working on it (3); With difficulty (1); Poor (0)

_____12. Do you sleep well (for at least seven hours a night)?
Almost every night (3); Frequently (2); Occasionally (1); Never (0)

_____13. Are you able to say no to demands on you when this is appropriate?
Always (3); Mostly (2); Seldom (1); Never (0)

_____14. Do you set realistic goals for your life, both short term and long term?
Regularly (5); Occasionally (3); Seldom (1); Never (0)

_____15. Are you careful to eat a balanced diet?
Always (5); Most of the time (3); Not often (1) ; A lot of "junk food" (0)

_____16. Is your weight appropriate for your height?
Consistently (3); Yes, with difficulty (2); Overweight (0)

_____17. How would you describe the amount of touch you get in your life?
As much as you need (5); Frequent (4); Occasional (1); Seldom (0)

_____18. Can you deal with anger without repressing it or dumping it on others?
Always (5); Mostly (4); Occasionally (2); Rarely (1); Never (0)

_____19. How often do you have a good "belly laugh"?
At least daily (3); Frequently (2); Seldom (1); Never (0)

_____20. Do you have a creative hobby time (gardening, reading, music, etc.)?
Weekly (4); Occasionally (2); Rarely (1); Never (0)

_____21. Do you nurture your self-esteem (e.g.. with self affirmations)?
Regularly (5); Frequently (3); Occasionally (1); Rarely/never (0)

_____22. Do you practise forgiveness of those who have hurt you?
Regularly (5); Occasionally (3); Rarely (1); Never (0)

_____23. Have you dealt with old hurts and "baggage" from the past?
Yes (5); Most of them (3); Much remains to do (0)

TOTAL SCORE _____

Significance of score:

80 – 100	Good skills
70 – 80	Moderately good skills
50 – 70	Lifestyle changes needed
Below 50	In trouble!

Appendix 2:

Recommended reading

Literature relating to the care and support of international humanitarian workers has been steadily increasing in recent years. The books listed below provide an excellent foundation for any reader wishing to understand the issues and advances in knowledge and understanding. The list draws on material written for the international missions community as well as the wider NGO world. Principles and much of the practice discussed would be applicable to most first-world public health and community welfare organisations, as well as international environments. The list is not comprehensive, but these books themselves contain further reading lists.

Danieli, Y. 2002. *Sharing the Front Lines and the Back Hills: Peacekeepers, Humanitarian Aid Workers and the Media in the Midst of Crisis.* Amityville, N.Y.: Baywood Publishing Company.

Danieli, Y., N. Rodley and L. Weisaeth, eds. 1996. *International Responses to Traumatic Stress.* Amityville, N.Y.: Baywood Publishing Company.

de haan, B. 1994. *Humanitarian Action in Conflict Zones: Coping with Stress. International Red Cross Guidelines.* Geneva: International Committee of the Red Cross Publications.

DeWolfe, D. J. 2000. *Training Manual for Disaster Mental Health Workers.* 2d ed. Rockville, Md.: Center for Mental Health Services.

Ehrenreich, J. H. 2001. *Coping with Disaster: A Guidebook to Psychosocial Intervention.* Old Westbury, N.Y.: Center for Psychology and Society.

———. 2002. *A Guide for Humanitarian Health Care, Human Rights Workers.* Old Westbury, N.Y.: Center for Psychology and Society.

Everly, G. S., and J. T. Mitchell, 1999. *Critical Incident Stress Management.* 2d ed. Ellicott City, Md.: Chevron Publishing Co.

Fawcett, G. 1999. *Ad-Mission: The Briefing and Debriefing of Teams of Missionaries and Aid Workers.* Great Britain: YWAM.

Figley, C. R., ed. 1995. *Compassion Fatigue: Coping with Secondary Traumatic Stress Disorder in Those Who Treat the Traumatized.* New York: Brunner/Mazel.

Gourevitch, P. 1998. *We Wish to Inform You That Tomorrow We Will Be Killed with Our Families: Stories from Rwanda.* New York: Farrar, Straus and Giroux.

Grant, R. 1999. *Living and Working in Environments of Violence and Trauma: A Resource Manual for Humanitarian Workers.* Burlingame, Calif.

Jensen, S. B. 1999. *Taking Care of the Care-Takers Under War Conditions; Who Cares?* European University Centre for Mental Health and Human Rights.

Mitchell, J. T., and G. Bray. 1990. *Emergency Services Stress.* Englewood Cliffs, N.J.: Prentice-Hall.

Mitchell, J. T., and G. S. Everly. 1996. *Critical Incident Stress Debriefing: An Operations Manual for the Prevention of Traumatic Stress Among Emergency Services and Disaster Workers.* 2d ed., rev. Ellicott City, Md.: Chevron Publishing Company.

O'Donnell, K. S., ed. 1997. *Too Valuable to Lose: Exploring the Causes and Cures of Missionary Attrition.* Pasadena, Calif.: William Carey Library.

———. 2002. *Doing MemberCare Well: Perspectives and Practices from Around the World.* New York: Gabriel Resources.

Paton, D., and J. Violanti. "Responding to International Needs: Critical Occupations as Disaster Relief Agencies." In *Traumatic Stress in Critical Occupations: Recognition, Consequences and Treatment,* edited by D. Paton and J. Violanti, 139-72. Springfield, Ill.: Charles C. Thomas.

Rapheal, B., and J. P. Wilson. 2000. *Psychological Debriefing: Theory, Practice and Evidence.* London: Cambridge University Press.

Shalev, A. Y., R. Yehuda and A. C. McFarlane. 2000. *International Handbook of Human Response to Trauma.* New York: Kluwer Academic/Plenum Publishers.

Vaux, A. 2001. *The Selfish Altruist.* London: Earthscan Publications.

Appendix 3

A review of the professional psychological literature

GARY TRICE

This literature review is both extensive and comprehensive. It is also relatively technical in nature and of most interest to professionals in the area of stress and trauma management. The intent is to collate information relating to stress and trauma in humanitarian work. This is not an annotated bibliography. Readers will need to follow up on references to determine the applicability of the information to their specific situations. Because there are some similarities with other professions such as social work, counselling, therapy, law enforcement, paramedic services and the military, studies on these groups have also been included. While some of this material is highly specialized, there are excellent books summarising the latest understanding of this topic; a list of these appears in the first section.

It is not our intent that all the material referenced here be read. However, we do believe that this literature review in itself is a major resource for any organisation or individual who wishes to investigate further.

The review is divided into three sections.

Gary Trice completed a B.A. in psychology and in Bible/theology at Wheaton College and an M.A. in psychology at Fuller Theological Seminary's Graduate School of Psychology. He is currently completing a Psy.D. and a M.A.C.L. at Fuller. As former business owners, he and his wife of eight years, Kristy, are passionate about the application of integrated psychology and integrated management, and they plan to practise these in international contexts.

- Psychological debriefing and its efficacy
- Christian humanitarian work
- Psychological trauma in international relief work and in similar populations

Psychological Debriefing and the Efficacy of Such Procedures

Armstrong, K., W. O'Callahan and C. Marmar. 1991. "Debriefing Red Cross Personnel: The Multiple Stressor Debriefing Model. *Journal of Traumatic Stress* 4/4, 581-93.

Armstrong, K. R., D. F. Zatick, T. J. Metzler, D. S. Weiss, C. R. Marmar, S. Garma, H. M. Ronfeldt and L. Roepke. 1998. "Debriefing American Red Cross Personnel: Pilot Study on Participants' Evaluations and Case Examples From the 1994 Los Angeles Earthquake Relief Operation." *Social Work in Health Care* 27/1, 33-50.

Bisson, J. I., P. L. Jenkins, J. Alexander and C. Bannister. 1997. "Randomised Controlled Trial of Psychological Debriefing for Victims of Acute Burn Trauma." *British Journal of Psychiatry* 171, 78-81.

Bisson, J. I., A. C McFarlane and S. Rose. 2000. "Psychological Debriefing." In *Effective Treatments for PTSD: Practice Guidelines from the International Society for Traumatic Stress Studies* edited by E. Foa, T. Keane and M. Friedman, 39-59. New York: Guilford Press.

Budd, F. 1997. "Helping the Helpers After the Bombing in Dharan: Critical-incident Stress Services Services for an Air Rescue Squadron." *Military Medicine* 162/8, 515-20.

Bunn, T. A., and A. M. Clarke. 1979. "Crisis Intervention: An Experimental Study of the Effects of a Brief Period of Counselling on the Anxiety of Relatives of Seriously Injured or Ill Hospital Patients. *British Journal of Medical Psychology* 52, 191-95.

Carlier, I. V. E., A. E. Voerman and B. P. R. Gersons. 2000. "The influence of Occupational Debriefing on Post-traumatic Stress Symptomology in Traumatized Police Officers." *British Journal of Medical Psychology* 73, 87-98.

Chemtob, C. M., S. Tomas, W. Law and D. Cremniter. 1997. "Postdisaster Psychosocial Intervention: A Field Study of the Impact of Debriefing on Psychological Distress." *American Journal of Psychiatry* 154, 415-17.

Deahl, M. 2000. "Psychological Debriefing: Controversy and Challenge." *Australian New Zealand Journal of Psychiatry* 34/6, 929-39.

de Haan, B. 1998. "Le debriefing emotionnel collectif des intervenants humanitaires L'experience du CICR" [Emotional group debrief-

ing of humanitarian aid workers: The experience of ICRC].
Schweizer Archiv fur Neurologie und Psychiatrie 149/5, 218-28.

Dyregrov, A. 1989. "Caring for Helpers in Disaster Situations: Psychological Debriefing." *Disaster Management* 2, 25-30.

Everly, G. S. 1995. *Innovations in Disaster and Trauma Psychology.* Vol. 1. Ellicott City, Md.: Chevron Publishing Co.

Everly, G. S., and J. T. Mitchell. 1999. *Critical Incident Stress Management.* 2d ed. Ellicott City, Md.: Chevron Publishing Co.

Fullerton, C. S., R. J. Ursano, K. Vance and L. Wang. 2000. "Debriefing Following Trauma." *Psychiatric Quarterly* 71/3, 259-76.

Gist, R., and S. J. Woodall. 1998. "Social Science Versus Social Movements: The Origins and Natural History of Debriefing." *The Australasian Journal of Disaster and Trauma Studies* 1.

Griffiths, J., and R. Watts. 1992. *The Kempsey and Grafton Bus Crashes: The Aftermath.* Northern Rivers, N. S. W., Australia: University of New England.

Herman, J. L. 1992. *Trauma and Recovery.* New York: Basic Books.

Hytten, K., and A. Hasle. 1989. "Fire Fighters: A Study of Stress and Coping." *Journal of Community Health Nursing* 13, 43-49.

Jones, C. A. 2000. "Trauma Debriefing and Perceived Organizational Support with Bank Robbery Victims." *Dissertation Abstracts International Section A: Humanities and Social Sciences* 60/7-A, 2679.

Kenardy, J. A., R. A. Webster, T. J. Lewin, V. J. Carr, P. L. Hazell and G. L. Carter. 1996. "Stress Debriefing and Patterns of Recovery Following a Natural Disaster." *Journal of Traumatic Stress* 9, 37-49.

Lindemann, E. 1971. *Beyond Grief: Studies in Crisis Intervention.* New York: Jason Aronson.

Mayou, R. A., A. Ehlers and M. Hobbs. 2000. "Psychological Debriefing for Road Traffic Accident Victims: Three-year Follow-up of a Randomised Controlled Trial." *British Journal of Psychiatry* 176, 589-93.

McCammon, S. L. 1995. "Debriefing and Treating Emergency Workers." In *Compassion Fatigue: Coping with Secondary Traumatic Stress Disorder in Those Who Treat the Traumatized*, edited by C. R. Figley, 115-30. New York: Brunner/Mazel.

Miskiman, D. 1988. "The Crrtical Incident Stress Debriefing Programme: Stress and the Rural Emergency Responder." *Canadian Emergency News* 12, 23-35.

Mitchell, J. T. 1983. "When Disaster Strikes." *Journal of Emergency Medical Services* 8, 36-39.

———. 1988. "Stress: The History, Status and Future of Critical Incident Stress Debriefings." *Journal of Emergency Medical Services*, 47-51.

Mitchell, J. T., and G. Bray. 1990. *Emergency Services Stress.* Englewood Cliffs, N.J.: Prentice-Hall.

Mitchell, J. T., and G. S. Everly. 1996. *Critical Incident Stress Debriefing: An Operations Manual for the Prevention of Traumatic Stress Among Emergency Services and Disaster Workers.* 2d ed., rev. Ellicott City, Md.: Chevron Publishing.

Neria, Y., and Z. Solomon. 2000. "Prevention of Posttraumatic Reactions: Debriefing and Frontline Treatment." In *Posttraumatic Stress Disorder: A Comprehensive Text*, edited by P. Saigh and J. Bremner. Boston: Allyn and Bacon.

Pickett, M., A. M. W. Brennan, H. S. Greenberg, L. Licht and J. D. Worrell. 1994. "Use of Debriefing Techniques to Prevent Compassion Fatigue in Research Teams." *Nursing Research* 43, 250-52.

Raphael, B., ed. 1986. *When Disaster Strikes.* New York: Basic Books.

Robbins, I. 1999. "The Psychological Impact of Working in Emergencies and the Role of Debriefing." *Journal of Clinical Nursing* 8/3, 263-69.

Robinson, R. C., and J. T. Mitchell. 1993. "Evaluation of Psychological Debriefings." *Journal of Traumatic Stress* 11, 367-82.

Rose, S., and J. Bisson. 1998. "Brief Early Psychological Intervention Following Trauma: A Systematic Review of the Literature." *Journal of Traumatic Stress* 6, 697-710.

Shalev, A. Y., and R. Tuval-Mashiach. 1999. "Early Interventions and Debriefing Following Traumatic Events: Sihot/Dialogue." *Israel Journal of Psychotherapy* 13/3, 206-19.

Shalev, A. Y., and R. J. Ursano. 1990. "Group Debriefing Following Exposure to Traumatic Stress." In *Wartime Medical Services*, edited by J. Lundeberg, U. Otto and B. Rybeck, 192-207. Stockholm: Forsvarets Forskningsanstalt.

Townsend, C. J., and J. M. Loughlin. 1998. "Critical Incident Stress Debriefing in International Aid Workers." *Journal of Travel Medicine* 5, 226-27.

van der Kolk, B., A. McFarlane and L. van der Hart. 1996. *Traumatic Stress: The Effects of Overwhelming Experience on Mind, Body and Society.* New York: Guildford Press.

Wessely, S., S. Rose and J. Bisson. 2000. "Brief Psychological Interventions ('debriefing') for Trauma-related Symptoms and the Prevention of PTSD (Cochran Review)." In *The Cochran Library*, Issue 3. Oxford, England: Update Software, The Cochrane Library.

Wraith, R. 2000. "Children and Debriefing: Theory, Interventions and Outcomes." In *Psychological Debriefing: Theory, Practice and Evidence*, edited by B. Raphael and J. Wilson, 195-212. Cambridge: Cambridge University.

Christian Humanitarian Work

Barney, S. T. 1998. "The Relationship Between Christian Religious Beliefs, Attributions, World Views and Psychological Symptoms in a Population with a History of Significant Negative Life Events." *Dissertation Abstracts International: Section B: The Sciences and Engineering* 59/1-B, 0410.

Bricker, P. L., and C. G. Fleischer. 1993. "Social Support as Experienced by Roman Catholic Priests: The Influence of Occasionally Imposed Network Restrictions." *Issues in Mental Health Nursing* 14, 219-34.

Carr, K. F. 1994. "Trauma and Post-traumatic Stress Disorder Among Missionaries." *Evangelical Missions Quarterly* 30/3, 246-55.

———. 1997. "Crisis Intervention for Missionaries." *Evangelical Missions Quarterly* 3/4, 450-58.

Chinnici, R. 1985. "Pastoral Care Following a Natural Disaster." *Pastoral Psychology* 33/4, 245-54.

Gardner, L. 1987. "Proactive Care of Missionary Personnel." *Journal of Psychology and Theology* 15, 308-14.

Grosch, W. N., and D. C. Olsen. 2000. "Clergy Burnout: An Integrative Approach." *Journal of Clinical Psychology* 56/5, 619-32.

Jones, M. 1995. *Psychology of Missionary Adjustment.* Springfield, Mo.: Logion Press.

Miersma, P. K. 1993. "Understanding Missionary Stress from the Perspective of a Combat-related Stress Theory." *Journal of Psychology and Theology* 21/1, 93-101.

O'Donnell, K., and O'Donnell, M., eds. 1988. *Helping Missionaries Grow: Readings in Mental Health and Missions.* Pasadena, Calif.: William Carey Library.

———. 1992. *Missionary Care: Counting the Cost for World Evangelization.* Pasadena, Calif.: William Carey Library.

Schubert, E. 1999. "A Suggested Prefield Process for Missionary Candidates." *Journal of Psychology and Theology* 27, 87-97.

Psychological Trauma in International Relief and Development Work and in Similar Populations

Aguilera, D. M., L. A. and Planchon. 1995. "The American Psychological Association-California Psychological Association Disaster Response Project: Lessons from the Past, Guidelines for the Future." *Professional Psychology: Research and Practice* 26/6, 550-57.

Alexander, D. A. 1990. "Psychological Intervention for Victims and Helpers After Disasters." *British Journal of General Practice* 40, 337, 345-48.

Alexander, D. A., and S. Klein. 2001. "Ambulance Personnel and Critical Incidents: Impact of Accident and Emergency Work on Mental Health and Emotional Well-being." *British Journal of Psychiatry* 178/1, 76-81.

Alexander, D. A., and A. Wells. 1991. "Reactions of Police Officers to Body-handling After a Major Disaster: A Before and After Comparison." *British Journal of Psychiatry* 159, 547-55.

American Psychiatric Committee on Nomenclature and Statistics. 1980. *Diagnostic and Statistical Manual of Mental Disorders.* 3d ed. Washington, D.C.: American Psychiatric Association.

———. 1994. *Diagnostic and Statistical Manual of Mental Disorders.* 4th ed. Washington, D.C.: American Psychiatric Association.

Anderson, D. G. 2000. "Coping Strategies and Burnout Among Veteran Child Protection Workers." *Child Abuse and Neglect* 24/6, 839-48.

Artiss, K. L. 1963. "Human Behavior Under Stress: From Combat to Social Psychiatry." *Military Medicine* 128, 1011-15.

Ballone, E., M. Valentino, L. Occhiolini, C. Di Mascio, D. Cannone and F. S. Schioppa. 2000. "Factors Influencing Psychological Stress Levels of Italian Peacekeepers in Bosnia." *Military Medicine* 165/12, 911-15.

Bamber, M. 1994. "Providing Support for Emergency Service Staff." *Nursing Times* 90, 22, 32-33.

Bartone, P., R. J. Ursano, L. H. Ingraham and K. Saczynski-Wright. 1987. "The Impact of Military Air Disaster on Family Assistance Workers." Paper presented at the meeting of the American Psychological Association, New York.

Bartone, P. T., and K. M. Wright. 1990. "Grief and Group Recovery Following a Military Air Disaster." *Journal of Traumatic Stress* 33/4, 523-29.

Beaton, R., S. Murphy, C. Johnson, K. Pike and W. Corneil. 1998. "Exposure to Duty-related Incident Stressors in Urban Firefighters and Paramedics." *Journal of Traumatic Stress* 11/4, 821-28.

Belenky G. L., S. Noy and Z. Solomon. 1987. "Battle Stress, Morale, "Cohesion," Combat Effectiveness, Heroism and Psychiatric Casualties: The Israeli Experience." In *Contemporary Studies in Combat Psychiatry*, edited by G. Lucas, 11-20. Westport, Conn.: Greenwood Press.

Berk, J. H. 1998. "Trauma and Resilience During War: A Look at the Children and Humanitarian Aid Workers of Bosnia." *The Psychoanalytic Review* 85/4, 639-56.

Billings, A. G., and R. H. Moos. 1981. "The Role of Coping Responses and Social Resources in Attenuating the Impact of Stressful Life Events." *Journal of Behavioral Medicine* 4, 139-57.

Bolton, E. E. 2001. "An Exploration of the Impact of Self-disclosure on the Development of Psychological Distress Among Somalia

Peacekeepers." Dissertation Abstracts International: Section B: The Sciences and Engineering 61/7-B, 3831.

Boudreaux, E. and Mandry, C. 1996. Sources of stress among emergency medical technicians (Part I): What does the research say? *Prehospital and Disaster Medicine, 11*, 296-301.

Boudreaux, E., C. Mandry and P. J. Brantley. 1998. "Emergency Medical Technician Schedule Modification: Impact and Implications During Short- and Long-term Follow-up." *Academic Emergency Medicine* 5, 128-33.

Brady, J. L., J. D. Guy, P. L. Poelstra and B. F. Brokaw. 1999. "Vicarious Traumatization, Spirituality, and the Treatment of Sexual Abuse Survivors: A National Survey of Women Psychotherapists." *Professional Psychology: Research and Practice* 30, 386-93.

Bramsen, I., A. J. E. Dirkzwager and H. M. Van der Ploeg. 2000. "Predeployment Personality Traits and Exposure to Trauma as Predictors of Posttraumatic Stress Symptoms: A Prospective Study of Former Peacekeepers." *American Journal of Psychiatry* 157/7, 1115-19.

Bramsen, I., I. E. Reuling and H. M. van der Ploeg. 2000. "Indirect Traumatization of Spouses of Dutch War Victims" (in Dutch). *Ned Tijdschr Geneeskd* 11.

Brandt, G. T., et al. 1995. "Disasters: Psychological Responses in Health Care Providers and Rescue Workers." *Nordic Journal of Psychiatry* 49/2, 89-94.

Brende, J. O. 1998. "Coping with Floods: Assessment, Intervention and Recovery Processes for Survivors and Helpers." *Journal of Contemporary Psychotherapy* 28/2, 107-39.

Britt, T. W., and A. B. Adler. 1999. "Stress and Health During Medical Humanitarian Assistance Missions." *Military Medicine* 164/4, 275-79.

Brown, J. M., and E. A. Campbell. 1991. "Stress Among Emergency Personnel: Progress and Problems." *Journal of the Society of Occupational Medicine* 41, 149-50.

Bryant, R. A., and A. G. Harvey. 1996. "Posttraumatic Stress Reactions in Volunteer Firefighters." *Journal of Traumatic Stress* 9/4, 51-62.

Burkle, F. M. 1983. "Coping with Stress Under Conditions of Disaster and Refugee Care." *Military Medicine* 148, 800-803.

Butler, R. W., D. W. Foy, L. Snodgrass, J. Hurwicz and J. Goldfarb. 1988. "Combat-related Posttraumatic Stress Disorder in a Nonpsychiatric Population." *Journal of Anxiety Disorders* 2, 11-120.

Caplan, G. 1961. *An Approach to Community Mental Health.* New York: Grune and Stratton.

Carlier, I. V., R. D. Lamberts and B. P. Gersons. 2000. "The Dimensionality of Trauma: A Multidimensional Scaling Comparison of Police Officers with and Without Posttraumatic Stress Disorder." *Psychiatry Research* 97/1, 29-39.

Carr, V. J., T. J. Lewin, R. A. Webster and J. A. Kenardy. 1997. "A Synthesis of the Findings from the Quake Impact Study: A Two-year Iinvestigation of the Psychosocial Sequelae of the 1989 Newcastle Earthquake." *Social Psychiatry and Psychiatric Epidemiology* 32/3, 123-36.

Carr, V. J., et al. 1997. "Psychosocial Sequelae of the 1989 Newcastle Earthquake: II. Exposure and Morbidity Profiles During the First Two Years Post-disaster." *Psychological Medicine* 27/1, 167-77.

Charney, A. E., and L. A. Pearlman. 1998. "The Ecstasy and the Agony: The Impact of Disaster and Trauma Work on the Self of the Clinician." In *Emergency Psychological Services: The Evaluation and Management of Life-threatening Behavior,* edited by P. Kleespies, 418-35. New York: The Guilford Press.

Chung, M. C., J. Werrett, S. Farmer, Y. Easthope and C. Chung. 2000. "Responses to Traumatic Stress Among Community Residents Exposed to a Train Collision." *Stress Medicine* 16/1, 17-25.

Clay, R. 1999. "Healing the Scars from Rwanda's War." *APA Monitor* 30 (April), 28.

Coalson, R. "The Trauma of War: Homecoming After Afghanistan." *Journal of Humanistic Psychology* 33/4, 48-62.

Cook, J. D., L. and Bickman, L. 1990. "Social Support and Psychological Symptomatology Following a Natural Disaster." *Journal of Traumatic Stress* 3/4, 541-56.

Creamer, M., W. J. Buckingham and P. M. Burgess. 1991. "A Community Based Mental Health Response to a Multiple Shooting." *Australian Psychologist* 26/2, 99-102.

Dabelstein, N. 1996. "Evaluating the International Humanitarian System: Rationale, Process and Management of the Joint Evaluation of the international Response to the Rwanda Genocide." *Disasters* 20, 287-91.

Danieli, Y. 1984. "Psychotherapists' Participation in the Conspiracy of Silence About the Holocaust." *Psychoanalytic Psychology* 1, 23-42.

———. 1988. "Confronting the Iunimaginable: Psychotherapists' Reactions to Victims of the Nazi Holocaust." In *Human Adaptation to Extreme Stress: From the Holocaust to Vietnam,* edited by J. P. Wilson, Z. Harel and B. Kahan. New York: Plenum.

Danieli, Y. 2002. *Sharing the Front Lines and the Back Hills: Peacekeepers, Humanitarian Aid Workers and the Media in the Midst of Crisis.* Amityville, N.Y.: Baywood Publishing Company.

Davidson, J. R. 2000. "Pharmacotherapy of Posttraumatic Stress Disorder: Treatment Options, Long-term Follow-up, and Predictors of Outcome." *Journal of Clinical Psychiatry* 61/5: 52-59.

Davidson, J. R. T., and E. B. Foa, eds. 1993. *Posttraumatic Stress Disorder: DSM-IV and Beyond*. Washington, D.C.: American Psychiatric Press.

de Haan, B. 1994. *Humanitarian Action in Conflict Zones: Coping with Stress. International Red Cross Guidelines*. Geneva: ICRC Publications.

DeJong, K., N. Ford and R. J. Kleber. 1999. "Mental Health Care for Refugees from Kosovo: The Experience of Medecins Sans Frontieres." *Lancet*.

Derry, P., and Baum, A. 1994. "The Role of the Experimenter in Field Studies of Distressed Populations." *Journal of Traumatic Stress* 7, 625-35.

DeSilva, P. 1993. "Post Traumatic Stress Disorder: Cross-cultural Aspects." *International Review of Psychiatry* 5, 217-19.

DeWolfe, D. J. 2000. *Training Manual for Disaster Mental Health Workers*. 2d ed. Rockville, Md.: Center for Mental Health Services.

Diminic, I. T., B. Delic and I. Serdarevic. 1992. "Traumatization of Group Leaders in Their Work with Refugees." *Psychologische Beitrage* 34, 184-88.

Ditzler, T. 2001. "Mental Health and Aid Workers: The Case for Collaborative Questioning." *The Journal of Humanitarian Assistance*. Available online.

Duckworth, D. H. 1991. "Facilitating Recovery from Disaster-work Experiences." *British Journal of Guidance and Counselling* 19/1, 13-22.

———. 1991. "Information Requirements for Crisis Intervention After Disaster Work." *Stress Medicine* 7/1, 19-24.

Dunning, C. 1990. "Mental Health Sequelae in Disaster Workers: Prevention and Intervention." *International Journal of Mental Health* 19/2, 91-103.

Dunning, C. M., and M. N. Silva. 1980. "Disaster-induced Trauma in Rescue Workers." *Victimology* 5, 287-97.,

Durham, T. W., S. L. McCammon and E. J. Allison Jr. 1985. "The Psychological Impact of Disaster on Rescue Personnel. *Annals of Emergency Medicine* 14, 664-68.

Dutton, L. M., et al. 1978. "Psychological Stress Levels in Paramedics." *Emergency Medical Services* 7, 88, 90-94, 113.

Dyregrov, A. 1995. "Effects of Traumatized Children on the Rescuer." In Everly, *Innovations in Disaster and Trauma Psychology*, 1:26-41.

———. 2000. "Refugee Families' Experience of Research Participation." *Journal of Traumatic Stress* 13/3, 413-26.

Dyregrov, A., J. I. Kristoffersen, R. Gjestad. 1996. "Voluntary and Professional Disaster-workers: Similarities and Differences in Reactions. *Journal of Traumatic Stress* 9/3, 541-55.

Eagle, G. T. 1998. "Promoting Peace by Integrating Western and Indigenous Healing in Treating Trauma, Peace and Conflict." *Journal of Peace Psychology* 4/3, 271-82.

Eby, D. L. 1985. "Healing the Helper: A Disaster Worker's Response." In *Role Stressors and Supports for Emergency Workers,* 119-25. Rockville, Md.: National Institute of Mental Health.

Egge, B., M. S. Mortensen and L. Weisaeth. 1996. "Soldiers for Peace: Ordeals and Stress." In *International Responses to Traumatic Stress,* edited by Y. Danieli, N. Rodley and L. Weisaeth, 257-82. Amityville, N.Y.: Baywood Publishing Company.

Ehlich, P. J., L. Roemer and B. T. Litz. 1997. "PTSD After A Peace-keeping Mission." *The American Journal of Psychiatry* 154, 1319-20.

Eisenman, D. P., S. Bergner and I. Cohen. 2000. "An Ideal Victim: Idealizing Trauma Victims Causes Traumatic Stress in Human Rights Workers." *Human Rights Review* 1, 106-14.

Elsass, P., J. Andersen and H. Fuglsang. 1997. *Treating Victims of Torture and Violence: Theoretical, Cross-Cultural and Clinical Implications.* New York: New York University Press.

Englund, H. 1998. "Death, Trauma and Ritual: Mozambican Refugees in Malawi." *Social Science and Medicine* 46/9, 1165-74.

Eriksson, C. B. 1997. *Traumatic Exposure and Reentry Symptomatology in International Relief and Development Personnel,* Dissertation. Pasadena, Calif.: Fuller Theological Seminary.

Eriksson, C. B., et al. 2001. "Trauma Exposure and PTSD Symptoms in International Relief and Development Personnel." *Journal of Traumatic Stress* 14/1, 205-12.

Fairbank, J. A., W. E. Schlenger, P. A. Saigh and J. R. T. Davidson. 1995. "An Epidemiologic Profile of Post-Traumatic Stress Disorder: Prevalence, Comorbidity and Risk Factors." In *Neurobiological and Clinical Consequences of Stress: From Normal Adaptation To PTSD,* edited by M. J. Friedman, D. S. Charney and A. Y. Deutch, 415-27. Philadelphia: Lippincott-Raven.

Farberow, N. L. 1983. *Training Manual for Human Service Workers in Major Disasters.* Rockville, Md.: National Institute of Mental Health.

Fawcett, J. 2000. "Caring for Staff in Complex Humanitarian Emergencies." In *Complex Humanitarian Emergencies: Lessons from Practitioners,* edited by M. Janz and J. Slead. Monrovia, Calif.: World Vision.

Figley, C. R. 1989. *Helping Traumatized Families.* San Francisco: Jossey-Bass.

————. 1995. "Compassion Fatigue: Toward a New Understanding of the Costs of Caring." In Stamm, *Secondary Traumatic Stress*, 3-28.

Figley, C. R., ed. 1995. *Compassion Fatigue: Coping with Secondary Traumatic Stress Disorder in Those Who Treat the Traumatized.* New York: Brunner/Mazel.

Firth-Cozens, J., and Burges, C. 1999. "Questionnaire Survey of Posttraumatic Stress Disorder in Doctors Involved in the Omagh Bombing." *British Medical Journal.*

Fischman, Y. "Metaclinical Issues in the Treatment of Psychopolitical Trauma." *American Journal of Orthopsychiatry* 68/1, 27-38.

Flannery, R. B. 1990. "Social Support and Psychological Trauma: A Methodological Review." *Journal of Traumatic Stress* 3, 593-611.

Follette, V. M., M. M. Polusny and K. Milbeck. 1994. "Mental Health and Law Enforcement Professionals: Trauma History, Psychological Symptoms and Impact of Providing Services to Child Sexual Abuse Survivors." *Professional Psychology: Research and Practice* 25, 275-82.

Foreman, C. 1994. "Immediate Post-Disaster Treatment of Trauma." In *Handbook of Post-Traumatic Therapy*, edited by M. B. Williams and J. F. Sommer, 267-82. Westport, Conn.: Greenwood Press.

Foreman, C., and L. Eraenen. 1999. "Trauma of World Policing: Peacekeeping Duties." In *Police Trauma: Psychological Aftermath of Civilian Combat*, edited by J. M. Violanti and D. Paton, 189-200. Springfield, Ill.: Charles C Thomas.

Foy, D. W., et al. 1984. "Etiology of Posttraumatic Stress Disorder in Vietnam Veterans: Analysis of Premilitary, Military and Combat Exposure Influences." *Journal of Consulting and Clinical Psychology* 52, 79-87.

Foy, D. W., et al. 1987. "Premilitary, Military and Postmilitary Factors in the Development of Combat-Related Posttraumatic Stress Disorder." *Behavior Therapist* 10, 3-9.

Foy, D. W., et al. 1997. "Trauma Focus Group Therapy for Combat-Related PTSD." In *Psychotherapy in Practice* 3, 59-73.

Foy, D. W., et al. 2000. "Group Therapy." In *Effective Treatments for PTSD: Practice Guidelines from the International Society for Traumatic Stress Studies*, edited by E. Foa, T. Keane and M. Friedman, 155-75, 336-38. New York: Guilford Press.

Fraser, J., and Spicka, D. 1981. "Handling the Emotional Response to Disaster: The Case for American Red Cross/Community Mental Health Collaboration. *Community Mental Health Journal* 17, 255-64.

Freinkel, A., C. Koopman and D. Spiegel. 1994. "Dissociative Symptoms in Media Eyewitnesses of an Execution." *American Journal of Psychiatry* 151, 1335-39.

Friedman, M. J. 1996. "PTSD Diagnosis and Treatment for Mental Health Clinicians." *Community Mental Health Journal* 32/2, 173-89.

Friedman, M. J. and P. P. Schnurr. 1995. "The Relationship Between Trauma, Post-Traumatic Stress Disorder and Physical Health." In *Neurobiological and Clinical Consequences of Stress: From Normal Adjustment to PTSD*, edited by M. J. Friedman, D. S. Charney and A. Y. Deutch. Philadelphia: Lippincott-Raven Publishers.

Fullerton, C. S., et al. 1992. "Psychological Responses of Rescue Workers: Firefighters and Trauma." *American Journal of Orthopsychiatry* 62, 371-78.

Fullerton, C. S., et al. 1993. "Social Support for Disaster Workers After a Mass-Casualty Disaster: Effects on the Support Provider." *Nordic Journal of Psychiatry*, 47/5, 315-24.

Fullerton, C. S., and Ursano, R. J. 1997. "Posttraumatic Responses in Spouse/Significant Others of Disaster Workers." In Fullerton and Ursano, *Posttraumatic Stress Disorder*, 59-75.

Fullerton, C. S, and R. J. Ursano, eds. 1997. *Posttraumatic Stress Disorder: Acute and Long-Term Responses to Trauma and Disaster.* Washington, D.C.: American Psychiatric Press.

Furukawa, T. 1997 "Cultural Distance and Its Relationship to Psychological Adjustment of International Exchange Students." *Psychiatry and Clinical Neurosciences* 51, 87-91.

———. 1997. "Depressive Symptoms Among International Exchange Students and Their Predictors." *Acta Psychiatrica Scandinavica* 96, 242-46.

———. 1997. "Sojourner Readjustment: Mental Health of International Students After Oneyear's Foreign Sojourn and Its Psychosocial Correlates." *Journal of Nervous and Mental Disease* 185, 263-68.

Furukawa, T., I. G. Sarason and B. R. Sarason. 1998. "Social Support and Adjustment to a Novel Social Environment." *International Journal of Social Psychiatry* 44, 56-70.

Garbarino, J. 1996. "The Spiritual Challenge of Violent Trauma." *American Journal of Orthopsychiatry* 66/1, 162-63.

Gibbs, M. S., J. Drummond and J. R. Lachenmeyer. 1993. "Effects of Disasters on Emergency Workers: A Review, with Implications for Training and Postdisaster Interventions." *Journal of Social Behavior and Personality* 8, 189-212.

Golan, N. 1959. "When Is a Client in Crisis?" *Social Casework* 50, 389-94.

Gonzalez, R. 1996. "Education As a Means of Prevention for Cross-Cultural Stress." *Humanitarian Aid Quarterly* 262, 56-63.

Graham, N. K. 1981. "Done In, Fed Up, Burned Out: Too Much Attrition in EMS." *Journal of Emergency Medical Services* 6, 24-28.

————. 1981. "How to Avoid a Short Career." *Journal of Emergency Medical Services* 6, 25-31.

Grant, R. 1999. *Living and Working in Environments of Violence and Trauma: A Resource Manual for Humanitarian Workers.* Burlingame, Calif.

Greenaway, S., A. J. and Harris. 1998. "Humanitarian Security: Challenges and Responses." Paper presented at the Forging Peace Conference, Harvard University, Cambridge, Massachusetts, March 13-15.

Grieger, T. A., et al. 2000. "Acute Stress Disorder and Subsequent Post-Traumatic Stress Disorder in a Group of Exposed Disaster Workers." *Depress Anxiety* 11/4, 183-84.

Grevin, F. 1996. "Posttraumatic Stress Disorder, Ego Defense Mechanisms, and Empathy Among Urban Paramedics." *Psychological Reports* 79, 483-95.

Grigsby, D. W., and M. A. Mcknew. 1988. "Work-Stress Burnout Among Paramedics." *Psychological Reports* 63, 55-64.

Grossman, L. 1973. "Train Crash: Social Work and Disaster Services." *Social Work* 18, 38-44.

Haight, W. L. 1998. "'Gathering the Spirit' at First Baptist Church: Spirituality As a Protective Factor in the Lives of African American Children." *Social Work* 43, 213-21.

Halilovic, S. 1998. "Psycho-Social Help As a Coping Skill for Non-Professionals Who Are Themselves Refugees." In *War Violence, Trauma and the Coping Process: Armed Conflict in Europe and Survivor Response*, edited by L. T. Arcel, 86-92. Zagreb, Croatia: Nakladnistvo Lumin.

Hammer, J. S., et al. 1985. "Measurement of Occupational Stress in Hospital Settings: Two Validity Studies of Measure of Self-Reported Stress in Medical Emergency Rooms." *General Hospital Psychiatry* 7, 156-62.

Hartsough, D. M., and D. G. Myers. 1985. *Disaster Work and Mental Health: Prevention and Control of Stress Among Workers.* Rockville, Md.: National Institute of Mental Health.

Heller, F. 1983. *Perceived Social Support Survey.* Cambridge: Oxford Press.

Herman, J. L. 1992. *Trauma and Recovery.* New York: Basic Books.

Hodgkinson, P. E., and M. A. Shepherd. 1994. "Impact of Disaster Support Work." *Journal of Traumatic Stress* 7/4, 587-600.

Holaday, M., et al. 1995. "A Preliminary Investigation of on-the-Scene Coping Mechanisms Used by Disaster Workers." *Journal of Mental Health Counseling* 17/3, 347-59.

Holmes, C. B. 1994. *Like a Lasting Storm: Helping with Real-Life Problems.* Brandon, Vt.: Clinical Psychology Publishing Company.

Horowitz, et al. 1979. "Impact of Event Scale: A Measure of Subjective Stress." *Psychosomatic Medicine* 41, 209-18.

Howard, G. 1995. "Occupational Stress and the Law: Some Current Issues for Employers." *Journal of Psychosomatic Research* 39, 707-19.

Hytten, K., and A. Hasle. 1989. "Fire Fighters: A Study of Stress and Coping." *Acta Psychiatrica* (Scandinavia) 355, 50-55.

Jacobs, G. 1990. "Lessons from the Aftermath of Flight 232: Practical Considerations for the Mental Health Professions Response to Air Disasters." *American Psychologist* 45/12, 1329-35.

Jacobs, G. 1995. "The Development of a National Plan for Disaster Mental Health." *Professional Psychology: Research and Practice* 26/6, 543-49.

James, A. 1988. "Perceptions of Stress in British Ambulance Personnel." *Work and Stress* 2, 319-26.

Janik, J. 1992. "Addressing Cognitive Defenses in Critical Incident Stress." *Journal of Traumatic Stress* 5, 497-503.

Jiggetts, S. M., and D. P. Hall. 1995. "Helping the Helper: 528th Combat Stress Center in Somalia." *Military Medicine* 160/6, 275-77.

Johnson, P. R., and J. Indvik. 1994. "The Impact of Unresolved Trauma on Career Management." *International Journal of Career Management* 6/2, 12.

Jones, D. R. 1985. "Secondary Disaster Victims: The Emotional Effects of Recovering and Identifying Human Remains." *American Journal of Psychiatry* 142, 303-7.

Jones, S. 1998. "Missionary Attrition: A Survey of the Seven Leading Senders." *Missions Today* 106, 23-28.

Joushepperd, M., and P. Hodgkinson. 1990. "The Hidden Victims of Disaster: Helper Stress." *Stress Medicine* 6/1, 29-35.

Kim, S. E. 2000. "Vicarious Traumatization: The Impact of Therapists of Treating Trauma Clients." *Dissertation Abstracts International: Section B: The Sciences and Engineering* 60/9-B, 4892.

King, D. W., et al. 1995. "Prewar Factors in Combat-Related Posttraumatic Stress Disorder: Structural Equation Modeling with a National Sample of Male and Female Vietnam Veterans." *Journal of Consulting and Clinical Psychology* 64, 520-31.

King, L. A., et al. 1995. "The Los Angeles Symptom Checklist: A Self-Report Measure of Posttraumatic Stress Disorder." *Assessment* 2, 1-17.

King, L. A., et al. 1998. "Resiliency-Recovery Factors." *Journal of Personality and Social Psychology* 74/2, 420-34.

Klein, R. H., and V. L. Schermer. 2000. "Introduction and Overview: Creating a Healing Matrix." In *Group Psychotherapy for Psychological Trauma*, edited by R. H. Klein and V. L. Schermer. New York: Guilford Press.

Kocijan-Hercigonja, D., et al. 1997. "Psychosocial Support in War Areas Using Community-Based Rehabilitation Strategy."

Scandinavian Journal of Social Medicine 25/1, 14-16.

Kramer, G. 1999. "Traumatized Women Working with Traumatized Women: Reflections upon Life and Work in a War Zone." *Women and Therapy* 22/1, 107-20.

Kroon, M. B. R., and W. I. E. Overdijk. 1993. "Psychosocial Care and Shelter Following the Bijlmermeer Air Disaster." *Crisis* 14/3, 117-25.

Kulka, R. A., et al., eds. 1990. *Trauma and the Vietnam War Generation: Report on the Findings from the National Vietnam Veterans Readjustment Study.* New York: Brunner/Mazel.

Lamerson, C. D., and E. K. Kelloway. 1996. "Towards a Model of Peacekeeping Stress: Traumatic and Contextual Influences." *Canadian Psychology* 37/4, 195-204.

Landry, L. P. 1999. "Secondary Traumatic Stress Disorder in the Therapists from the Oklahoma City Bombing." Dissertation, University of North Texas. *Dissertation Abstracts International 61/07-B*: 3849 (January 2001).

Lansen, J. 1993. "Vicarious Traumatization in Therapists Treating Victims of Torture and Persecution." *Torture* 3/4, 138-40.

Lesaca, T. 1996. "Symptoms of Stress Disorder and Depression Among Trauma Counselors After an Airline Disaster." *Psychiatric Services* 47/4, 424-26.

Lima, B., J. Santacruz and J. Luna. 1987. "Screening for the Psychological Consequences of a Major Disaster in a Developing Country: Aremero, Colombia." *Acta Psychiatrica Scandinavia* 76/5, 561-67.

Lima, B., et al. 1989. "Disaster Severity and Emotional Disturbance: Implications for Primary Mental Health Care in Developing Countries." *Acta Psychiatrica Scandinavia* 79, 74-82.

Lima, B., et al. 1990. "The Stability of Emotional Symptoms Among Disaster Victims in a Developing Country." *Journal of Traumatic Stress* 3/4, 1990.

Lima, B., et al. 1990. "Disasters and Mental Health: Experience in Colombia and Ecuador and Its Relevance for Primary Care in Mental Health in Latin America." *International Journal of Mental Health* 19/2, 3-20.

Lima, B., et al. 1991. "Psychiatric Disorders in Primary Health Care Clinics One Year After a Major Latin American Disaster." *Stress Medicine* 7/1, 25-32.

Lima, B., et al., 1993. "Emotional Distress in Disaster Victims." *The Journal of Nervous and Mental Disease* 181/6, 388-93.

Lima, B., and S. Pai. 1992-93. "Response to the Psychological Consequences of Disasters in Latin America." *International Journal of Mental Health* 21/4, 59-71.

Lindeman, M., et al. 1996. "Traumatic Stress and Its Risk Factors Among Peripheral Victims of the M/S Estonia Disaster." *European Psychologist* 1/4, 255-70.

Linton, J. C. 1995. "Acute Stress Management with Public Safety Personnel: Opportunities for Clinical Training and Pro Bono Community Service." *Professional Psychology: Research and Practice* 26/6, 566-73.

Litz, B. T. 1996. "The Psychological Demands of Peacekeeping for Military Personnel." *National Center for Post-Traumatic Stress Disorder Clinical Quarterly* 6 (Winter), 1-8.

Litz, B. T., et al. 1997. "Posttraumatic Stress Disorder Associated with Peacekeeping Duty in Somalia for US Military Personnel." *American Journal of Psychiatry* 154, 178-84.

Litz, B. T., et al. 1997. "Warriors As Peacekeepers: Features of the Somalia Experience and PTSD." *Journal of Consulting and Clinical Psychology* 65, 1001-1010.

Lundin, T., and M. Bodegard. 1993. "The Psychological Impact of An Earthquake on Rescue Workers: A Follow-Up Study of the Swedish Group of Rescue Workers in Armenia, 1988." *Journal of Traumatic Stress* 6, 129-39.

Lundin, T., and V. Otto. 1992. "Swedish UN Soldiers in Cyprus, UNFICYP: Their Psychological and Social Situation." *Psychotherapy and Psychosomatics* 57, 187-93.

Luthar, S., D. Chiccetti and B. Becker. 2000. "The Construct of Resilience: A Critical Evaluation and Guidelines for Future Work." *Child Development* 71, 543-62.

Madsen, J. P. 1995. "Stresspavirking Under FN-Tjeneste." *Militaert Tidsskrift* 1, 4-10.

Marmar, C. R., et al. 1996. "Stress Responses of Emergency Services Personnel to the Loma Prieta Earthquake Interstate 880 Freeway Collapse and Control Traumatic Incidents." *Journal of Traumatic Stress* 9/1, 63-85.

Marmar, C. R., et al. 1996. "Characteristics of Emergency Services Personnel Related to Peritraumatic Dissociation During Critical Incident Exposure." *American Journal of Psychiatry* 153/7, 94-102.

Marmar, C. R., et al. 1999. "Longitudinal Course and Predictors of Continuing Distress Following Critical Incident Exposure in Emergency Services Personnel." *Journal of Nervous and Mental Disease* 187/1, 15-22.

Maslach, C., and S. Jackson. 1981. "The Measurement of Experienced Burnout." *Journal of Occupational Behavior* 2, 99-113.

Mazor, A., Y. Gampel and G. Horowitz. 1997. "Interviewers' Reactions to Holocaust Survivors' Testimony." *Echoes of the Holocaust* 5, 31-54.

Mccall, M., and P. Salama. 1999. "Selection, Training and Support of Relief Workers: An Occupational Health Issue." *British Medical Journal* 318 (January 9).

Mccammon, S., et al. 1988. "Emergency Workers' Cognitive Appraisal and Coping with Traumatic Events." *Journal of Traumatic Stress* 1, 353-72.

Mccammon, S. L. 1995. "Painful Pedagogy: Teaching About Trauma in Academic and Training Settings." In Stamm, *Secondary Traumatic Stress*, 105-20.

———. 1996. "Emergency Medical Service Workers: Occupational Stress and Traumatic Stress." In Paton and Violanti, *Traumatic Stress in Critical Occupations*, 58-86.

Mccann, I. L., and L. A. Pearlman. 1990. "Vicarious Traumatization: A Framework for Understanding the Psychological Effects of Working with Victims." *Journal of Traumatic Stress* 3/1, 131-49.

Mccarroll, J. E., A. S. Blank and K. Hill. 1995. "Working with Traumatic Material: Effects on Holocaust Memorial Museum Staff." *American Journal of Orthopsychiatry* 65, 66-75.

Mccarroll, J. E., R. Ursano and C. Fullerton. 1993. "Symptoms of Posttraumatic Stress Disorder Following the Recovery of War Dead." *American Journal of Psychiatry* 150/12, 1875-77.

Mcfarlane, A. C., and B. Raphael. 1984. "Ash Wednesday: The Effects of a Fire." *Australian and New Zealand Journal of Psychiatry* 18, 341-51.

Mclaren, S., W. Gollan, W. and C. Horwell. 1998. "Perceived Stress As a Function of Occupation." *Psychological Reports* 82, 794.

Meichenbaum, D. 2000. "Helping the Helpers." In Scott and Palmer, *Trauma and Post-Traumatic Stress Disorder*, 117-21.

Miller, L. 1995. "Tough Guys: Psychotherapeutic Strategies with Law Enforcement and Emergency Services Personnel." *Psychotherapy* 32/4, 592-600.

———. 1998. "Helping the Helpers: Psychotherapeutic Strategies with Law Enforcement and Emergency Services Personnel." In *Shocks to the System: Psychotherapy of Traumatic Disability Syndromes*, edited by L. Miller, 215-48. New York: Norton.

Mitchell, J. T. 1982. "The Psychological Impact of the Air Florida 90 Disaster on Fire-Rescue, Paramedic and Police Officer Personnel." In *Mass Casualties: A Lessons Learned Approach*, edited by R. A. Crowley, 239-44. Washington, D.C.: U.S. Government Printing Office.

Mitchell, J. T., and G. Bray. 1990. *Emergency Services Stress: Guidelines for Preserving the Health and Careers of Emergency Service Personnel.* Englewood Cliffs, N.J.: Prentice-Hall.

Moran, C., and N. Britton. 1994. "Emergency Work Experience and Reactions to Traumatic Incidents." *Journal of Traumatic Stress* 7/4, 575-85.

Morgan, T., and A. L. Cummings. 1999. "Change Experienced During Group Therapy by Female Survivors of Childhood Sexual Abuse." *Journal of Consulting and Clinical Psychology* 671, 28-36.

Munro, L., J. Rodwell and L. Harding. 1998. "Assessing Occupational Stress in Psychiatric Nurses Using the Full Job Strain Model: The Value of Social Support to Nurses." *Journal of Advanced Nursing* 26, 120-25.

Murphy, S. A., et al. 1999. "Occupational Stressors, Stress Responses and Alcohol Consumption Among Professional Firefighters: A Prospective, Longitudinal Analysis." *International Journal of Stress Management* 6/3, 179-96.

Mwiti, G. 1999. "Trauma in the War Zone." *Christian Counseling Today* 7, 9-11, 34-35.

Myers, C. S. 1915. "A Contribution to the Study of Shell Shock." *Lancet*, 316-20.

Myers, D. G. 1985. "Helping the Helpers: A Training Manual." In Hartsough and Myers, *Disaster Work and Mental Health*, 45-149.

———. 1995. "Worker Stress During Long Term Disaster Recovery Efforts: Who Are These People and What Are They Doing Here?" In Everly, *Innovations in Disaster and Trauma Psychology* 158-91.

Neale, A. V. 1991. "Work Stress in Emergency Medical Technicians." *Journal of Occupational Medicine* 33, 991-97.

Neumann, D. A., and S. J. Gamble. 1995. "Issues in the Professional Development of Psychotherapists: Countertransference and Vicarious Traumatization in the Newtrauma Therapist." *Psychotherapy* 32, 341-47.

Nocera, A. 2000. "Prior Planning to Avoid Responders Becoming 'Victims' During Disasters." *Prehospital Disaster Med* 15/1, 46-48.

Norwood, A. E., R. J. Ursano and C. S. Fullerton. 2000. "Disaster Psychiatry: Principles and Practice." *Psychiatry Quarterly* 71/3, 207-26.

Nurmi, L. A. 1999. "The Estonia Disaster: National Interventions, Outcomes and Personal Impacts." In *When a Community Weeps: Case Studies in Group Survivorship*, edited by E. S. Zinner and M. B. Williams, 48-71. Philadelphia: Brunner/Mazel.

Ono, M. 1994. "Another Cost of Ministry on Foreign Soil: Stress." *Journal of Psychology and Religion* 451, 140-56.

O'Rear, J. 1992. "Post Traumatic Stress Disorder: When the Rescuer Becomes the Victim." *JEMS: A Journal of Emergency Medical Services* 30, 30-38.

Orsillo, S. M., et al. 1998. "Psychiatric Symptomatology Associated with Contemporary Peacekeeping: An Examination of Post-Mission Functioning Among Peacekeepers in Somalia." *Journal of Traumatic Stress* 11, 611-25.

Ostodic, E. 1999. "Some Pitfalls for Effective Caregiving in a War Region." *Women and Therapy* 22/1, 161-65.

Paramjit, T. J. 1998. "Guidelines for International Trauma Work." *International Review of Psychiatry* 10/3, 179.

Passey, G., and D. Crocket. 1995. "Psychological Consequences of Canadian UN Peacekeeping in Croatia and Bosnia." Paper presented At the annual meeting of the International Society of Traumatic Stress Studies, Boston, Massachusetts, November.

Paton, D. 1989. "Disasters and Helpers: Psychological Dynamics and Implications for Counselling." *Counselling Psychology Quarterly* 2/3, 303-21.

———. 1990. "Assessing the Impact of Disasters on Helpers." *Counselling Psychology Quarterly* 3/2, 149-52.

———. 1994. "Disaster Relief Work: An Assessment of Training Effectiveness." *Journal of Traumatic Stress* 7/2, 275-88.

———. 1996. "Responding to International Needs: Critical Occupations As Disaster Relief Agencies." In Paton and Violanti, *Traumatic Stress in Critical Occupations*, 139-72.

Paton, D., and B. Kelso. 1991. "Disaster Rescue Work: The Consequences for the Family." *Counselling Psychology Quarterly* 4/2-3, 221-27.

Paton, D., and J. Violanti, eds. 1996. *Traumatic Stress in Critical Occupations: Recognition, Consequences and Treatment.* Springfield, Ill.: Charles C. Thomas.

Pearlman, L. A. 1995. "Self-Care for Trauma Therapists: Ameliorating Vicarious Traumatization." In Stamm, *Secondary Traumatic Stress*, 51-64.

Pearlman, L. A., and P. S. Mac Ian, 1993. "Vicarious Traumatization Among Trauma Therapists: Empirical Findings on Self-Care." *Traumatic Stresspoints: News for the International Society for Traumatic Stress Studies* 7/3 (summer), 5.

———. 1995. "Vicarious Traumatization: An Empirical Study of the Effects of Trauma Work on Trauma Therapists." *Professional Psychology: Research and Practice* 26/6, 558-65.

Pearlman, L. A., and K. W. Saakvitne. 1995. *Trauma and the Therapist: Countertransference and Vicarious Traumatization in Psycho-Therapy with Incest Survivors.* New York: Norton.

———. 1995. "Treating Therapists with Vicarious Traumatization and Secondary Traumatic Stress Disorders." In Figley, *Compassion Fatigue: Coping with Secondary Traumatic Stress Disorder in Those Who Treat the Traumatized*, 150-77. New York: Brunner/Mazel.

Pearlstein, L. 2000. "Antidepressant Treatment of Posttraumatic Stress Disorder." *Journal of Clinical Psychiatry* 61/7: 40-43.

Pickens, J., et al. 1995. "Posttraumatic Stress, Depression and Social Support Among College Students After Hurricane Andrew." *Journal of College Student Development* 36/2, 152-61.

Pines, A. 1993. "Burnout." In *Handbook of Stress*, edited by L. Goldberger and S. Bresnitz, 386-402. New York: The Free Press.

Procidano, M. E., and K. Heller. 1983. "Measures of Perceived Social Support from Friends and from Family: Three Validation Studies." *American Journal of Community Psychology* 11, 1-24.

Pynoos, R. S., et al. 1987. "Life Threat and Posttraumatic Stress in School Age Children." *Archives of General Psychiatry* 44, 1057-63.

Raphael, B., B. Singh and L. Bradbury. 1980. "Disaster: The Helper's Perspective." *The Medical Journal of Australia* 2, 445-47.

Raphael, B., et al. 1983. "Who Helps the Helper? The Effects of Disaster on the Rescue Workers." *Omega* 14/1, 9-20.

Reeker, J., D. Ensing and R. Elliott. 1997. "A Meta-Analytic Investigation of Group Treatment Outcomes for Sexually Abused Children." *Child Abuse and Neglect* 21, 669-80.

Resnick, H. S., et al. 1992. "Vulnerability – Stress Factors in Development of Posttraumatic Stress Disorder." *Journal of Nervous and Mental Disease* 180, 424-30.

Resnick, M. D. 2000. "Protective Factors, Resiliency and Healthy Youth Development." *Adolescent Medicine, State of the Art Review* 11, 157-64.

Reuven, G. 1998. "Colleagues in Distress: 'Helping the Helpers.'" *International Review of Psychiatry* 10/3, 234-38.

Revicki, D. A., et al. 1988. "Organizational Characteristics, Occupational Stress and Depression in Rural Emergency Medical Technicians." *Journal of Rural Health* 4, 73-83.

Revicki, D. A., and R. R. M. Gershon. 1996. "Work-Related Stress and Psychological Distress in Emergency Medical Technicians." *Journal of Occupational Health Psychology* 1, 391-96.

Richards, D. 1994. "Traumatic Stress at Work: A Public Health Model." *British Journal of Guidance and Counselling* 22, 51-64.

Riordan, R. J., and S. K. Saltzer. 1992. "Burnout Prevention Among Health Care Providers Working with the Terminally Ill: A Literature Review." *Omega* 25, 17-24.

Robb, N. 1999. "After Swissair 111, the Helpers Needed Help." *Canadian Medical Association Journal* 160/3, 394.

Rodgers, L. M. 1998. "A Five Year Study Comparing Early Retirements on Medical Grounds in Ambulance Personnel with Those in Other Groups of Health Service Staff. Part II: Causes of Retirements." *Occupational Medicine* 48, 119-32.

Roemer, L., et al. 1998. "Increases in Retrospective Accounts of War-Zone Exposure Over Time: The Role of PTSD Symptom Severity." *Journal of Traumatic Stress* 11/3, 597-605.

Rosebush, P. A. 1998. "Psychological Intervention with Military Personnel in Rwanda." *Military Medicine* 163/8, 559-63.

Rosenbloom, D. J., A. C Pratt and L. A. Pearlman. 1995. "Helpers' Responses to Trauma Work: Understanding and Intervening in An Organization." In Stamm, *Secondary Traumatic Stress*, 65-79.

Rosser, R. M. 1997. "Effects of Disasters on Helpers." In *Psychological Trauma: A Developmental Approach*, edited by D. Black et al., 326-38. London: Gaskell.

Ruzek, J. I. 1993. "Professionals Coping with Vicarious Trauma." *National Center for PTSD Clinical Newsletter* 3/2, 12-13, 17.

Saakvitne, K. W., and L. A. Pearlman, eds. 1996. *Transforming the Pain: A Workbook on Vicarious Traumatization*. New York: Norton.

Saigh, P. A. 1991. "The Development of Posttraumatic Stress Disorder Following Four Different Types of Traumatization." *Behaviour Research and Therapy* 29/3, 213-16.

Salama, P. 1999. "The Psychological Health of Relief Workers: Some Practical Suggestions." *Relief and Rehabilitation Network Newsletter* (November).

Salb, T. J. 1998. "Disaster Workers: Coping and Hardiness." Ph.D. dissertation, Texas Tech University, *Dissertation Abstracts International* 59/11B, 6108.

Salmon, T. W. 1919. "War Neuroses and Their Lesson." *New York Medical Journal* 109, 993-94.

Sannes, P. H., and B. W. Walcott. 1983. "Stress Reactions Among Participants in Mass Casualty Simulations." *Annals of Emergency Medicine* 12, 426-28.

Schauben, L. J., and P. A. Frazier. 1995. "Vicarious Trauma: The Effects on Female Counselors of Working with Sexual Violence Survivors." *Psychology of Women Quarterly* 19, 49-64.

Schnurr, P. P., et al. 2001. "Design of Department of Veterans Affairs Cooperative Study No. 420: Group Treatment of Posttraumatic Stress Disorder." *Controlled Clinical Trials* 22, 74-88.

Schumm, W. R., D. B. Bell and B. Knott. 2000. "Factors Associated with Spouses Moving Away from Their Military Installation During an Overseas Deployment." *Psychological Reports* 86/3, 1275-82.

Schutzwohl, M. 2000. "Early Intervention Following Trauma: An Overview of Programs and Their Effectiveness" (in German). *Fortschr Neurol Psychiatry Sep* 68/9, 423-30.

Schwam, K. 1998. "The Phenomenon of Compassion Fatigue in Perioperative Nursing." *AORN Journal* 68/4, 642-48.

Scott, M. J., and S. Palmer, eds. 2000. *Trauma and Post-Traumatic Stress Disorder*. New York: Cassell.

Sewell, J. D., and L. Crew. 1984. "The Forgotten Victim: Stress and the Police Dispatcher." *FBI Law Enforcement Bulletin* 53, 7-11.

Shah, G. 1985. "Social Work in Disaster." *Indian Journal of Social Work* 45, 462-71.

Shalev, A. Y., R. Yehuda and A. C. Mcfarlane. 2000. *International Handbook of Human Response to Trauma*. New York: Kluwer Academic/Plenum Publishers.

Sharp, T. W., et al. 1995. "Illness in Journalists and Relief Workers Involved in International Humanitarian Ssistance Efforts in Somalia, 1992-93." *Journal of Travel Medicine* 1/2, 70-76.

Shepherd, M. A., and P. E. Hodgkinson. 1990. "The Hidden Victims of Disaster: Helper Stress." *Stress Medicine* 6/1, 29-35.

Simon, B. 1993. "Obstacles in the Path of Mental Health Professionals Who Deal with Traumatic Violations of Human Rights." *International Journal of Law and Psychiatry* 16, 427-40.

Slusarcick, A. L., et al. 1999. "Stress and Coping in Male and Female Health Care Providers During the Persian Gulf War: The USNS Comfort Hospital Ship." *Military Medicine* 164, 166-73.

Smith, B., et al. 1996. "Health Activities Across Traumatized Populations: Emotional Responses of International Humanitarian Aid Workers." In *International Responses to Traumatic Stress*, edited by Y. Danieli, N. Rodley and L. Weisaeth, 397-423. Amityville, N.Y.: Baywood Publishing Company.

Smith, J. 1972. "Cross-Cultural Adjustment: Are Our Troops Thriving Or Surviving?" *U.S. Government Journal of Psychology* 152, 150-58.

Solomon, S. D. 1986. "Mobilizing Social Support Networks in Times of Disaster." In *Trauma and Its Wake*, vol. 2, *Traumatic Stress Theory, Research and Intervention*, edited by C. R. Figley, 232-63. New York: Bruner/Mazel.

Solomon, S. D., et al. 1987. "Social Involvement As a Mediator of Disaster-Induced Stress." *Journal of Applied Social Psychology* 17, 1092-1112.

Solomon, S. D., D. A. Regier and J. D. Burke. 1989. "Role of Perceived Control in Coping with Disaster." *Journal of Social and Clinical Psychology* 8/4, 376-92.

Solomon, Z., and R. Benbenishty. 1986. "The Role of Proximity, Immediacy and Expectancy in Frontline Treatment of Combat Stress Reaction Among Israelis in the Lebanon War." *American Journal of Psychiatry* 143, 613-17.

Sparrius, S. K. 1992. "Occupational Stressors Among Ambulance and Rescue Service Workers." *South African Journal of Psychology* 22, 87-91.

Spiers, C. 1997. "Counselling and Crisis Intervention Training for Humanitarian Aid Workers." *International Journal of Stress Management* 4/4, 309-13.

Stalker, C. A., and R. Fry. 1999. "A Comparison of Short-Term Group and Individual Therapy for Sexually Abused Women." *Canadian Journal of Psychiatry* 44/2, 168-74.

Stamm, B. H. 1997. "Work-Related Secondary Traumatic Stress." *PTSD Research Quarterly* 8, 1-6.

———. 2002. "Measuring Compassion Satisfaction As Well As Fatigue: Developmental History of the Compassion Fatigue and Satisfaction Test." In *Treating Compassion Fatigue*, edited by C. R. Figley. Philadelphia: Taylor and Francis.

Stamm, B. H., ed. 1995. *Secondary Traumatic Stress: Self-Care Issues for Clinicians, Researchers and Educators*. Lutherville, Md.: Sidran Press.

Stauffer, L. B., and E. Deblinger. 1996. "Cognitive Behavioral Groups for Nonoffending Others and Their Young Sexually Abused Children: A Preliminary Treatment Outcome Study." *Child Maltreatment* 1, 65-76.

Stearns, S. D. 1993. "Psychological Distress and Relief Work: Who Helps the Helpers?" *Refugee Participation Network* 15, 3-8.

Stuart, G., and E. Huggins. 1990. "Caring for Caretakers in Time of Disaster: The Hurricane Hugo Experience." *Journal of Child and Adolescent Psychiatric and Mental Health Nursing* 3/4, 144-47.

Summerfield, D. 1999. "A Critique of Seven Assumptions Behind Psychological Trauma Programmes in War-Affected Areas." *Social Science Medicine* 48/10, 1449-62.

Sutker, P. B., et al. 1994. "Psychopathology in War-Zone Deployed and Nondeployed Operation Desert Storm Troops Assigned Graves Registration Duties." *Journal of Abnormal Psychology* 103, 383-90; abstracted in *PTSD Research Quarterly* 7/1 (1996).

Tarrier, N., and L. Humphreys. 2000. "Subjective Improvement in PTSD Patients with Treatment by Imaginal Exposure Or Cognitive Therapy: Session by Session Changes." *British Journal of Clinical Psychology* 39, 27-34.

Taylor, A., and D. Frazer. 1982. "The Stress of Post-Disaster Body Handling and Victim Identification." *Journal of Human Stress* 39, 19-40.

Taylor, A. J. W., and A. G. Frazer. 1982. "The Stress of Post-Disaster Body Handling and Victim Identification Work." *Journal of Human Stress* 8, 4-12.

Taylor, S., J. Wood and R. Lechtman. 1983. "It Could Be Worse: Selective Evaluation As a Response to Victimization." *Journal of Social Issues* 39, 719-40.

Taylor, W. D., ed. 1997. *Too Valuable to Lose: Exploring the Causes and Cures of Missionary Attrition*. Pasadena, Calif.: William Carey Library.

Terry, M. J. 1995. "Kelengakutelleghpat: An Arctic Community-Based Approach to Trauma." In Stamm, *Secondary Traumatic Stress*, 149-78.

Theorell, T., et al. 1994. "'Person Under Train' Incidents from the Subway Driver's Point of View? A Prospective 1-Year Follow-Up

Study: The Design, and Medical and Psychiatric Data." *Social Science and Medicine* 38, 471-75.

Tierney, K. J., and B. Baisden. 1979. *Crisis Intervention Program for Disaster Victims.* Washington, D.C.: U.S. Department of Health, Education and Welfare.

Tierney, K. J., and V. A. Taylor. 1977. "EMS Delivery in Mass Emergencies: Preliminary Research Findings." *Mass Emergencies* 2, 205-17.

Turner, C. 1998. "Humanitarian U.N. Work Is Risky Business." *Los Angeles Times*, August 2, A1, A8, A9.

Ursano, R. J., et al. 1999. "Posttraumatic Stress Disorder and Identification in Disaster Workers." *American Journal of Psychiatry* 156/3, 353-59.

Valent, P. 1995. "Survival Strategies: A Framework for Understanding Secondary Traumatic Stress and Coping in Helpers." In Figley, *Compassion Fatigue: Coping with Secondary Traumatic Stress Disorder in Those Who Treat the Traumatized*, 21-50.

Van Der Kolk, B., A. Mcfarlane and L. Van Der Hart. 1996. *Traumatic Stress: The Effects of Overwhelming Experience on Mind, Body and Society*. New York: Guilford Press.

Van Der Veer, G. 1992. "The Consequences of Working with Refugees for the Helping Professional." In *Counselling and Therapy with Refugees: Psychological Problems of Victims of War, Torture and Repression*, editd by G. Van Der Veer, 241-48. Chichester, England: Wiley.

Vera, E. 1982. "Effects of Disaster on Emergency Care Providers." Third National Symposium on Psychosocial Factors in Emergency Medicine, Chicago.

Wagner, D., M. Heinrichs and V. Ehlert. 1998. "Prevalence of Symptoms of Posttraumatic Stress Disorder in German Professional Firefighters." *American Journal of Psychiatry* 155/12.

Wahlen, S. D. 1997. "Secondary Victimization Among Learners of Violence Issues." *Journal of Aggression, Maltreatment and Trauma* 1/2, 307-19.

Warheit, G. J. 1970. "Fire Departments: Operations During Major Emergencies." *American Behavioral Scientist* 13, 262-68.

Washington, K. 1994. *Harvard Trauma Questionnaire*. Cambridge: Harvard Press.

Weaver, A. J., H. G. Koenig and F. M. Ochberg. 1996. "Posttraumatic Stress, Mental Health Professionals, and the Clergy: A Need for Collaboration, Training and Research." *Journal of Traumatic Stress* 9/4, 847-56.

Weaver, J. D. 1995. *Disasters: Mental Health Interventions*. Sarasota, Fla.: Professional Resource Press.

Weisaeth, L., L. Mehlum and M. S. Mortensen. 1996. "Peacekeeper Stress: New and Different?" *National Center for Post-Traumatic Stress Disorder Clinical Quarterly* 6 (Winter), 1-8.

Weiss, D., et al. 1995. "Predicting Symptomatic Distress in Emergency Services Personnel." *Journal of Consulting and Clinical Psychology* 63/3, 361-68.

Weisz, J., et al. 1995. "Effects of Psychotherapy with Children and Adolescents Revisited: A Meta-Analysis of Treatment Outcome Studies." *Psychological Bulletin* 117, 450-68.

Welsh, J. 1995. "Violations of Human Rights: Traumatic Stress and the Role of NGOs: The Contribution of Non-Governmental Organizations." In *International Responses to Traumatic Stress*, edited by Y. Danieli, N. Rodley and L. Weisaeth. Amityville, N.Y.: Baywood Publishing Company.

Werner, E. 2000. "Protective Factors and Individual Resilience." In *Handbook of Early Childhood Intervention*, 2d ed., edited by J. Shonkoff and S. Meisels, 115-33. Cambridge: Cambridge University Press.

White, G. D. 1998. "Trauma Treatment Training for Bosnian and Croatian Mental Health Workers." *American Journal of Orthopsychiatry* 68/1, 58-62.

White, R. 1979. "Supporting Foreign Embassy Workers with More Than Dollars." *U.S. Government Journal of Psychology* 236, 15-18.

Wilson, J., and J. Lindy. 1994. *Countertransference in the Treatment of PTSD.* New York: Guilford Press.

Wilson, J. P., and B. Raphael, eds. 1993. *International Handbook of Traumatic Stress Syndromes.* New York: Plenum.

Wilson, J. P., et al. 2000. "Preventing PTSD in Trauma Survivors." *Bulletin Menninger Clin* 64/2, 181-96.

Wolff, B., M. Romero Facey and D. Burke. 1988. "Responder Wellness: This One's for You." *Journal of Emergency Medical Services* 13, 24-27.

Yalom, I. D. 1995. *The Theory and Practice of Group Psychotherapy.* New York: Basic Books.

Young, B. H., et al. 1998. *Disaster Mental Health Services: A Guidebook for Clinicians and Administrators.* Palo Alto, Calif./White River Junction, Vt.: National Center for PTSD.

Yutrzenka, B. 1990. "Psychological Impact of Disaster Response Among Diverse Emergency Response Providers." Paper presented at the 98th annual convention of the American Psychological Association, Boston, Massachusetts, August.

Zimmerman, G., and W. Weber. 2000. "Care for the Caregivers: A Program for Canadian Military Chaplains After Serving in NATO and United Nations Peacekeeping Missions in the 1990s." *Military Medicine* 165/9, 687-90.